LOCAL JOURNALISM

The Reuters Institute for the Study of Journalism at the University of Oxford aims to serve as the leading international forum for a productive engagement between scholars from a wide range of disciplines and practitioners of journalism. As part of this mission, we publish work by academics, journalists, and media industry professionals focusing on some of the most important issues facing journalism around the world today.

All our books are reviewed by both our Editorial Committee and expert readers.

LOCAL JOURNALISM

THE DECLINE OF NEWSPAPERS AND THE RISE OF DIGITAL MEDIA

Edited by RASMUS KLEIS NIELSEN

REUTERS
INSTITUTE for the
STUDY of
JOURNALISM

Published by I.B.Tauris & Co. Ltd in association with
the Reuters Institute for the Study of Journalism, University of Oxford

Published in 2015 by
I.B.Tauris & Co. Ltd
London • New York
www.ibtauris.com

References to websites were correct at the time of writing.

ISBN: 978 1 78453 320 5 (HB)
ISBN: 978 1 78453 321 2 (PB)
eISBN: 978 0 85773 980 3

A full CIP record for this book is available from the British Library
A full CIP record is available from the Library of Congress

Library of Congress Catalog Card Number: available

Typeset by Riverside Publishing Solutions, Salisbury SP4 6NQ
Printed and bound in Great Britain by T.J. International, Padstow, Cornwall

Contents

Tables and Figures

Tables

Figures

Contributors

C. W. Anderson is Associate Professor in the Department of Media Culture at City University of New York, College of Staten Island (United States).

Olivier Baisnée is Associate Professor in Political Science at Sciences Po, Toulouse (France).

Piet Bakker is Professor at the Utrecht University of Applied Sciences, School of Journalism (the Netherlands).

Franck Bousquet is Senior Lecturer in Information-Communication at the University of Toulouse (France).

Stephen Coleman is Professor of Political Communication in the School of Media and Communication at the University of Leeds (United Kingdom).

David Domingo is Chair of Journalism at Université libre de Bruxelles (Belgium).

Bengt Engan is Associate Professor in the Social Science Faculty, School of Journalism, at the University of Nordland (Norway).

Julie Firmstone is Lecturer in Media and Communication at the University of Leeds (United Kingdom).

Dave Harte is Senior Lecturer in Media and Communications at Birmingham City University (United Kingdom).

Marco van Kerkhoven is Researcher at the Utrecht University of Applied Sciences, School of Journalism (the Netherlands).

Rasmus Kleis Nielsen is Director of Research at the Reuters Institute for the Study of Journalism at the University of Oxford (United Kingdom).

Florence Le Cam is Chair of Journalism at Université libre de Bruxelles (Belgium).

Emmanuel Marty is Lecturer in Information and Communication Sciences at the University of Nice Sophia Antipolis (France).

Matthew Powers is Assistant Professor in the Department of Communication, University of Washington, Seattle (United States).

Nikos Smyrnaios is Senior Lecturer in Information-Communication at the University of Toulouse (France).

Nancy Thumim is Lecturer in Media and Communication at the University of Leeds (United Kingdom).

Jerome Turner is Research Assistant on the Media, Community, and the Creative Citizen Project and a PhD student at Birmingham City University (United Kingdom).

Andy Williams is Lecturer at the School of Journalism, Media, and Cultural Studies, Cardiff University (United Kingdom).

Sandra Vera Zambrano is Researcher at Sciences Po, Toulouse (France).

Preface

This book deals with local journalism. This is not a sexy topic. But it is an important topic, one that is intellectually interesting, often overlooked, and deserves more attention.

The book is structured as follows. The introduction presents an overview of existing research on local journalism as well as the structural changes currently underway. Part I (Chapters 1, 2, and 3) focuses on the role of local journalism as part of the *news media ecosystem* in a range of different communities in Denmark, France, the United Kingdom, and the United States. Part II (Chapters 4, 5, and 6) focuses on *local journalism and its interlocutors* with studies from Belgium, Norway, and the United Kingdom. Part III (Chapters 7, 8, and 9) focuses on *new forms of local media* emerging that offer various degrees of and kinds of support for online-only forms of journalism and has studies from France, the Netherlands, and the United Kingdom.

Several of the chapters included were initially presented at a conference 'Local Journalism around the World: Professional Practices, Economic Foundations, and Political Implications' hosted at the Reuters Institute for the Study of Journalism in Oxford in February 2014. It was an interesting and wide-ranging event with papers from 16 different countries, underlining the many differences and similarities not only between local journalism in different countries, but also local journalism in different communities, and the differences between local journalism and national and international journalism.

We would like to thank everyone who took part in the conference for two days of discussion that has done much to inform and improve much of what is presented in this book. In addition to the contributors to the book, the participants included Aleksandra Krstic, Ana Milojevic, André Haller, Annika Bergström, Annika Sehl, Birgit Røe Mathisen, Daniel H. Mutibwa, David Ryfe, Diana Bossio, Dimitri Prandner, Dobin Yim, Helle Sjøvaag, Ingela Wadbring, Ioannis Angelou, Jonathan Albright,

Kirsi Hakaniemi, Kristy Hess, Lenka Waschkova Cisarova, Lisa Waller, Mato Brautovic, Penelope Abernathy, Saba Bebawi, Sanne Hille, Sonja Kretzschmar, Vasileios Katsaras, and Verena Wassink.

Beyond the authors and the conference participants, I as editor would like to thank Robert G. Picard (who led the work on organising the conference), Kate Hanneford-Smith and Monique Ricketts (for expert logistical assistance), Alex Reid (who has helped shepherd the book to publication), and especially David Levy, David Ryfe, Ian Hargreaves, and Katrin Voltmer for their constructive comments on the manuscript.

Rasmus Kleis Nielsen, November 2014

Introduction: The Uncertain Future of Local Journalism

Rasmus Kleis Nielsen

For more than a century, most people in the Western world have taken local journalism for granted. From small rural communities covered by weeklies to larger towns covered by their own daily, newspapers have been an integral part of local life, and their journalists have chronicled events from the mundane to the monumental, publicised local debates, and kept a more or less watchful eye on those in positions of power. Local media have represented their area and helped people imagine themselves as part of a community, connected in part through their shared local news medium, bound together by more than geographic proximity or politically defined administrative boundaries.

Journalists and journalism scholars alike are and have been ambivalent about the quality of local journalism. On the one hand, local journalism seems *terrible* to many. It is frequently seen as superficial and deferential, as skirting controversy, and as catering to advertisers and affluent audiences over the wider community. Commentator George Monbiot, for example, sees the local press as one of the 'most potent threats to British democracy, championing the overdog, misrepresenting democratic choices, defending business, the police and local elites from those who seek to challenge them' (Monbiot, 2009). On the other hand, local journalism is also seen as *terribly important*. It provides information about local public affairs, it holds local elites at least somewhat accountable, it provides a forum for discussion, and it ties communities together. The reality of local journalism probably lies not between these two extremes, but in their combination. Like journalism more broadly, local journalism may well be frequently terrible and yet also terribly important.

Local journalism does not always play its roles well, but the roles it plays are important.

It is because it is important and imperfect that we – whether as journalists, as journalism scholars, or as readers, viewers, users – should try to understand local journalism, how it operates, what its consequences are, and where it is heading. The first thing to recognise is that local journalism, like journalism more generally, is changing today as part of a wider structural transformation of our media environment, driven in large part by the rise of digital media (but also other factors). This unfinished media revolution involves changes in how we communicate, share content, get informed, are advertised to, and entertain ourselves (e.g. Grueskin et al., 2011; Levy and Nielsen, 2010; Nielsen, 2012). The changes are not identical from case to case, community to community, or country to country, but they are profound and share certain commonalities across most high-income democracies: print, the mainstay of the newspaper business, is in decline, broadcasting has been transformed by the growth of multi-channel television, and digital media provide new ways for accessing, finding, and sharing media content that challenge the inherited business models and journalistic routines of established news media.

This book takes these changes as its starting point and focuses on the uncertain future of local journalism. Much has been written about how these changes affect the news media and journalism generally (e.g. Fenton, 2010; Lee-Wright et al., 2012; Russell, 2011). But the emphasis has been overwhelmingly on national media, on the most prominent newspapers, the biggest broadcasters, and the most successful digital start-ups. Though local journalism actually accounts for the majority of the journalistic profession, and though much of the news media industry is local and regional rather than national or international, less attention has been paid to how contemporary changes are affecting local journalism and local media specifically (for exceptions see Abernathy, 2014; Fowler, 2011; Ryfe, 2012). In several countries, legislatures, media regulators, and advocacy groups have all noted the serious challenges facing local and regional news media. There has been much less independent research into these issues. This limits our understanding of journalism (most of it is local), of the news media (much of the industry is local), and of local communities (tied together in part by local journalism and local news media). The chapters collected here push beyond these limitations and advance our understanding of the distinct characteristics of local media ecosystems, local journalism and its various interlocutors, and new forms of local media, providing a fuller and more nuanced picture not only of local journalism around the world, but also journalism more generally.

The uncertain future of local journalism

The premise of the book is twofold.

First, while we have in the past been able to take the *existence* of local journalism, its practical feasibility and its commercial sustainability, for granted, this is no longer the case. The business models that local newspapers have been based on are under tremendous pressure today as readership is eroding, advertising declining, and overall revenues plummeting. Digital growth has far from made up for what has been lost on the print side of the business. Most newspaper companies have responded by cutting costs to remain profitable or at least limit the operating losses. Seeing little potential for growth, investors have lost interest in the sector, as demonstrated by the collapsing market value of publicly traded local newspaper companies. While broadcasting has so far weathered the digital transition better as a business, both radio and television are more often organised regionally than locally, and in any case they typically make at best limited investments in local journalism. (The US has a more robust local television industry than most other countries, with a greater emphasis on local news. Yet research there has suggested that the coverage is often inadequate, episodic, and superficial – and rarely genuinely local. See for example Fowler et al., 2007.) Public media, especially licence-fee-funded public service broadcasters in Western Europe, face fewer challenges to their resource base (though in some cases well-known political pressures). But, like their commercial counterparts, they generally provide more regional news than genuinely local news.[1] The emergence of new digital forms of local media has occasioned much optimism about the future of local journalism. But so far, the evidence that digital-only operations can sustain local journalism on a significant scale is inconclusive. And after the cyclical challenges that have come with the global financial crisis and prolonged recessions in many countries, the advertising business is changing in ways that make it harder to fund local content production – Facebook, Google, and other large digital players are increasingly offering locally targeted forms of advertising, making specifically local media less distinct. As one advertising executive has put it, 'Local isn't valuable anymore. Anyone can sell local' (quoted in Suich, 2014). So this is the first premise: developments

3

in media business across print, broadcasting, and digital media mean that we cannot take the existence of local journalism for granted any more.

Second, while the structural transformation that has challenged the economic and organisational underpinnings of local journalism is tied in with the larger change in our media environment affecting national and international media, we cannot simply deduce from studies of national media what will happen at the local level, or indeed assume that local journalism is the same throughout a given country. Journalism at the national level is, for example, increasingly oriented towards a non-stop 24/7 breaking-news cycle and characterised by intensified competition between multiple news organisations covering the same stories and appealing to the same audiences. It is not clear that *any* of this is the case at the local level. Similarly, the *Guardian*, the *Banbury Guardian* (local paid daily), and the *Croydon Guardian* (free weekly) are all UK newspapers, are all affected by the changes in our media environment, and have all launched digital operations in response to these changes. That does not mean, however, that one can rely on the (many) analyses of the *Guardian* to understand how the *Banbury Guardian* and the *Croydon Guardian*, their place in local media ecosystems, their local journalism, and their position online, are changing. To understand the uncertain future of local journalism, we need to take into account the often pronounced differences not only *between* countries (international variation in, say, the structure of local media markets and the practice of local journalism) but also differences *within* countries (intranational variation between urban and rural areas, between different regions). French local journalism, for example, is different from US local journalism. But there are also considerable differences within France, between relatively strong and commercially robust regional newspaper chains like *Ouest France* in Brittany and weaker individual titles elsewhere in the country. Similarly, local journalism in a major metropolitan area is different from local journalism in a medium-size provincial town or a sparsely populated countryside. That is the second premise: we need to take the specificities of local journalism, the international and intranational differences between local journalism in different areas, seriously.

This introduction presents an overview of main trends in terms of what is happening to local news media, discusses different perspectives on the role of local journalism, and then proceeds to summarise key points from existing research to provide an overview of what we know about local journalism in terms of three areas, namely (1) accountability

4

and information, (2) civic and political engagement, and (3) community integration. It is important to underline from the outset that research on local journalism is neither as detailed, extensive, or systematically comparative as research on national news media. Much of what we know about local journalism is therefore based on individual case studies or research from one community or country, sometimes work completed well before the current changes in our media environment picked up pace. While we have reason to expect that many of these findings apply more generally, substantiating that, and fully understanding the practice and consequences of local journalism in different settings, will require more research than has been done so far. Nonetheless, key overall trends can be highlighted.

What is happening to local media?

Contemporary changes in local media are tied in with a wider change in the way in which we live our lives, the way in which the economy works, and the way in which politics works. At least since the 1990s, social scientists have increasingly stressed that we cannot take the idea of 'local communities' for granted, especially if we think of these as socially, economically, and politically self-contained. We still live local lives, but our lives are less locally bounded, as people move more often, as more and more people commute to work elsewhere, as more and more of the goods and services we consume are produced far away, and as some of the most important decisions impacting our lives and communities are taken elsewhere. The sociologist Anthony Giddens, for example, while underlining the continuing relevance of locality and community as enduring features of the modern world, also argues that many parts of social life have become 'disembedded', that social, economic, and political relations have been 'lifted out' of the local context of interaction (Giddens, 1990: 21; see also Castells, 2000). This is not simply a case of centralisation, of the increasing importance of financial centres, large multinational corporations, and national capitals, but also of developments where people, goods, services, and power circulate in new networks that cut across traditional distinctions between the local, the regional, the national, and the global (Sassen, 2006). These changes impact local media too. Transient populations represent a different kind of audience from long-term residents, local business news is less important for people who work and shop outside the community, and the incentive to follow local politics is reduced if power is perceived to be elsewhere. Local journalism increasingly faces the challenge not only of covering local affairs, but also of identifying in ways that resonate with their audience what is local, what makes it local, and why the local is even relevant.[2]

Local media themselves have changed significantly too since the 1990s. Already then, journalism scholars warned of a bleak present and worse future for local and regional media (Franklin and Murphy, 1998), noting how newspaper circulation was declining, advertising revenues were shrinking, and many local and regional media companies were responding by cutting investments in local newsrooms and often consolidating operations in regional centres, leading to media that were 'local in name only' (Franklin, 2006: xxi). There are considerable variations in how the local and regional media have developed even within the Western world in the postwar years – some countries, like Germany, have a media market characterised by very strong local and regional newspapers and public service broadcasters with a strong regional orientation, whereas others, like the United Kingdom, have much more nationally oriented media systems, dominated to a larger extent by media based in the capital. (These differences in part reflect wider structural difference between, for example, a federal political system in Germany versus a more centralised one in the United Kingdom.) But in most countries, local media markets have been highly concentrated for decades. Typically, local newspapers have enjoyed a dominant position within their circulation areas, facing only limited competition from regional and national media and in some cases from community media. Structural diversity has been low and incumbents often highly profitable due to their near-monopoly on local advertising.

The pace of change differs from country to country, and there are important variations, but the overall direction since has been the same. Private local and regional newspapers have lost whole categories of advertising (classifieds, much of automotive, jobs, and real estate) to online competitors and are going through a structural transformation as their historically profitable print product declines in importance and their digital operations cannot make up for the revenue lost (even in cases where they reach a considerable audience). Commercial broadcasters make limited investments in local news (with the US being a partial exception). Public service broadcasters are primarily regionally oriented. Forms of alternative, citizen, and community media increase media diversity in important ways in some areas, but their resources and reach are often limited, and most localities are primarily served by market-based and public service media. People everywhere rely on wide and diverse media repertoires to be entertained and stay informed. But when it comes to local news, local newspapers have historically played a central role. These newspapers are under tremendous pressure today.

These pressures are important not only for owners and employees of local newspapers, but also for the communities they cover, as a number of studies have shown how central newspapers are to local media ecosystems, especially in terms of the sheer volume and variety of locally oriented news they produce (Project for Excellence in Journalism, 2010; Lund, 2010; Anderson, 2013). In many countries, people more often identify television and sometimes radio as their main *source* of local news than they name newspapers. But in terms of news *production*, newspapers remain central. Their decline must raise concerns over a growing local 'news gap' between the information we would ideally want communities to have access to, and the information that is actually made available from independent sources of news (Currah, 2009). In areas where local newspapers are not only cutting back on coverage but closing altogether, and where broadcasters and digital media provide little substantial local coverage, we face the prospect of local 'news deserts' where communities are not covered at all, and have to rely on the local grapevine of interpersonal communication and information from self-interested parties (politicians, local government, businesses) to stay informed about local affairs (Friedland et al., 2012).

The growth of digital media has been accompanied by considerable optimism that new forms of local media would thrive online, where low entry and operating costs could potentially allow lean, efficient operations to focus on local communities and cover them in depth and in detail and thus produce distinct content and carve out their own niche in an increasingly competitive media environment. The ease with which digital media could potentially allow people to collaborate and produce new forms of alternative media, citizen journalism, or community media has also given rise to hopes that non-market forms of local news provision would thrive online (similar to the hopes that once formed around community radio and public-access television). Faced with growing concern over the future of established, legacy local and regional media, this optimism has been embraced by policy-makers in several countries. In the US, the Federal Communications Commission has stated that 'independent non-profit websites are providing exciting journalistic innovation on the local level' (FCC, 2011: 191). In the UK, the media regulator Ofcom

(2012: 103) has highlighted how digital media have 'the potential to support and broaden the range of local media content available to citizens and consumers at a time when traditional local media providers continue to find themselves under financial pressure'.

So far, however, the evidence is very uneven and the optimism and high hopes surrounding digital local media are not always well-supported. A number of impressive new local media initiatives – some professionally organised and commercially run, others non-profits, sometimes with a stronger volunteer component – have been launched (e.g. Barnett and Townend, 2014). But the wider field of new forms of local media is characterised by very uneven quality, a high turnover (as many new ventures rarely last long), and genuine concerns over their editorial autonomy and independence (e.g. Kurpius et al., 2010; Thurman et al., 2012; van Kerkhoven and Bakker, 2014). Furthermore, there seem to be pronounced national differences in the number and vitality of digital local news media. There have been very few launched in Denmark, despite high levels of internet use and a large share of advertising going to digital, in part probably because of the strength of legacy media, whereas there has been a substantial number of local start-ups in countries like France and the United Kingdom. Individual examples of local news start-ups from the US are often brought as reasons for optimism, but the most systematic review of the US scene produced so far provides a sombre picture. In it, Matthew Hindman (2011: 10) writes that 'there is little evidence [...] that the Internet has expanded the number of local news outlets'. He continues, 'while the Internet adds only a pittance of new sources of local news, the surprisingly small audience for local news traffic [also] helps explain the financial straits local news organizations now face'. Digital advertising is a volume game, dominated by large players like Google and Facebook who are increasingly offering geographically targeted advertising at low rates. Local news media, who in Hindman's study in the US on average attract well below 1% of all monthly page views in most media markets, have found it very hard to develop a profitable digital business. Freely accessible, advertising-supported online-only local news organisations – the most common form of new local news media – who typically have more limited audience reach than established newspapers and broadcasters and have no legacy business to subsidise digital operations, have had an especially hard time achieving sustainability.

Beyond the news media, digital media have underpinned the growth of new forms of social and interpersonal communication, online additions to existing forums for and networks of person-to-person communication at home, on the job, and elsewhere. Daily conversation with family, friends, and colleagues has been, is, and will continue to be an important part of how people follow local affairs (e.g. Huckfeldt and Sprague, 1995) and the 'story-telling networks' that tie local communities together are only partially intertwined with news media (Kim and Ball-Rokeach, 2006). Today, these conversations increasingly have online components and manifestations, on bulletin board debates, listservs, social networking sites, and the like. Even though, so far, research suggests these various sites produce little original news, they can facilitate communities of interest and in addition play an important role as 'alert systems', disseminating information produced by others and drawing people's attention to issues of common concern (Project for Excellence in Journalism, 2010). Digital media have also presented various organised actors in local communities, politicians, local governments, local businesses and community groups with new ways of communicating with people via websites, newsletters, and social media. (More broadly, many of these actors are increasingly investing in their own forms of communication, sometimes going beyond PR, marketing, and various digital platforms to include media like the so-called 'town-hall Pravdas', papers published by some city councils in the UK to announce council business.) These developments underline that even in communities where there is only one or only a few local news media, local journalism does not have a monopoly on providing local information. People have other sources. But so far, surveys suggest that local newspapers in most places still represent the most widely used sources and the most important source of independently produced information about local public affairs.

What is the role of local journalism?

Journalists and journalism scholars alike typically see journalism's most important role as holding power to account and keeping people informed about public affairs. This role is associated with the notion of journalism as a 'fourth estate' and reads journalism through the lens of liberal representative democracy. A frequently used metaphor for this role is the idea of journalism as a 'watchdog', and indeed, research has shown that many journalists in the Western world primarily see themselves as 'detached watchdogs' (Hanitzsch, 2011). The metaphor is particularly associated with investigative reporting, the work of independent journalists who toil diligently and often at length to unearth secrets and expose corruption.

Popular as the watchdog metaphor is for the autonomy, importance, and moral purpose it ascribes to journalism, it has never been a particularly good description of how the profession actually works. This is illustrated by the frequency with which it is invoked by critics as a way of highlighting how journalism often falls short of its own aspirations – 'the watchdog that didn't bark' – and it is contrasted with a negative metaphor of journalism as a 'lapdog' that uncritically follows the lead of local elites. The notion of journalism as a 'guard dog' has been suggested as a more appropriate canine metaphor by a team of researchers on the basis of years of extensive research on journalism in different communities in the United States (Donohue et al., 1995; Tichenor et al., 1980). In their view, journalism is not a watchdog working on behalf of the public at large or the whole community. But it is not a lapdog at the beck and call of the local elite either. Instead, they suggest we recognise that local news media are deeply influenced by local community structures, including local political fault lines, the relative strength of different community groups, and indeed the social structure in terms of class and ethnicity, and that it serves most effectively those groups in local communities who already have some influence, power, and resources. In their analysis, this is so not because journalists explicitly *aim* to serve these groups, but because journalists and the news media they work for *depend* on these groups as sources (for journalists) and as readers (both subscribers and as attractive to advertisers).

The guard dog metaphor still sees accountability and public affairs coverage as at the centre of what local journalism does, even though it comes with a more modest view of the extent to which, and the conditions under which, journalism can actually hold local elites to account. Guard dog journalism depends in part on local elite conflict and competition for its ability to effectively monitor people in positions of power, just as national news journalism often turns out to provide the most diverse, revelatory, and multi-perspectival coverage of issues when political elites disagree (Bennett, 2005). It presents journalism and local media with a more modest, but still important, role as an institution that publicises key aspects of local public affairs – especially elite competition and conflict – helping citizens understand the actors and the stakes and make decisions on whether and how this impacts them and whether and how they want to get involved.

If journalists and journalism scholars expect journalism to hold power to account and keep people informed about public affairs (or hope that it will), what do people themselves expect of (local) journalism? Here, research from the Netherlands and the United States identifies a significant overlap between what journalists and journalism scholars expect from local journalism and what people more broadly expect, but also a wider range of roles beyond those that professionals and academics normally associate with local media.

Qualitative research with local television audiences in the Netherlands suggests that people there expect local media to do seven things:

(1) supply relatively diverse, reliable, timely, and unbiased background *information* on community affairs;
(2) foster social *integration* by helping people navigate their local community;
(3) provide *inspiration* and good examples;
(4) ensure *representation* of different groups in the community;
(5) increase local intra-community *understanding* between different groups;
(6) maintain a form of *local memory* or chronicle of local affairs; and
(7) contribute to social cohesion, a sense of *belonging* to the locale (Costera Meijer, 2010).

The information role and to a lesser extent the representation role overlaps to a significant degree with the journalistic self-conception and the guard dog metaphor. But it is clear that people also expect much more from local media than a conventional focus on public affairs coverage would suggest. Journalists may prefer to see themselves as independent – detached – from the community they cover, even if in reality they are highly dependent on it, both in terms of sources for their reporting and resources to sustain the news organisations they work for. Their audiences may appreciate the ambition to be impartial and unbiased that lies behind the notion of detachment. But they also expect local media to be engaged with the community they cover.

Quantitative research from the United States further substantiates the idea that people expect more – and different – things from local media than accountability reporting and regular coverage of local public affairs. On the basis of a survey of local community members, a team of

American researchers suggest that people *do* expect their local media to provide accurate and unbiased regular local news coverage on a timely basis and to serve as a watchdog holding local elites to account. But, more than anything, they expect local media to be 'good neighbors' (Poindexter et al., 2006). They expect local journalists to care about the community, to understand and appreciate its values, and, crucially, to prioritise solutions as much as problems in their coverage – in the US surveys, especially ethnic minorities, less affluent and less well-educated groups, and women say they expect local journalism to emphasise solutions as well as problems (Heider et al., 2005). These broader conceptions of local journalism and its role overlap only partially with how the journalistic profession conventionally sees itself and its mission through the image of the detached watchdog. They represent a communitarian supplement to a liberal self-understanding, and are better aligned with what some community media have been aiming to do (Dickens et al., 2014) and are, especially in the emphasis on community values and solutions, reminiscent of what the public journalism movement called for in the 1990s in the US (Rosen, 1999).[3]

Both qualitative and quantitative research suggests that people have a positive image of what local news media are, or at least positive visions for what they might be. This is well in line with numerous surveys reporting that many people say that local news is important for them. But one should not exaggerate the bonds that tie local communities, local journalism, and local media together. In 2012, a majority (51%) of Americans said it would have *no* impact on their ability to keep up with information and news about their community if their local newspaper closed down (even as the same research project showed the multiple ways in which many actually depended on newspapers) (Rosenthiel et al., 2012). This is probably at least in part because the very social significance of what for example 'journalism' means may be changing as people access and get information from more and more different sources, also about local affairs. Not only the organisational, but also the cultural forms of news are changing today. Though most people clearly have certain expectations and ideals that local news media can leverage to define a broadly speaking positive and important role for themselves in local communities, local journalists cannot simply assume that their work is appreciated and valued, let alone that it will be so in the future. Especially when it comes to younger people and people who live less locally rooted lives, local news media and local journalism has to constantly prove its relevance and earn people's trust.

What do we know about local journalism?

What does existing empirical research on local journalism tell us in terms of how it performs the various roles assumed by journalists and assigned to it by others? The main points can be broken down in terms of three areas: (1) *accountability and information*, (2) *civic and political engagement*, and (3) *community integration*. These areas all combine a normative concern with the ideal role of journalism in local communities with an analytical ambition to assess its actual implications. (They all also take more or less for granted the existence of local journalism, a relatively clearly defined journalistic profession, and a shared understanding of what constitutes (local) news. All these seem less stable today.) Within each, there are several insights into the actual practice and consequences of local journalism that have been well-substantiated across a number of studies in different contexts.

Accountability and information

Local journalists often work at news media with limited editorial staff, a wide number of potential stories to cover in the community, and a considerable news hole to fill (especially with the growth of additional digital publishing platforms). It is therefore no surprise that a number of studies from different countries and contexts have all found that local journalism is mostly reactive and often based on single sources, frequently self-interested ones like politicians, local government officials, or businesses (Franklin and Richardson, 2002b; O'Neill and O'Connor, 2008; Örebro, 2002). More proactive reporting based on multiple sources and points of view makes up only a minority of local news, and is mostly produced by local daily newspapers, much less so by regional broadcasters and local weeklies (Lund, 2010; Project for Excellence in Journalism, 2010). Local journalists, as much as their national and international peers, 'co-produce' the news in collaboration with sources (Cook, 1998).

Locally, politicians and government officials have in many cases been found to be the most frequently cited local sources, with local businesses frequently coming second, community activists much less frequently, and ordinary citizens rarely making it into the news (Kaniss, 1991; O'Neill and O'Connor, 2008). In individual cases, media-savvy community activists can help drive a story (Anderson, 2010). But routine coverage is typically organised around a limited number of privileged sources that occupy

13

key positions in local politics, local government, and local business. This pattern is an old one, found as often in the 1970s as in the 2000s (see Lund, 2012; Svendsen, 1979). These institutionalised forms of co-production, characterised by routine interactions with a limited number of local elite sources, rarely results in the independent, investigative reporting associated with autonomous accountability journalism.

This does not mean, however, that local journalism offers no substantial coverage of local public affairs. Though critics have lamented a rising focus on sensationalist accounts of crime and softer, more entertainment- and lifestyle-oriented local stories (e.g. Franklin, 2006), systematic large-scale content analysis has in several countries shown that local journalism on the whole is in fact both informative and wide-ranging (Franklin and Richardson, 2002a), plays an important role in publicising what local authorities are doing (Ekström et al., 2006), and also offers some degree of critical debate and scrutiny, especially in those communities where local elites disagree amongst themselves (Tichenor et al., 1980). More generally, research has shown that news coverage helps reduce government corruption (Brunetti and Weder, 2003) and make elected officials more responsive to their constituents (Snyder and Strömberg, 2008).

We also know from a growing number of studies that local journalism is genuinely informative. The positive side of this is that people who follow local news know more about local public affairs (Shaker, 2009; Tichenor et al., 1970). (This is in line with a growing body of research that documents that news media users more generally are more informed about public affairs than those of their peers who do not regularly use news, e.g. Aalberg and Curran, 2012.) The more negative side of this is the persistent 'knowledge gap' between regular news users and those who do not regularly follow news, a gap that, because of the socio-economic profile of local news users, tends to reinforce pre-existing differences between the relatively more affluent, well-educated, and locally engaged (who know more about public affairs) and the relatively less affluent, well-educated, and locally engaged (who know less) (Donohue et al., 1995; Tichenor et al., 1970). (This too is in parallel with research showing growing differences in political information levels driven in part by many people opting not to follow the news regularly, e.g. Prior, 2007, and with research suggesting many young people – even if they express an interest in politics – do not feel that conventional forms of journalism speak to them, follow the news less, and know less about some aspects of public affairs, e.g. Buckingham, 2000.)

Civic and political engagement

While local media could no doubt often do more to mobilise people to take part in local public affairs, a growing number of studies have also documented that local journalism significantly increases people's civic and political engagement. Studies have shown that local newspaper use, controlling for socio-economic variables and interest, has a positive influence on involvement in local politics (Scheufele et al., 2002). Across print, broadcast, and digital, attention to local news has been found to influence civic engagement more broadly (Shah et al., 2001). The closure of local newspapers in various American cities has been shown to be followed by significant drops in civic engagement (Shaker, 2012). A range of studies from different countries has also shown that local news media have a positive effect on local election turnout specifically (e.g. Baekgaard et al., 2014; Gentzkow et al., 2009). Conversely, the absence of local news leads to lower turnout than in comparable communities (Filla and Johnson, 2010) and a reduction in the number of newspapers covering a community can reduce political participation even when other local media continue to cover the area (Schulhofer-Wohl and Garrido, 2012).

Clearly, many factors influence overall levels of civic and political engagement, including socio-economic resources, individual motivation, as well as mobilisation efforts, just as many other organisations beyond local news media mobilise people to get involved in local public affairs. But despite fears that superficial journalism and possibly more immediately appealing alternatives like entertainment might depress political participation, most studies seem to suggest that, even with its shortcomings, news generally has a net positive effect on levels of civic engagement. As with the effects of local journalism on political information levels, there is likely to be an 'engagement gap' parallel to the 'knowledge gap' discussed above, where the positive net effects of media use combined with differences in media use result in a growing difference between those who are attentive and engaged and those who do not follow local news and are less engaged in local public affairs (e.g. Jeffres et al., 2002).

Community integration

Finally, researchers have long highlighted the important role that local journalism has played in defining and tying together local communities, and many local media have been as attuned as any social scientist to the intimate connection between communication and community. The great American newspaper editor Horace Greeley famously likened a local newspaper to 'the printed diary of the home town'. Walter Lippmann (1997: 210), working off Greeley's analogy, highlighted how coverage of prosaic aspects of daily life as much as news about public affairs could help people develop a sense of community through shared experience that goes beyond what comes from simply living near each other in an area administratively defined as this or that district, municipality, or canton. Local media help 'orient' us towards each other within a shared geography, they mark the weddings, anniversaries, and funerals of those around us as relevant; they provide a common set of references that goes beyond news to include social events, sports, and the offers of local businesses.

A long tradition of research has substantiated that the connection between local journalism and local community is a significant one. Sociologists have shown how local community papers help people define and maintain neighbourhood identities in large metropolitan areas (Janowitz, 1952) and connect and identify with each other in sparsely populated rural areas (Kirkpatrick, 1995), just as national news media are seen as having been integral to the development of the 'imagined communities' of nation-states (Anderson, 1991). Recently, one team of researchers has shown empirically how what they call 'local media connectedness' increases not only information levels and civic and political engagement but also gives people a sense of community belonging (Kim and Ball-Rokeach, 2006). Even as more and more media – competing for attention in a crowded field, often available over vast distances and differences, in the case of digital media, almost globally – are perhaps more closely tied to distributed communities of interest or commercially attractive segments of consumers than to geographically delineated and localised communities, journalism scholars have highlighted the role of specifically *local* news media in offering people a 'sense of place', something that sets their locale apart from the seeming boundlessness and openness of the wider world (Hess, 2013; Hess and Waller, 2014). Having a local news medium dedicated to covering you and people around you helps mark the identity of the place where you live as *somewhere* and helps mark people there as *someone*. The close ties between local journalism and community integration are not unalloyed boons. Local news helps cultivate consensus, coherence, and stability within a community (Janowitz, 1952) – whether that is a good thing or a bad thing depends on your personal perspective and position in the status quo. In either case, local news media help create what one scholar has called 'communicatively integrated communities' (Friedland, 2001).

Conclusion

Local journalism today is changing in part because of the larger changes underway in our media environments. This transformation puts the future of local journalism as we have known it in question because the business models that have for more than a century supported the profession are under tremendous pressure, and because the very social significance of categories like 'news' and 'journalism' that we have taken for granted sometimes seem in flux. The digital media environment undoubtedly represents considerable potential for inspiring new forms of local journalism, but so far few have managed to realise that potential and establish sustainable forms of born-digital local journalism. Both market and non-market forms of online-only local news production have so far struggled to survive. It is possible that various forms of distributed information production, sharing, and networked journalism in the future can provide many of the same kinds of things local journalism and local news media organisations offer and have offered without having to build similar kinds of organisations with all the costs associated with them. But so far that is largely hypothetical. Meanwhile, newspapers continue to see their print circulation decline, readership decrease, revenues erode, and often in turn cut their investment in local journalism.

Ten years ago, Bob Franklin could conclude in his review of local media in the UK that 'local newspapers are increasingly a business success but a journalistic failure' (2006: 4). Today, not only their journalism, but also the businesses that sustain and sometimes constrain it face an uncertain future. As Clay Shirky (2009) has noted, this is what revolutions are like – 'the old stuff gets broken faster than the new stuff is put in its place'. Sometimes nothing takes the place of that which is broken. This goes for both organisational forms (news media) and social categories (journalism, news). The consequences depend on what one thinks of local journalism as we know it (with variations from case to case, community to community, and country to country). Critics may say that, romanticised images of quaint old hometown papers aside, actually existing local

17

journalism is in fact often superficial and deferential in its reporting, distant from the communities covered, and no longer an integral part of community life. These are important criticisms, whether raised amongst colleagues or by outsiders, as there is certainly always room for improvement. But empirical research suggests that, while far from ideal, local journalism, even with all its imperfections, has served a number of important functions in many local communities. This is more than a 'legitimist vision' of local news media and their social implications (Kuhn and Neveu, 2002). There is compelling evidence that local journalism, despite its shortcomings, is actually often informative and helps people follow local public affairs. Much work suggests that local journalism also helps generate higher levels of civic and political engagement. Finally, researchers have shown how local journalism contributes to community integration, represents communities, and helps tie people together.

Most people would see these demonstrable impacts of local journalism as we know it as broadly speaking positive. Insofar as local journalism is in peril, these effects too are imperilled. Of course, they are not essentially or necessarily tied to local journalism. We can imagine, and surely identify, forms of local journalism more likely to spread misinformation, depress engagement, and divide communities. Similarly, others, beyond local media and local journalism, can help people stay informed about local public affairs, mobilise them to get engaged, and help people maintain a sense of locally rooted community. But today, local journalism in most places seems to contribute to these areas. These contributions are thrown into question as the profession, and the local news media that have historically sustained it, change. The changes currently underway in local journalism point to an uncertain future where people will have access to more and more media, but may well have access to less and less independently reported genuinely *local* news, and where the differences will grow between a shrinking minority who seek out local news and a growing majority who do not regularly follow it. They point towards a future in which, if the trends continue and existing research is anything to go by, we risk seeing much weaker local news media that do less in terms of holding power to account and keeping people informed, less to encourage civic and political engagement, and less to foster community integration than they have in the past (even as digital media offer both individual citizens and local communities many other benefits in other areas beyond news and journalism).

Different aspects of these changes are in focus in the rest of this book. It proceeds in three sections. Part I deals with local media ecosystems and presents different analyses of the interplay between different types of actors and media in the circulation of information in various communities. Part II shifts the focus to local journalism and its interlocutors, and examines the actors involved in how stories come about and how different actors in various communities see each other and evaluate each other's roles. Part III is dedicated to analysis of new forms of local media and looks at the business models and motivations behind various kinds of hyperlocal news sites as well as the kinds of content they produce. Each of these parts starts with a short introduction and overview. Each of them can be read in connection with this book as a whole or as a standalone set of analyses of one particular aspect of local journalism today. They take as their starting point what we know about local journalism as an important source of information, a part of civic and political engagement, and as something that ties communities together, but move beyond this to focus on how local journalism is changing today, and on its uncertain future tomorrow.

Notes

1 In the UK, for example, the BBC operates 12 regions and 43 smaller local radio stations across England, and the Conservative–Liberal Democrat government in 2013 issued 19 local TV licences in their attempt to foster a locally oriented commercial television industry. By comparison, more than 300 local websites are part of the network Openly Local, and more than 1,000 local newspapers are part of the Newspaper Society, all serving much smaller areas than the broadcasters.

2 The definition of local media used throughout this book is tied to territory, that is, local media and regional media are media primarily oriented towards covering more circumscribed geographic areas than national and international media. Historically, their orientation has in large part been defined by their circulation or broadcast area, a seemingly 'natural' delineation that is losing meaning as people can access digital editions of local media from elsewhere. But their identity is still primarily constructed with reference to geography, as is both the business of local commercial media and the political rationale and legitimacy behind local/regional public media. The 'local' in local media is thus revealed not as a given but as a construct, a particular orientation and sense of place of what Kristy Hess (2013) calls 'geo-social news'.

3 Interestingly, recent research on the role-perceptions of local journalists in Australia suggest that they see themselves as both advocates for the local community and as hosting a forum for debate – see Hanusch, 2014.

Bibliography

Aalberg, Toril, and James Curran (eds). 2012. *How Media Inform Democracy: A Comparative Approach*. Routledge New Developments in Communication and Society. New York: Routledge.

Abernathy, Penelope Muse. 2014. *Saving Community Journalism: The Path to Profitability*. Chapel Hill, NC: University of North Carolina Press.

Aldridge, Meryl. 2007. *Understanding the Local Media*. Maidenhead: Open University Press.

Anderson, Benedict R. 1991. *Imagined Communities: Reflections on the Origin and Spread of Nationalism*. Rev. edn. London: Verso.

Anderson, C. W. 2010. 'Journalistic Networks and the Diffusion of Local News: The Brief, Happy News Life of the "Francisville Four"', *Political Communication*, 27(3): 289–309. doi:10.1080/10584609.2010. 496710.

Anderson, C. W. 2013. *Rebuilding the News: Metropolitan Journalism in the Digital Age*. Philadelphia: Temple University Press.

Baekgaard, Martin, Carsten Jensen, Peter B. Mortensen, and Søren Serritzlew. 2014. 'Local News Media and Voter Turnout', *Local Government Studies*, 40(4): 1–15. doi:10.1080/03003930.2013.834253.

Barnett, Steven, and Judith Townend. 2014. 'Plurality, Policy and the Local', *Journalism Practice*: 1–18. doi:10.1080/17512786.2014.943930.

Bennett, W. Lance. 2005. *News: The Politics of Illusion*. 6th edn. New York: Pearson/ Longman.

Brunetti, Aymo, and Beatrice Weder. 2003. 'A Free Press is Bad News for Corruption', *Journal of Public Economics*, 87(7–8): 1801–24. doi:16/S0047-2727(01)00186-4.

Buckingham, David. 2000. *The Making of Citizens: Young People, News and Politics*. London: Routledge.

Castells, Manuel. 2000. *The Rise of the Network Society*. 2nd edn. Oxford: Blackwell Publishers.

Cook, Timothy E. 1998. *Governing with the News: The News Media as a Political Institution*. Chicago: University of Chicago Press.

Costera Meijer, Irene. 2010. 'Democratizing Journalism? Realizing the Citizen's Agenda for Local News Media', *Journalism Studies*, 11(3): 327–42. doi:10.1080/14616700903500256.

Currah, Andrew. 2009. 'Navigating the Crisis in Local and Regional News: A Critical Review of Solutions'. Working Paper. Oxford: Reuters Institute for the Study of Journalism. http://reutersinstitute.politics.ox.ac.uk/sites/default/

files/Navigating%20the%20Crisis%20in%20Local%20%26%20Regional%20 News.pdf.

Dickens, Luke, Nick Couldry, and Aristea Fotopoulou. 2014. 'News in the Community?', *Journalism Studies*, 16(1): 1–18. doi:10.1080/146167 0X.2014.890339.

Donohue, George A., Phillip J. Tichenor, and Clarice N. Olien. 1995. 'A Guard Dog Perspective on the Role of Media', *Journal of Communication*, 45(2): 115–32. doi:10.1111/j.1460-2466.1995.tb00732.x.

Ekström, Mats, Bengt Johansson, and Larsåke Larsson. 2006. 'Journalism and Local Politics', *Journalism Studies*, 7(2): 292–311. doi:10.1080/14616700500533627.

FCC. 2011. *Information Needs of Communities*. www.fcc.gov/info-needs-communities.

Fenton, Natalie (ed.) 2010. *New Media, Old News: Journalism and Democracy in the Digital Age*. London: SAGE.

Filla, Jackie, and Martin Johnson. 2010. 'Local News Outlets and Political Participation', *Urban Affairs Review*, 45(5): 679–92. doi:10.1177/1078087409351947.

Firmstone, Julie, and Stephen Coleman. 2014. 'The Changing Role of the Local News Media in Enabling Citizens to Engage in Local Democracies', *Journalism Practice*, 8(5): 1–11. doi:10.1080/17512786.2014.895516 (accessed June 2014).

Fowler, Erika Franklin, et al. 2007. 'Does Local News Measure Up?', *Stanford Law and Policy Review*, 18: 411.

Fowler, Neil. 2011. *Have They Got News for You? The Past, Present and Future of Local Newspapers in the UK*. Oxford: Nuffield College. http://www.nuffield. ox.ac.uk/Resources/Guardian/Documents/Nuffield%20Guardian%20 Lecture%202011.pdf.

Franklin, Bob. 2006. 'Preface', in Bob Franklin (ed.), *Local Journalism and Local Media: Making the Local News*. London: Routledge, xvii–xxii.

Franklin, Bob, and David Murphy (eds). 1998. *Making the Local News: Local Journalism in Context*. London and New York: Routledge.

Franklin, Bob, and John Richardson. 2002a. 'A Journalist's Duty? Continuity and Change in Local Newspaper Reporting of Recent UK General Elections', *Journalism Studies*, 3(1): 35–52. doi:10.1080/14616700120107329.

Franklin, Bob, and John E. Richardson. 2002b. 'Priming the Parish Pump', *Journal of Political Marketing*, 1(1): 117–47. doi:10.1300/J199v01n01_07.

Friedland, Lewis A. 2001. 'Communication, Community, and Democracy toward a Theory of the Communicatively Integrated Community', *Communication Research*, 28(4): 358–91. doi:10.1177/009365001028004002.

Friedland, Lewis, Philip Napoli, Katherine Ognyanova, Carola Weil, and Ernest J. Wilson. 2012. *Review of the Literature Regarding Critical Information Needs of the American Public.* Washington, DC: FCC. http://transition.fcc.gov/bureaus/ocbo/Final_Literature_Review.pdf.

Gentzkow, Matthew, Jesse M. Shapiro, and Michael Sinkinson. 2009. *The Effect of Newspaper Entry and Exit on Electoral Politics.* Working Paper 15544. National Bureau of Economic Research. http://www.nber.org/papers/w15544.

Giddens, Anthony. 1990. *The Consequences of Modernity.* Stanford, CA: Stanford University Press.

Grueskin, Bill, Ava Seave, and Lucas Graves. 2011. *The Story So Far: What We Know about the Business of Digital Journalism.* New York: Tow Center for Digital Journalism, Columbia Journalism School. http://towcenter.org/wp-content/uploads/2012/11/TOWCenter-Post_Industrial_Journalism.pdf.

Hanitzsch, Thomas. 2011. 'Populist Disseminators, Detached Watchdogs, Critical Change Agents and Opportunist Facilitators: Professional Milieus, the Journalistic Field and Autonomy in 18 Countries', *International Communication Gazette*, 73(6): 477–94. doi:10.1177/1748048511412279.

Hanusch, Folker. 2014. 'A Different Breed Altogether?', *Journalism Studies*: 1–18. doi:10.1080/1461670X.2014.950880.

Heider, Don, Maxwell McCombs, and Paula M. Poindexter. 2005. 'What the Public Expects of Local News: Views on Public and Traditional Journalism', *Journalism and Mass Communication Quarterly*, 82(4): 952–67. doi:10.1177/107769900508200412.

Hess, Kristy. 2013. 'Breaking Boundaries', *Digital Journalism* 1(1): 48–63. doi:10.1080/21670811.2012.714933.

Hess, Kristy, and Lisa Waller. 2014. 'Geo-Social Journalism', *Journalism Practice*, 8(2): 121–36. doi:10.1080/17512786.2013.859825.

Hindman, Matthew. 2011. *Less of the Same: The Lack of Local News on the Internet.* Washington, DC: FCC. https://apps.fcc.gov/edocs_public/attachmatch/DOC-307476A1.pdf.

Huckfeldt, R. Robert, and John D. Sprague. 1995. *Citizens, Politics, and Social Communication: Information and Influence in an Election Campaign.* Cambridge: Cambridge University Press.

Janowitz, Morris. 1952. *The Community Press in an Urban Setting.* Glencoe, IL: Free Press.

Jeffres, Leo W., David Atkin, and Kimberly A. Neuendorf. 2002. 'A Model Linking Community Activity and Communication with Political Attitudes and

Involvement in Neighborhoods', *Political Communication,* 19(4): 387–421. doi:10.1080/01957470290055574.

Kaniss, Phyllis C. 1991. *Making Local News.* Chicago and London: University of Chicago Press.

Kim, Yong-Chan, and Sandra J. Ball-Rokeach. 2006. 'Community Storytelling Network, Neighborhood Context, and Civic Engagement: A Multilevel Approach', *Human Communication Research,* 32(4): 411–39. doi:10.1111/j.1468-2958.2006.00282.x.

Kirkpatrick, Rod. 1995. 'The Mirror of Local Life: Country Newspapers, Country Values and Country Content', in Perry Share (ed.), *Communication and Culture in Rural Areas.* Wagga Wagga: Centre for Rural Social Research, 219–38.

Kuhn, Raymond, and Erik Neveu (eds). 2002. *Political Journalism: New Challenges, New Practices.* London: Routledge.

Kurpius, David D., Emily T. Metzgar, and Karen M. Rowley. 2010. 'Sustaining Hyperlocal Media', *Journalism Studies,* 11(3): 359–76. doi:10.1080/14616700903429787.

Lee-Wright, Peter, Angela Phillips, and Tamara Witschge (eds). 2012. *Changing Journalism.* Abingdon and New York: Routledge.

Levy, David A. L., and Rasmus Kleis Nielsen (eds). 2010. *The Changing Business of Journalism and its Implications for Democracy.* Oxford: Reuters Institute for the Study of Journalism, University of Oxford.

Lippmann, Walter. 1997. *Public Opinion.* New Brunswick, NJ: Transaction Publishers.

Lund, Anker Brink. 2002. *Den Redigerende Magt: Nyhedsinstitutionens Politiske Indflydelse.* Århus: Aarhus Universitetsforlag.

Lund, Anker Brink. 2010. *De Lokale Nyhedsmedier Og Kommunikationsstrategien.* Copenhagen: KL. http://www.kl.dk/ImageVaultFiles/id_41050/cf_202/De_lokale_nyhedsmedier_og_kommunikationsstrategien.PDF.

Lund, Anker Brink, Ida Willig, and Mark Blach-Ørsten. 2009. *Hvor kommer nyhederne fra? Den journalistiske fødekæde i Danmark før og nu.* Århus: Ajour.

Metzgar, Emily T., David D. Kurpius, and Karen M. Rowley. 2011. 'Defining Hyperlocal Media: Proposing a Framework for Discussion', *New Media and Society,* 13(5): 772–87. doi:10.1177/1461444810385095.

Monbiot, George. 2009. 'I, Too, Mourn Good Local Newspapers: But This Lot Just Aren't Worth Saving', *Guardian,* 9 November. http://www.theguardian.com/commentisfree/2009/nov/09/local-newspapers-democracy (accessed August 2014).

Nielsen, Rasmus Kleis. 2012. *Ten Years that Shook the Media World*. Oxford: Reuters Institute for the Study of Journalism.

Ofcom. 2013. *The Communications Market Report: United Kingdom*. London: Ofcom.

O'Neill, Deirdre, and Catherine O'Connor. 2008. 'The Passive Journalist', *Journalism Practice*, 2(3): 487–500. doi:10.1080/17512780802281248.

Örebro, Larsåke Larsson. 2002. 'Journalists and Politicians: A Relationship Requiring Manoeuvring Space', *Journalism Studies*, 3(1): 21–33. doi:10.1080/14616700120107310.

Paulussen, Steve, and Evelien D'heer. 2013. 'Using Citizens for Community Journalism', *Journalism Practice*, 7(5): 588–603. doi:10.1080/17512786.2012.7 56667.

Poindexter, Paula M., Don Heider, and Maxwell McCombs. 2006. 'Watchdog or Good Neighbor? The Public's Expectations of Local News', *Harvard International Journal of Press/Politics*, 11(1): 77–88. doi:10.1177/1081180X05283795.

Prior, Markus. 2007. *Post-Broadcast Democracy: How Media Choice Increases Inequality in Political Involvement and Polarizes Elections*. New York: Cambridge University Press.

Project for Excellence in Journalism. 2010. 'How News Happens'. http://www. journalism.org/analysis_report/how_news_happens.

Rosen, Jay. 1999. *What are Journalists for?* New Haven and London: Yale University Press.

Rosenthiel, Tom, et al. 2012. '72% of Americans follow local news closely', *Pew Research Center*, 12 April. www.pewinternet.org/2012/04/12/72-of-americans-follow-local-news-closely.

Russell, Adrienne. 2011. *Networked: A Contemporary History of News in Transition*. Cambridge: Polity.

Ryfe, David. 2012. *Can Journalism Survive? An Inside Look at American Newsrooms*. Cambridge: Polity.

Sassen, Saskia. 2006. *Territory, Authority, Rights: From Medieval to Global Assemblages*. Princeton: Princeton University Press.

Scheufele, Dietram A., James Shanahan, and Sei-Hill Kim. 2002. 'Who Cares about Local Politics? Media Influences on Local Political Involvement, Issue Awareness, and Attitude Strength', *Journalism and Mass Communication Quarterly*, 79(2): 427–44. doi:10.1177/107769900207900211.

Schulhofer-Wohl, Sam, and Miguel Garrido. 2013. 'Do Newspapers Matter? Short-Run and Long-Run Evidence from the Closure of the *Cincinnati Post*', *Journal of Media Economics*, 26(2): 60–81. doi:10.1080/08997764.2013.785553.

Shah, Dhavan V., Jack M. McLeod, and So-Hyang Yoon. 2001. 'Communication, Context, and Community: An Exploration of Print, Broadcast, and Internet Influences', *Communication Research*, 28(4): 464–506. doi:10.1177/009365001028004005.

Shaker, Lee. 2009. 'Citizens' Local Political Knowledge and the Role of Media Access', *Journalism and Mass Communication Quarterly*, 86(4): 809–26. doi:10.1177/107769900908600406.

Shaker, Lee. 2014. 'Dead Newspapers and Citizens' Civic Engagement', *Political Communication*, 31(1): 131–48. doi:10.1080/10584609.2012.762817.

Shirky, Clay. 2009. 'Newspapers and Thinking the Unthinkable.' www.shirky.com/ weblog/2009/03/newspapers-and-thinking-the-unthinkable.

Snyder, James M., and David Strömberg. 2008. *Press Coverage and Political Accountability*. Working Paper 13878. National Bureau of Economic Research. www.nber.org/papers/w13878.

Stamm, Keith R., Arthur G. Emig, and Michael B. Hesse. 1997. 'The Contribution of Local Media to Community Involvement', *Journalism and Mass Communication Quarterly*, 74(1): 97–107. doi:10.1177/107769909707400108.

St John, Burton, Kirsten Johnson, and Seungahn Nah. 2014. 'Patch.com', *Journalism Practice*, 8(2): 197–212. doi:10.1080/17512786.2013.859835.

Suich, Alexandra. 2014. *Advertising and Technology*. London: The Economist.

Svendsen, Erik Nordahl. 1979. *Avisen i Lokalsamfundet: Skive Folkeblad Og Herning Folkeblad*. Århus: Institut for Presseforskning.

Thurman, Neil, Jean-Christophe Pascal, and Paul Bradshaw. 2012. 'Can Big Media Do Big Society? A Critical Case Study of Commercial, Convergent Hyperlocal News', *International Journal of Media and Cultural Politics*, 8(2–3): 269–85. doi:10.1386/macp.8.2-3.269_1.

Tichenor, P. J., G. A. Donohue, and C. N. Olien. 1970. 'Mass Media Flow and Differential Growth in Knowledge', *Public Opinion Quarterly*, 34(2): 159–70. doi:10.1086/267786.

Tichenor, Phillip J., George A. Donohue, and Clarice N. Olien. 1980. *Community Conflict and the Press*. Beverly Hills, CA: SAGE.

Van Kerkhoven, Marco, and Piet Bakker. 2014. 'The Hyperlocal in Practice', *Digital Journalism* [online]. doi:10.1080/21670811.2014.900236 (accessed June 2014).

Part I

Local Media Ecosystems

Local news can be seen as circulating in local media ecosystems, systems associated with a geographic locale and defined by a population of actors (including media), the interactions between these actors, and their relation with a wider environment. As with other naturalistic analogies, the concept of ecosystem underlines the need to see individual actors as parts of a wider environment. It helps both journalists and journalism researchers see media structures, news production, and the circulation of information about public affairs as something that takes place in a specific and situated context.

As with any other notion of 'local' – local politics, local economy, local community – the precise definition of a 'local media ecosystem' is not a simple task. To delineate an ecosystem for analytical purposes, one can begin with administrative boundaries (a municipality defined by law), economic boundaries (a media market defined by media companies and advertisers), or often contested and rarely clearly demarcated social boundaries defining different communities (our neighbourhood, our town, our part of the city). These definitions of locality do not necessarily coincide (Stacey, 1969), but each can provide a starting point for analysis.

Drawing on the notion of ecosystems as developed in biology, local media ecosystems should be seen as defined by interaction, interdependence, and unequal relations between a wide range of different actors, by collaboration but also competition for often scarce resources, as generative and productive, and as something dynamic and potentially fragile that can be disturbed, radically altered, and ultimately destroyed.

Just like national media systems ('the French media', 'the US media', etc.), local media ecosystems are thus not self-contained or clearly separate from each other in a simple sense, no matter what definition one starts with. They are shot through with, for example, regional economic processes, national policies, and are in part reliant on transnational technological infrastructures. Ecosystems are shaped by both internal and external forces. Facebook and national media like public service broadcasters can be as important as a community radio station in structuring a local media ecosystem. Also, such systems should not be seen as internally homogeneous. A given local media ecosystem operates differently depending on whether you see it from the point of view of a dominant legacy media organisation or a new online-only start-up, from the point of view of an affluent media user coveted by advertisers or someone from a poor and marginalised community.

Seeing local news as part of local media ecosystems is useful in that it directs our attention to questions concerning similarities and differences in how these ecosystems are structured, in what kind of news is produced and made available in them, and how different kinds of news circulate within them. This perspective connects back to a long tradition of media and communication research exemplified by the Chicago School of Sociology, various kinds of community studies, and contemporary forms of institutional analysis (e.g. Janowitz, 1952; Lowrey, 2011; Park, 1938).

Its potential is demonstrated here by three chapters focused on different local media ecosystems. In Chapter 1, Matthew Powers, Sandra Vera Zambrano, and Olivier Baisnée analyse similarities and differences in the structure of local media in Seattle (US) and Toulouse (France) and show how differently they have developed over the last decade as they have dealt with the rise of digital media. In Chapter 2, Rasmus Kleis Nielsen uses a community study of Næstved municipality in Denmark to show how local newspapers, despite their diminished resources and reach, still play a role as 'keystone media' in political information environments. In Chapter 3, C. W. Anderson, Stephen Coleman, and Nancy Thumim analyse similarities and differences in how news circulates across a wider range of actors in two metropolitan areas, namely Philadelphia (US) and Leeds (UK), and identify the 'information ecosystem blockages' that continue to hamper diffusion even in an increasingly digital environment.

All these chapters show how the questions of structure, production, and circulation central to the notion of local media ecosystems in turn help us understand the social, economic, political, and ultimately democratic implications of local journalism and how it is changing.

References

Janowitz, Morris. 1952. *The Community Press in an Urban Setting*. Glencoe, IL: Free Press.

Lowrey, Wilson. 2011. 'Institutionalism, News Organizations and Innovation', *Journalism Studies*, 12(1): 64–79. doi:10.1080/1461670X.2010.511954.

Park, Robert E. 1938. 'Reflections on Communication and Culture', *American Journal of Sociology*, 44(2): 187–205. doi:10.2307/2768727.

Stacey, Margaret. 1969. 'The Myth of Community Studies', *British Journal of Sociology*, 20(2): 134. doi:10.2307/588525.

1

The News Crisis Compared: The Impact of the Journalism Crisis on Local News Ecosystems in Toulouse (France) and Seattle (US)

Matthew Powers, Sandra Vera Zambrano,
and Olivier Baisnée

Introduction

In this chapter, we present a cross-national study of two local news ecosystems: Toulouse (France) and Seattle (US). We ask how and in what ways the news media of these two interestingly similar cities have been impacted by the economic and technological transformations of the past decade (as measured by changes in audience size, newsroom employment, and revenue sources). We then examine how news organisations – print, audiovisual, and online outlets – have responded to these changes (in terms of strategies taken to raise revenues and new journalism ventures that have been started). Finally, we ask journalists in both cities to clarify the sorts of journalism to which they aspire (in terms of their evaluations of journalistic excellence). Throughout, we consider the political, economic, and professional factors shaping similarities and differences between the two news ecosystems.

Our aims are twofold. First, we use cross-national analysis to broaden the scope of local news scholarship. While sophisticated studies of local news exist in both the US and Europe (e.g. Anderson, 2013; Ryfe, 2012; Smyrnaios and Bousquet, 2011), this research is typically confined to a single nation. As a result, local news scholarship precludes analysis of how cross-national variations in market structure, political systems, and professional histories shape the development of local news ecosystems. As we detail below, comparative scholarship helps bring visibility to these otherwise taken-for-granted forces. Second, we use local news to deepen comparative understandings of media systems (Hallin and Mancini, 2004) themselves. To date, comparative research has generally confined itself to a small number of agenda-setting news outlets, which in turn stand in for a country's media system. Whether and how local news media fit within these established media system models thus constitutes an important theory-building opportunity for comparative scholarship.

Drawing on statistical data and interviews, we find that while news media in both cities struggle to find a stable financial footing and adapt to online platforms, the effects of economic and technological change have generally been less severe in Toulouse than Seattle on several measures (job losses, circulation declines) as a result of both government aid and market developments (especially the introduction of free daily newspapers). To an important degree, these forces – themselves rooted in the particular history of the French journalistic field – insulate local news media from upheavals (Benson and Neveu, 2005; Ferenczi, 1993; Neveu, 2009). At the same time, we find that French resilience coexists with low levels of new journalistic ventures and increasingly precarious employment conditions, while in Seattle instability produces very high levels of churn (e.g. the loss of one print newspaper, many newsroom layoffs) but also a surprisingly high number of online initiatives, many of which fail to endure. In neither city do professional ideals correspond to dominant national visions of journalistic excellence as represented in the existing comparative literature. Taken together, these findings suggest that national media systems shape – but do not mechanistically control – how local media ecosystems experience economic and technological transformations.

In what follows, we first introduce the case studies of Toulouse and Seattle and situate them within the larger comparative literature on French–US media scholarship. This approach allows us to analyse impacts on local news ecosystems in terms of cross-national differences while keeping in mind possible contrasts between the local level and national media models. We link these two levels of analysis by discussing how the literature predicts news media in both cities will experience the economic and technological transformations and the degree to which the two cases may diverge from national media models. We then present our comparative analysis of how the two news ecosystems have been impacted by and responded to the economic and technological changes, while also detailing the varying visions of journalism to which professionals in both cities aspire. We conclude by reviewing our findings in light of the extant literature on both local news and comparative research and suggest prospects for future research.

A French–US perspective on local news

Toulouse and Seattle are comparably sized cities located on the geographic periphery of their respective countries (south-western France and north-western US, respectively). Average levels of education and computer use in both are as high, if not higher, than national averages. Economically, large aeronautics and information technology sectors have helped drive a sustained period of economic growth (Toulouse is home to Airbus, Seattle to Boeing). Partly as a result, populations in both cities have boomed over the past several decades. Large universities in both cities also provide sizeable student populations. Thus, while no two cities are strictly equivalent, we can be reasonably sure that by holding roughly constant these demographic and economic features any differences or similarities will be due to the respective news media ecosystems under analysis, rather than other confounding variables.

Over the past decade, media in both Toulouse and Seattle have been subject to the same economic and technological shocks that have wreaked havoc on news media throughout Western Europe and North America. Audiences for legacy media have both aged and shrunk, revenues and staff size for these media have turned downwards, and online technologies have presented a new arena in which legacy and emergent actors compete for growing audiences (Downie and Schudson, 2009; Levy and Nielsen, 2010). As we detail below, Seattle saw one print newspaper stop its print edition entirely and Toulouse saw its main private television channel go out of business. At the same time, in both cities there have been developments within and beyond the traditional newsroom to respond to these changing conditions. In an attempt to capture this empirical heterogeneity, we designate the conglomeration of all news outlets – print, audiovisual, and online – within the geographic boundaries of both cities, an 'ecosystem'.

In selecting Toulouse and Seattle, we aim to build on a large body of comparative research examining similarities and differences in the French and US media (Alexander, 1981; Benson, 2013; Neveu, 2009; Padioleau, 1985). This scholarship consistently finds the two countries' news media to vary considerably in their relationship to both the market and state (with the US media more commercialised and advertising-driven and the French media more reliant on government revenues to fund or subsidise news production). Research also suggests that the two countries' media vary in their professional logics and evaluations of journalistic excellence. Together, these differences form a key component of Hallin and Mancini's (2004) influential theoretical account of comparative media systems. According to Hallin and Mancini, media systems encompass the economic (level of newspaper readership, forms of ownership, etc.), political (level of party pluralism, form of political representation, etc.), and professional (e.g. historical development of journalism) forces that shape journalism in different countries. They conceptualise France and the US as providing opposing media system models, with France's more deliberative and opinion-oriented press contrasted to the US's more commercialised, objectivity-oriented model. Whether and how local news media reflect these models is an important, and to our knowledge underexplored, question.

In order to explore these questions, our chapter proposes three dimensions wherein the news ecosystems of Toulouse and Seattle can be compared: first, in terms of the impact of economic and technological transformations; second, in terms of how news ecosystems respond to these changes; and third, in terms of how journalists in both cities evaluate visions of professional worth. As we review below, the literatures on comparative media and local news suggest slightly different trends and outcomes on each of these three dimensions. Therefore the case studies of Toulouse and Seattle can help empirically adjudicate these accounts while also offering insight into the relative factors shaping how local news media respond to their rapidly changing environment.

The first dimension compares the impact of economic and technological transformations on both local news ecosystems (e.g. figures for audience size, newspaper circulation, newsroom employment, etc. over time). Comparative research suggests the impact to be greater in the more commercially driven US media, while local news scholarship suggests similar cross-national effects as a result of the unique properties of local news media. From a comparative perspective, previous French–US comparisons note how much more exposed US news outlets are to economic cataclysms than their French counterparts (Benson, 2013). The US press is among the world's most commercialised: newspapers draw between 60 and 80% of revenues from advertising (World Association of Newspapers, 2007); audiovisual media are almost entirely commercial entities, apart from a small number of publicly funded television and radio stations. By contrast, the French press relies on a mixture of advertising, sales, and press subsidies, which may serve as a buffer in the face of unfavourable economic conditions. Furthermore, the French audiovisual sector includes a greater mixture of public channels relative to its American counterpart (even though these channels are themselves less popular than their commercial competitors): nationally, seven French television channels are public, while 25 are privately owned (2014 figures). For these reasons, and especially because of the different roles of the public and private actors (Baisnée and Balland, 2011; Benson and Powers, 2011), while we might expect both cities to experience declines in revenue, circulation, audience share, and workforce, comparative insights suggest that the impacts will be felt more acutely in Seattle than in Toulouse.

Local news scholarship offers a slightly different reading of how changing economic and technological conditions will impact local ecosystems. Local media ecosystems tend to be less economically competitive than national news markets, both in terms of audiences and advertising (Picard, 2009). In both Seattle and Toulouse, leading print and television news providers need to cater to and symbolically link geographically proximate but socially diverse audiences: past research suggests that news outlets achieved this goal by focusing news coverage on broad issues of regional identity (Kaniss, 1991; Le Floch, 1997). Given economically and technologically driven trends towards niche news, some have argued that omnibus local news media – especially print newspapers – are imperilled (Jones, 2009). For these reasons, we would expect the impacts to be broadly similar in both cities, especially for legacy news outlets (as indicated by comparable percentage declines in newspaper circulation, television audience share, and newsroom employment).

A second dimension of analysis pertains to the responses made to these economic and technological changes. Comparative scholarship has focused much of its attention in this realm on questions of funding. Scholars note, for example, the role played by the French government in supporting the press (Baisnée and Balland, 2011). In the most recent crisis, the French government provided nearly $1 billion in support to existing news organisations (Wauters, 2009). By contrast, US government policy generally shies away from active intervention in the media business (though it does little to discourage media mergers and corporate consolidation). The loss of a third of the workforce, for example, drew no US government response and government funding of public media is a fraction of what Western European countries provide (Benson and

Powers, 2011). Instead, the US relies primarily on a mix of commercial or non-profit ventures, typically funded through philanthropic foundations (Waldman, 2011). Past partial measures, like Joint Operating Agreements, have largely gone away (Picard, 2007). Because these figures are typically aggregate national totals, the cases here present an opportunity to examine the relative prevalence of these funding strategies as a local response (e.g. number of non-profits, amount of state support) and assess their correspondence to national trends.

Local news scholarship has generally discussed responses in terms of journalism practice, rather than sources of funding. Scholars have noted that some legacy news outlets tend to see digital as a challenge or a threat, thus shaping a reactive and defensive position towards online platforms (e.g. Boczkowski, 2004; Ryfe, 2012). Others have stressed the opportunities that digital technologies present both to legacy news outlets and new journalism start-ups interested in playing a role in news production (Abernathy, 2014; Charon, 2011). Whether different funding structures enable or constrain these different modes of journalism practice is an important, and as yet unaddressed, question. We thus aim to survey the different responses in terms of both funding and practice and ask whether any relationship exists between the two.

Finally, a third dimension on which local news can be analysed is in terms of professional ideals regarding 'quality' journalism. Here, too, we find divergent suggestions in the comparative and local news literatures. Comparative scholars argue that, because national journalistic fields shape specific visions of what constitutes 'good journalism', cross-national evaluations of journalistic excellence will differ accordingly. Specifically, in the US, we expect a stronger emphasis on investigative, public affairs journalism (in keeping with the 'informational' model of American journalism) (Schudson, 2011). In France, we might expect a greater emphasis on deliberation and a particularly Parisian vision of journalism that valorises the role of the press, as seen in journalism oriented to international conflicts or political issues (Gatien, 2012; Neveu, 2009).

Conversely, local news scholarship suggests that the conditions shaping news production differ substantially between local and agenda-setting news media. Because of their geographic proximity, some suggest that local media maintain, or should maintain, a closer connection to their audience – and that this community orientation shapes evaluations of journalistic excellence (Abernathy, 2014; Kaniss, 1991). On this view, journalism practice that is lionised at the national level (e.g. literary orientation in France, a watchdog orientation in the US) might become partially submerged as efforts to engage the community through dialogue and forums prove more popular. Interestingly, these arguments tend to be made across national borders, suggesting a convergence in journalistic visions of excellence at the level of local news.

In sum, local media ecosystems can be analysed along three dimensions: (1) impact, (2) response, and (3) professional journalistic orientations. Comparative research suggests that these dimensions will broadly reflect those found at the national level while local news scholarship posits cross-national similarities across the two cases as a result of the unique economic, political, and professional contexts in which local media ecosystems operate. To be sure, it is possible that media in Seattle and Toulouse do not follow either pattern and are instead marked by local specificities not reducible to either local news or comparative media models. We aim here simply to capture an initial comparison of the two cases and situate them within these two important bodies of scholarship.

Data and methods

This study examines the impacts of economic and technological changes on local media ecosystems. By 'local media ecosystems', we mean any self-identified news outlets – print, audiovisual, or online – in the Toulouse or Seattle region. For Toulouse, we use geographical boundaries (the *département*) defined by the French government, covering the areas of Toulouse-Muret-Saint Gaudens (Haute-Garonne) and comprising roughly 1.3 million inhabitants (2012 figure). For Seattle, we rely on geographic boundaries used by the US census, covering the Seattle-Tacoma-Bellevue area and comprising roughly 3.5 million inhabitants. In both areas, we aim to survey the entire universe of news outlets: daily and weekly newspapers, television and radio, as well as online pure players. For Seattle, we rely on a survey conducted by the Washington News Council which oversees news outlets in the region. We also draw on the expertise of local informants to help identify news organisations omitted from the survey. We rely similarly on the expertise of local informants in Toulouse to ensure that we include all news organisations. In both cases, we include any news outlet that has been in existence at any time since 2008 (where organisations have gone defunct, we note it in the text).

To examine the impact of economic and technological trans-formations on local news ecosystems, we present several indicators.

Drawing on publicly available reporting, we examine over time newspaper circulation and newspapers per capita in both Seattle and Toulouse (including community daily newspapers as well as the major urban newspapers). For both, we present aggregate totals for the metropolitan region, which serve as indicators of the general direction of the daily newspaper industry between the mid-2000s and the present day. We then use these circulation figures to calculate the number of newspapers per 1,000 inhabitants, a commonly used indicator of newspaper density (e.g. Starr, 2004). In subsequent versions of this project, we aim to provide comparable indicators for the audiovisual sector. Given the difficulty – and incomplete nature – of these data at the metropolitan level (especially in Seattle), we are regretfully unable to provide such data at present. Finally, we present data on newsroom employment. These figures count only full-time newsroom staff (journalists, editors, photographers, etc.). This undoubtedly under-reports the total number of individuals working in journalism, as both cities employ a battery of freelance staff. Data for these figures are drawn from publicly available reports; we complement them wherever possible with data from interviews with journalists and local informants.

We examine the response of news actors to economic and technological changes at several levels. Drawing on interview data, we examine the business and professional strategies of legacy news media in their transition to online platforms (e.g. use of paywalls, participation in partnerships with other news outlets, general view on the prospects and threats of online for their media outlets). We complement these interviews with an overview of the revenue sources news media draw upon to fund their work (e.g. government aid, philanthropic funding, commercial ventures). Finally, we survey the number of new online outlets to emerge in the past decade in each city. Together, these data paint an initial picture of the responses taken across the breadth of the local media ecosystem.

Lastly, to examine the role of professional values in shaping journalistic evaluations of quality, we rely on interviews with journalists, editors, and news entrepreneurs in both Seattle and Toulouse. Interview subjects were contacted by email and conducted in person unless otherwise specified. Interviewees were asked to talk about how – or if – the changing economic and technological context shaped their work and, more broadly, how their news organisations were responding to these economic conditions. Finally, interviewees were asked to talk about their notions of 'quality journalism' (typically by talking about stories they or their news organisation had done and about which they were especially proud). At present, we have conducted 15 interviews in total. In addition to these interviews, ongoing informal conversations with Seattle and Toulouse journalists have allowed us to sharpen our understanding of the changing economic contexts in both metropolitan areas.

Findings

Impact of economic and technological transformations

News media, especially print newspapers, in both cities have been adversely impacted over the past decade: print revenue, circulation, and newsroom staffing are all down, while the audiovisual sectors have proven more resilient. These findings confirm local news predictions about secular declines in print news at the local level. At the same time, and in keeping with comparative hypotheses, the effects of economic and technological change have not been equally experienced across the two cities. On most measures, the impacts have been far greater in Seattle, where both per capita newspaper circulation and newsroom employment have been reduced considerably. By contrast, in Toulouse aggregate per capita newspaper circulation has actually increased due to the introduction of free dailies, while newsroom employment has dipped more moderately (even as employment conditions grow increasingly precarious). We suggest that these differences stem from the presence of – and fallout from – more direct competition and greater advertising reliance in Seattle, particularly in the realm of print newspapers.

In both cities, print newspapers have experienced – and continue to experience – substantial circulation and revenue declines. In Toulouse, *La Dépêche du Midi* has seen weekday circulation erode by roughly 17% from 2007 to 2013 (197,751 to 163,897) (OJD, 2014). In Seattle, two newspapers vied for dominance until 2009, when one – the *Post-Intelligencer* – ceased print publication (though it retains an online website). The remaining paper – the *Seattle Times* – now serves the entire metropolitan market. After a brief boost in 2009 (see below), its circulation has declined each year. In both cities, newspapers report declining revenues as news consumption habits and advertising dollars shift to online publishing platforms (Boardman, 2013). As a result, both newspapers have cut jobs in an attempt to cut costs and regain profitability (Fancher, 2011; Smyrnaios and Bousquet, 2011: 3).

The audiovisual sector has proven more resilient than print newspapers in both cities. Informants and interviewees suggest that major news stations in both countries have retained their business profitability and seen audiences diminish only marginally (interview with Mark Briggs, KING 5 Seattle, 13 January 2014; interview with Carlos Bellinchon, France 3, 14 November 2013). In Toulouse, the regional public television provider – France 3 – retains a newsroom staff of approximately 70 journalists. The region's primary private channel – whose audience share is small and declining over time – was recently purchased at 60% by the City Council (see below for details). In Seattle, each of the three commercial news providers – KING 5, KIRO, and KOMO – have roughly 30 newsroom staff. In just the past year, large media conglomerates have acquired two channels (Gannett and Sinclair Broadcast Group). What effects, if any, these ownership changes will have on newsroom staff and news content are at the moment unclear.

In both cities, the radio industry includes a mix of public and commercial operators. All face economic difficulties, though not at the same level as is experienced by print newspapers (in part because they never played the role of primary news provider and thus had smaller newsrooms). In Toulouse, most stations have between 5 and 15% market share. In Seattle, public radio has traditionally been a strong provider of local news programming, though its market share is similarly small (Friedland, 2014). Several commercial providers also offer news. Employment data is as yet unavailable for radio newsrooms.

If Toulouse and Seattle share similar tendencies, the aggregate impacts of economic and technological changes have been, on most measures, far greater in Seattle. In Seattle, total newspaper circulation has dropped 32.7% in the past decade (from 564,773 in 2006 to 380,325 in 2013) while increasing 7.6% in Toulouse (from 160,673 in 2008 to 172,867 in 2012). These shifts have reversed per capita circulation figures in the two cities. In 2006, Seattle had 171 newspapers per 1,000 inhabitants while Toulouse had 129. Today, Toulouse has 136 newspapers per 1,000 inhabitants while Seattle has just 109.

The primary driver of growth in Toulouse is the emergence of free daily newspapers. As with many Western European cities, free dailies like *Metronews* have rapidly gained in circulation over the past decade by distributing their product free of charge and using an advertising model that relies primarily on national advertisements (and thus does not compete with local newspapers for advertising). In *Metronews* or *20 Minutes*, only a third of the advertising inserts deal with regional companies or issues; the remainder are selected, negotiated, and chosen from Paris (Garcia, 2006).

The circulation decline in Seattle stems in large part from the *Post-Intelligencer*'s decision to cease publication of its print edition. Without the loss of that newspaper, we expect circulation declines would have been comparable to those seen at Toulouse's main daily newspaper. At the same time, and somewhat paradoxically, the removal of the *Post-Intelligencer*'s print edition may have provided a temporary boost to the circulation figures of its primary competitor. When the *Post-Intelligencer* ceased publication, its 116,572 print subscriptions were transferred automatically to the *Seattle Times*. Initially, those transferred subscriptions boosted overall figures significantly (from 198,741 in 2008 to 289,000 in 2009). However, the *Times'* circulation has fallen each year since (as of 2013, it is 229,764). Smaller daily newspaper regions, like the *Kitsap Sun*, report declining print circulations over time (interview with David Nelson, *Kitsap Sun*, 14 January 2014). It seems quite likely that circulation figures will continue to drop in the near future.

Both cities have experienced substantial reductions in newsroom employment, though the extent and trajectory of the trend varies. In absolute terms, Seattle has lost a far greater number of journalists than Toulouse (335 versus 50). This number stems from several factors. First, the number of full-time journalists in Seattle was far greater a decade ago. Because the two newspapers competed directly for audiences, both required relatively well-staffed newsrooms. When the *Post-Intelligencer* switched to an online-only format, it cut staff from 165 to 20. After the move, the *Times* also cut staff from a high of 375 in 2004 to about 200 today. While historical employment data is missing, it is likely that percentage declines are less stark in the two cities (because 50 journalists constitutes more than a third of the current workforce in Toulouse). Second, *La Dépêche du Midi* relies heavily on freelance reporters. Cuts to those staff are not counted in our data, though interviewees suggested freelancers and budgets have been slashed in recent years. Third, in France the distribution of journalists is heavily concentrated in Paris as a result of the field's Parisian orientation, leaving fewer journalists in geographically distant cities the possibility of getting hired in a national (Parisian) media outlet (Marchetti and Ruellan, 2001).

Response to economic and technological transformations

In both Toulouse and Seattle, legacy news media seek to transition to online platforms and search for reliable revenue sources. In Toulouse, government aid has been an important source of revenue. Its economic contributions insulate, to a degree, news outlets from technological and economic shocks, even as these contributions tend to reinforce the status quo (e.g. by minimising the development of new news ventures). By contrast, in Seattle, news outlets receive no comparable financial support from the state. This creates more churn but also gives rise to a number of content-sharing partnerships across news outlets as well as a veritable explosion of new online-only ventures, many of which fail to endure.

In neither city have legacy media converged on a single response to economic and technological changes. In Toulouse, some outlets like *La Dépêche du Midi* generally see online as a threat: their business strategies, whose success is unclear, seek to retain audience and build revenue. Others, like France 3, seem to see online as an opportunity to compete with local news outlets in new ways and, perhaps, partially escape the rigid and centralised structure of the public television organisation. In Seattle, the *Times* has implemented an online paywall and sought to partner with local news providers (Boardman, 2013; Fancher, 2011). Other legacy sites have become hosts for online news ventures, as occurred when a magazine (*Seattle Met*) began hosting a news blog (PubliCola). The television stations have invested in mobile platforms (Mark Briggs, KING 5, 13 January 2014). The public radio station has assumed a greater role as a news provider. As one person at the station put it, when the city had two competing newspapers, the radio newsroom saw itself as 'fringe' and 'supplementary to daily newspapers'. Now, she argues, 'our audience ceased to think of us as fringe, and started to think of us more as mainstream' (Carolyn Adolph, KUOW, 8 January 2014).

One primary difference between how the two cities have responded to these changes pertains to the role played by the state as an economic contributor. In Toulouse, the state provides financial support as a way to insulate public and commercial outlets from adverse economic conditions. According to official figures, 7% of each copy of *La Dépêche du Midi* (7 cents per euro) is guaranteed by direct or indirect government subsidies (Data.gouv.fr, 2014). The local private television station remains on air, despite going bankrupt, due to an infusion of public funds (Toulouse City Hall is the majority funder with 60% of the corporate stocks and aid from the Conseil Général under a three-year, €1.5 million package) (Arutunian, 2014). The public station, France 3, remains a major newsroom employer. In Seattle, the state plays no similar role in providing financial support: the loss of one newspaper provoked no government response, nor did the acquisition of local television news stations by large conglomerates. City government does provide infrastructural support to citizen-led efforts for neighbourhood communication (see Friedland, 2014: 105–7) but this is directed primarily at civic ventures, not media outlets.

The effects of this French government aid to media are multiple and somewhat contradictory. On the one hand, the support undoubtedly insulates news outlets during periods of economic turmoil. In both print and television, the state operates to ensure a degree of press pluralism even when the market proves incapable of supporting such a system. On the other hand, this aid also tends to reinforce the status quo and crowd out new journalistic entities and voices. In Toulouse, several different online ventures have been started in the last decade. Several displayed a strong commitment to quality public affairs reporting through in-depth articles and reports (see Chapter 7, this volume). At least one reported achieving a small but dedicated audience (interview with Xavier Lalu, Carré d'info, 19 December 2013). Yet most have closed down due to lack of revenue. Two online ventures – Toulouse7 and ToulouseNews – remain: the first is primarily oriented to local news coverage while the latter aggregates coverage produced by other news outlets.

By contrast, in Seattle there are fewer impediments to starting an online news venture. Indeed, Seattle has seen a veritable explosion of online news sites in the past five years. According to a 2011 count by the Washington News Council, there are at least 90 online ventures within the city limits alone (Fancher, 2011). There are several cases of former journalists (print or television) starting online ventures. A former journalist at the *Post-Intelligencer* started a public affairs reporting site (InvestigateWest). A former television news reporter started a neighbourhood news blog (West Seattle Blog) that has achieved national recognition. The founder of an alternative weekly newspaper helped found a local public affairs site (Crosscut). For all, financial viability remains a key question. Of the 90 sites, many are effectively walking zombies. While their websites exist, they are rarely updated and the journalism on offer is relegated to a part-time hobby. Several key sites have shut down completely due to lack of revenue.

The absence of government funding in Seattle gives new ventures two revenue options: non-profit status (which makes them tax-exempt but limits the amount of advertising they can use) and commercial status (which relies primarily on advertising revenues). While the US has seen much discussion about the non-profit model of journalism (Waldman, 2011), in Seattle the number of such ventures is quite small. In fact, we count only four non-profit outlets in our sample. Those non-profits tend to be reliant on foundations for revenue. Several non-profits discussed pressure from those foundations to find a 'sustainable' business model, suggesting that foundation support aims primarily to build successful business ventures, not supplement the marketplace with media that are not commercially viable. As one person put it: 'Foundations tend to think that two or three years is enough and don't want you dependent [on their support]' (David Brewster, Crosscut, 13 January 2014). Another person expressed a similarly critical sentiment, though from the view of a for-profit site: 'We stopped wasting our time on funders like Knight years ago, when for multiple years in a row, it was made abundantly clear they don't want to help people who are already sort of successful, they just want to give money to people who have "ideas" for something they "might" do' (personal email communication with Tracy Record, West Seattle Blog, 2 January 2014).

For the most part, Seattle's new online ventures are funded by advertising revenue. Unsurprisingly, this proves difficult for most sites to generate. What makes a particular site more or less likely to generate revenues depends on a number of factors, though the successful cases to date suggest the need for a specific neighbourhood or topical niche. West Seattle Blog, for example, serves as a traffic news source – though it of course reports on many other things – for a neighbourhood with only one bridge connecting it to the rest of the city. The majority of its revenue comes from neighbourhood businesses that purchase display advertising. Crosscut, a public affairs site, initially began as a commercial entity but quickly switched to not-for-profit status when it realised that advertiser funds were insufficient to support the venture.

Visions of quality journalism

We find substantial and surprising cross-national differences in how journalists envision their craft. In Seattle, journalists place a strong emphasis on audience engagement, whether this entails talking with their audience online, meeting them at events, or relying on them for news tips. In Toulouse, by contrast, journalists evince a 'peer orientation' that privileges national, rather than local, topics. These findings depart in important ways from traditional French/US distinctions that highlight the literary character of French journalism and the informational character of American models.

Every journalist interviewed in Seattle discussed ways they worked to serve and grow their audiences. This service ranges from providing weather and traffic updates, identifying topical issues of interest to the community, to engaging the community in debate. While the specific nature of the audience relation varies from one outlet to the next, the prevalence and prominence of audience talk is striking. Thus, someone working in the digital department at the local television station says: 'We try to take a very user-centric approach to everything and so if we're going to do something that's going to be popular and useful, we grow that audience and hope it will turn into revenue for us at some point' (Mark Briggs, KING 5 Seattle, 13 January 2014). At the public radio station, a journalist stressed that 'people here really like their listeners. And other forms of media that I've been with, people have, they have not liked their readers. They feel that their readers are stupid, they are callous, they mistake their trolls for being their readers' (Isolde Rafferty, KUOW, 8 January 2014). Importantly, for all interviewees, serving the audience was tightly linked with their evaluation of what constitutes quality journalism.

In Toulouse, it is quite rare to hear journalists talk about audiences in this way, when they talk about them at all. Instead, journalists tend to evaluate notions of journalistic quality vis-à-vis their relations with other journalists. This vision of quality privileges national topics and de-emphasises local journalism as a site for quality journalism per se. Put bluntly: the more local a media outlet (and the journalist working for it), the less legitimate it appears within the journalistic field. At France 3, for instance, one journalist discussed how the regional office had little autonomy vis-à-vis the national office. 'France is still a very Jacobin country: it's Paris, Paris, and Paris again' (Carlos Bellinchon, France 3, 14 November 2013). In comparison with Seattle, it is striking that no Toulouse news organisations, including the few online-only ventures, engaged in hyperlocal journalism, even though the advertising potential for such a venture seems to exist.

To be sure, Seattle journalists sometimes discuss their relationships with other news organisations. Yet these discussions typically refer to other local journalists, not national newspapers based in New York or Washington, DC. For the most part, such discussions focus on how Seattle news outlets can partner with one another to provide content to audiences in a way that maximises visibility for all partners. This, for example, is the logic behind the *Seattle Times'* use of local blog partners. On its online home page, the paper features news from verified local bloggers, giving the *Times* needed content in the face of staff cuts and the bloggers visibility they would otherwise struggle to achieve. The implications of these partnerships for the broader news ecology – that is, who and what moves through these networks – has yet to be explored.

In our view, it seems that the *expression* of journalistic quality changes at the local level vis-à-vis the national one, even as their structural positions remain similar. That is, in neither Toulouse nor Seattle do we hear journalists talking about 'literary' or 'informational/objective' models of journalism. Nor, however, do we find cross-national convergence due to some unique features of local news production. Instead, Seattle journalists talk about audiences, in part because the journalistic field as a whole is more dominated by market logics (and thus questions of audience satisfaction appear intuitive to all its actors, even as differentially situated actors pursue different strategies through which to achieve such satisfaction). Conversely, the combined insulation of the French journalistic field and its centralised orientation leads most journalists in Toulouse to evaluate quality in terms and topics that originate in Paris.

Conclusion

Our analysis suggests the news ecosystems of both Toulouse and Seattle have been adversely impacted by the economic and technological transformations of the past decade. In both cities, audiences, newsroom employment, and revenues are all on the decline. Yet our analysis also finds that the effects of these shocks have been less severe in Toulouse than Seattle as a result of government aid and the entrance of free dailies into the market. To an important degree, these forces – themselves rooted in the particular history of the French journalistic field – insulate local news media somewhat from economic and technological changes. At the same time, this insulation corresponds to low levels of journalistic innovation as well as increasingly precarious employment conditions. In Seattle, these same shocks have produced a great deal of churn and lots of uncertainty – but also a surprisingly high level of journalism innovation, as evidenced in the number and variety of online ventures.

Taken together, these findings suggest that local news ecosystems do indeed differ cross-nationally, but not always in the ways that comparative research predicts. While the extent and nature of changing economic and technological contexts has been lesser in Toulouse, it is not only because of government support: the emergence of free dailies, which boost per capita circulation, constitute a market-driven innovation made possible in part by the centralised nature of the French journalistic field. In Seattle, city government provides infrastructural support for civic communication, suggesting that while state aid to media outlets remains a political non sequitur, local governments may play an important role in shaping the depth and range of local news ecosystems. Further, the evaluations of journalistic excellence clearly differ in form from those posited at the national level.

At the same time, it is important not to overstate these deviations from the cross-national literature. In Seattle, city support remains targeted at civic ventures, not media outlets (Friedland, 2014). Further, non-profit status constitutes a small portion of the news players and is typically oriented towards a goal of future profitability. In general, commercial logics remain the dominant lens through which most Seattle journalists attempt to reinvigorate and reinvent their profession. More generally, in both cities national journalistic fields shape the range of possible responses to the economic and technological flux, but not always in ways that can be mechanically deciphered by knowing how news outlets operate and seek revenue at the national level. For all these reasons, further cross-national research on local news media – both within and beyond the two locales studied here – is needed.

This analysis offers a preliminary portrait of two cities with news ecosystems in transition. Moving forward, several lines of inquiry are important to develop a better sense of the changes. While we do not examine news content here, a more systematic analysis of news content is necessary to capture the degree to which news coverage has and has not changed over time – in both quantity and style of coverage. Such an analysis will further aid in problematising and refining extant national media system models. Moreover, and given the increasingly 'networked' (Russell, 2011) nature of journalism, analysing the relationship between different news actors is an important research problem to address. In Seattle, early evidence suggests that mainstream legacy sites espouse

47

some openness to partnering with online ventures, while this seems less prevalent in Toulouse (at least at its newspaper). More empirical and analytical detail of this process is needed in both cities. Finally, we know of very little research that examines where and how people actually consume local news. Assessing questions about the sufficiency of contemporary local ecosystems to address civic needs requires such an understanding.

Obviously, these are concerns that lie beyond the scope of this chapter. But they are concerns that point to the many opportunities the study of local news offers to comparative scholars (and vice versa). If comparative scholarship can help contextualise the developments of local news and make visible the various factors shaping those developments, then local news scholarship can also be used to refine, and perhaps problematise, extant theoretical models of media systems. Together, locally informed comparative scholarship can help provide both empirical and theoretical frameworks that are more sensitive to both the panoply of existing news media as well as the various civic needs they aim, however imperfectly, to support.

Bibliography

Abernathy, P. 2014. *Saving Community Journalism: The Path to Profitability*. Chapel Hill, NC: University of North Carolina Press.

Alexander, J. 1981. 'The Mass News Media in Systemic, Historical and Comparative Perspective', in E. Katz and T. Szecsko (eds), *Mass Media and Social Change*. Beverly Hills, CA: SAGE, 17–51.

Anderson, C. W. 2013. *Rebuilding the News: Metropolitan Journalism in the Digital Age*. Philadelphia: Temple University Press.

Arutunian, S. 2014. 'TLT, la Mairie de Toulouse dément vouloir fermer la chaîne locale mais fixe de nouveaux objectifs', *ObjectifNews*, 16 May. www.objectifnews.com/Business/tlt-toulouse-tele-moudenc-schwartzenberg-media-presse-com-15052014.

Association des journalistes de Toulouse et Midi-Pyrénées. 2013. 'Le Déclin continu de la presse écrite en Midi-Pyrénées.' www.ajt-mp.org/spip.php?article466.

Baisnée, O., and L. Balland. 2011. 'France: Much Ado About (Almost) Nothing?', in T. Eberwein, S. Fengler, E. Lauk, and T. Leppik-Bork (eds), *Mapping Media Accountability: In Europe and Beyond*. Cologne: Halem, 63–76.

Benson, R. 2013. *Shaping Immigration News: A French–American Comparison*. Cambridge: Cambridge University Press.

Benson, R., and E. Neveu (eds). 2005. *Bourdieu and the Journalistic Field.* Cambridge, MA: Polity.

Benson, R., and M. Powers. 2011. *Public Media and Political Independence.* Washington, DC: Free Press Policy Report.

Boardman, David. 2013. 'Digital Subscriptions Needed to Support Quality Journalism', *Seattle Times.* http://www.seattletimes.com/seattle-news/digital-subscriptions-needed-to-support-quality-journalism/.

Boczkowski, P. 2004. *Digitizing the News: Innovation in Online Newspapers.* Cambridge, MA: MIT Press.

Charon, J. M. 2011. *La Presse en ligne.* Paris: La Découverte.

Data.gouv.fr. 2014. 'Montants d'aides pour les 200 titres de presse les plus aidés.' www.data.gouv.fr/dataset/montants-d-aides-pour-les-200-titres-de-presse-les-plus-aides.

Downie, L., and M. Schudson. 2009. 'The Reconstruction of American Journalism', *Columbia Journal Review.* www.cjr.org/reconstruction/the_reconstruction_of_american.php?page=all.

Fancher, M. 2011. *Seattle: A New Media Case Study.* Pew Research Center's State of the News Media. http://stateofthemedia.org/2011/mobile-survey/seattle-a-new-media-case-study.

Ferenczi, T. 1993. *L'Invention du journalisme en France: naissance de la presse moderne à la fin du XIXème siècle.* Paris: Plon.

Friedland, L. 2014. 'Civic Communication in a Networked Society', in J. Girouard and C. Sirianni (eds), *Varieties of Civic Innovation: Deliberative, Collaborative, Network, and Narrative Approaches.* Nashville, TN: Vanderbilt University Press, 92–126.

Garcia, G. 2006. *La Presse gratuite: la production de l'information au service de l'économie. Une étude comparative du journal* 20 Minutes *en France et en Espagne.* Master's thesis under the advice of Olivier Baisnée, Institut d'Etudes Politiques.

Gatien, E. 2012. *Prix Albert Londres, prix journalistique et transformations du journalisme.* Paris: Fondation Varenne/LGDJ.

Hallin, D., and P. Mancini. 2004. *Comparing Media Systems: Three Models of Media and Politics.* Cambridge: Cambridge University Press.

Jones, A. 2009. *Losing the News.* New York: Oxford.

Kaniss, P. 1991. *Making Local News.* Chicago: University of Chicago Press.

Le Floch, Patrick. 1997. *Economie de la presse quotidienne régionale.* Paris: L'Harmattan.

Levy, D., and R. K. Nielsen (eds). 2010. *The Changing Business of Journalism and its Implications for Democracy.* Oxford: Reuters Institute for the Study of Journalism.

Marchetti, D., and D. Ruellan. 2001. *Devenir journalistes: Sociologie de l'entrée sur le marché du travail*. Paris: La Documentation Française.

Neveu, E. 2009. *Sociologie du journalisme*. Paris: La Decouverte.

OJD. 2014. 'Chiffres de diffusion de la presse payante grand public'. www.ojd.com/Support/la-depeche-du-midi.

Padioleau, J. G. 1985. *Le Monde et le Washington Post*. Paris: Presses Universitaires de France.

Picard, R. 2007. 'Natural Death, Euthanasia and Suicide: The Demise of Joint Operating Agreements', *Journal of Media Business Studies*, 4(2): 41–64.

Picard, R. 2009. 'Tremors, Structural Damage and Some Casualties, But No Cataclysm: The News about News Provision'. Background paper presentation at the US Federal Trade Commission Workshop. www.robertpicard.net/files/PicardFTCbackgroundpaper.pdf.

Russell, A. 2011. *Networked: A Contemporary History of Journalism in Transition*. Cambridge: Polity.

Ryfe, D. 2012. *Can Journalism Survive? An Inside Look at American Newsrooms*. Cambridge: Polity.

Schudson, M. 2011. *The Sociology of News*. New York: Norton.

Smyrnaios, N., and F. Bousquet. 2011. 'The Development of Local Online Journalism in South-Western France: The Case of *La Dépêche du Midi*', in R. Salaverría (ed.), *Diversity of Journalisms*. Proceedings of the ECREA Journalism Studies Section. Pamplona: University of Navarra, 347–58.

Starr, P. 2004. *The Creation of the Media: Political Origins of Modern Communications*. New York: Basic Books.

Waldman, S. 2011. *The Information Needs of Communication*. Washington, DC: FCC.

World Association of Newspapers. 2007. *World Press Trends*. Paris: World Association for Newspapers and Zenith Optimedia.

Wauters, C. 2009. 'State Aid and 10 Commandments to Revive the French Press', *European Journalism Centre*. http://ejc.net/magazine/article/state-aid-and-10-commandments-to-revive-french-press.

2

Local Newspapers as Keystone Media: The Increased Importance of Diminished Newspapers for Local Political Information Environments

Rasmus Kleis Nielsen

Introduction

Daily newspapers may become more important for local journalism and local political information environments even as their editorial resources and audience reach is diminished, because they are increasingly the only news organisations doing day-to-day reporting on local public affairs. They may no longer be *mainstream media* – as in many places the majority does not rely on local newspapers directly as a source of information. But they are *keystone media*, media that are the primary providers of a specific and important kind of information and enable other media's coverage, and thus have 'ecological' consequences that reach well beyond their own audience. That is my argument in this chapter, based on a mixed-method study of a strategically chosen case community in Denmark, a country characterised by comparatively high levels of digital media use, a strong tradition of newspaper journalism, and well-funded public service media organisations. On the basis of a combination of survey data, content analysis, and interviews with politicians, journalists, and citizens in the case community, Næstved (a provincial municipality with a population of 81,000), I examine the local political information environment and show that the local newspaper, *Sjællandske*, while reaching fewer people than it has historically, occupies an increasingly central position as a key provider of independent and professionally produced news about public affairs in an area where people have access to more and more media, but less and less local news.

Living in a highly and increasingly digitised media environment, citizens in Næstved can access media content from many different sources. They can peruse material from the local newspaper organisation, which operates a daily print paper, a website, a free weekly paper, and a commercial radio station. They can read one or more of several weekly home-delivered community freesheets. They enjoy the services of two different regional licence-fee-funded public service broadcasters (one organised around television, the other around radio, both with websites as well), a volunteer-driven community radio station, and a multitude of national and international media available on various platforms. They have access to a variety of online-only offerings including social media and a range of websites, amongst them the municipal government's own. (Despite the high levels of internet use and the generally high levels of participation in civic associations in Denmark, no hyperlocal or citizen journalism sites have emerged in the community, and bulletin boards with a local focus have very low levels of activity.[1]) But if citizens want independent and professionally produced news about local public affairs, closer scrutiny shows that most of what is available originates from a single source, the local newspaper, whose newsroom is still primarily funded by its eroding print business.

In the first part, I present the chapter's theoretical and methodological basis in the idea of political information environments, new institutionalist approaches to journalism, and in the community studies tradition that was so important in the early development of media and communication research. In the second part of the chapter, I explain the choice of the strategic case community examined here and present the main sources of data. In the third part, I show empirically how the local newspaper in the community at hand, despite its diminished reach in an increasingly digitised media environment, is occupying an increasingly important position in the local news environment as the main provider of independent, professionally produced news – content that other, more widely used, media in turn rely on when it comes to their coverage of local public affairs. In the final part, I discuss the wider implications of the study in terms of the central position occupied by the local newspaper, in terms of the relevance of the findings beyond Denmark, and in terms of the future prospects for local political information environments as newspapers continue to lose ground.

Local information environments, institutionalism, and the community studies tradition

People need access to information to engage with a complex world, in particular if they want to be equipped to be active citizens in a democracy. This is as true at the local level as it is at the regional, national, and international level, underlining the importance of understanding the political information environments that people live in locally. People need many different kinds of information in their daily lives, and only some of them are provided on a regular basis by journalists (Friedland et al., 2012). But amongst these are information about local politics (broadly conceived), and there, professionally produced news plays a central role. Scholars have defined *political* information environments in terms of the supply of information about public affairs routinely made available to and used by people in a given locale and a given media context (Aalberg et al., 2010; Curran et al., 2009; Esser et al., 2012). So far, the approach has mainly been used to advance our understanding of important *national* variations in how different media systems help people stay informed about public affairs (e.g. Aalberg and Curran, 2012). By transposing the concept to the local level, in this chapter I examine instead a *local* information environment in terms of the information available and actually used by people within a single municipality. I focus in particular on (1) the various *sources* of information people say are important for how they follow local politics and (2) the information actually *produced* and made available by these sources. On this basis, I identify the role of the local newspaper in the overall local political information environment.

In my analysis of the local political information environment, I draw on two intellectual inspirations in particular. The first inspiration is the work of Anker Brink Lund, who in a series of studies carried out with different collaborators has developed a specifically institutional approach to the naturalistic metaphors of 'ecology', 'environment', and 'ecosystem' that are widespread in media and communication studies. Based on a number of extensive empirical studies carried out in Denmark, Lund has shown how some news organisations play an outsize role in what he calls the news 'food chain', as stories published by these outlets tend to spread to a wider audience as they are copied, quoted, and elaborated on by other media (Lund, 2000; Lund et al., 2009). News agencies are the most obvious examples, but some radio and television shows and particular news websites and newspapers occupy a similar role in influencing how stories spread in the course of a news cycle. Here, I am interested in capturing a related dynamic, but in terms of the news available in a specific political information environment rather than in terms of how news spreads across platforms in the course of a news cycle. I define media organisations that occupy a critical role in political information environments as 'keystone media', drawing on the notion of 'keystone species' developed in conservation biology and zoology to capture the critical importance of particular species. Keystone species are those which, despite being only a small part of a larger interconnected ecology, play an outsize role in defining the state and structure of the wider environment.[2] In parallel, keystone media are characterised by their *systemic importance*, their importance not for the majority of media users, but for the wider information environment they live in. The key idea I take from Lund's institutionalist approach to political information environments is that to understand their true ecological role we should not look at news organisations in isolation but as part of an environment characterised by specific, empirically identifiable relations and interactions – in line with the idea of local media ecosystems shared throughout this section of the book. I define keystone media as media that in a particular media ecosystem (a) are the *main providers of specific and important types of information* and (b) *enable other media* to cover these issues. Keystone media are thus media that structure the local political information environment well beyond their own resources or reach. In the case analysed, a newspaper organisation occupies this role. In other media ecosystems, there might not be any keystone media, or there might be several. Other kinds of organisations or entities, like a broadcaster, a group blog, or the media outlets of a local civil society association, can of course occupy a similar role.

The second inspiration is the community studies tradition that played a key role in the early development of media and communication research through the work of the Chicago School, associated especially with Robert E. Park, and the Columbia School, led by Paul F. Lazarsfeld. Robert E. Park and his colleagues at the University of Chicago were interested in what they called 'human ecologies', relying on many of the same naturalistic metaphors currently enjoying a resurgence in media and communication studies. For Park, human ecology dealt with the relationship between man and his social, material, and natural environment, and was best studied as situated interwoven practices with a 'natural history' developing over time (Park, 1938). He and his students took as their object of study primarily the urban environment of the rapidly expanding and changing metropolis they lived in – the city of Chicago in the 1920s and 1930s. A former journalist and a scholar much influenced by pragmatist philosophy, early symbolic interactionism, and the ideas of Gabriel Tarde and Georg Simmel, Park was particularly interested in the role of communication in maintaining communities in space and time and in the news media's role in integrating individuals in different communities (Park, 1974). He was conscious both of the localising effect of some media – even going so far as to suggest that metropolitan regions in the US might best be defined in terms of the circulation area of particular newspapers – and the cosmopolitan orientation of others, such as the transnational communities that newcomers in Chicago and elsewhere could be part of through immigrant newspapers ('imagined communities' *avant la lettre*). Paul F. Lazarsfeld is today remembered as a pioneer in developing many key ideas in mass communication research and behaviouralist social science as well as a path-breaking survey researcher and quantitative analyst who has greatly influenced how media research, sociology, and political science are actually practised. What is often overlooked is how much his early, theoretically and empirically rich, work in the 1930s and 1940s had in common with the Chicago School of Sociology represented by, amongst others, Park. Lazarsfeld's enormously influential early studies of the formation of political attitudes, of the flow of information, and of voting decisions were in fact community studies based on close, multi-method studies of individual, spatially and socially situated towns similar to the Chicago tradition (Berelson et al., 1954; Katz and Lazarsfeld, 2006; Lazarsfeld et al., 1968). His ideas about media effects, two-step flows, and the social context of political behaviour were not developed from nationally representative samples of individuals, but on the basis of a combination of fieldwork, qualitative interviews, and community surveys in Erie County, Ohio, Elmira, New York, and Decatur, Illinois.

The key theoretical and methodological idea I take from the community studies tradition represented by Park and Lazarsfeld is that if we want to understand media and communication we cannot limit ourselves to studying on the one hand the individual media users, small primary groups, or individual media organisations at the centre of much of audience research and journalism studies or on the other hand the national media structures or nationally representative samples of much comparative media system research and political communication research. We *also* have to study the flow of information in actually existing socially and spatially situated communities – what is available, what is used, what do people make of it, and how do local political information environments develop and change over time? We cannot take locality or communities as unproblematic 'givens'; they do not simply exist out there as neatly demarcated objects of analysis. But we can take them as starting points, and examine the role of media in defining locales, connecting communities, and making it possible for those who live in them to stay informed about public affairs.

Mapping a local political information environment

The community in focus in this chapter, Næstved, is a critical case study for the state of local political information environments in Denmark (with possible wider implications that I discuss in the final part of the chapter). The community was chosen based on three criteria as part of a larger research project on local political communication and democracy in a changing media environment, pursued together with Nina Blom Andersen and Pernille Almlund from Roskilde University and conducted in the run-up to the November 2013 nationwide Danish municipal elections.[3] First, we wanted to study a community that was far enough away from the metropolitan region of greater Copenhagen that it could be meaningfully considered a distinct community rather than a suburb (about a quarter of the Danish population lives and/or works in the greater Copenhagen region). Second, we wanted a community in which there are still functioning local media (unlike some marginalised small provincial municipalities and many of the suburban municipalities adjacent to Copenhagen). Third, we wanted a municipality that was politically competitive so that citizens have higher incentives to follow local public affairs. Næstved fulfils all three criteria, making it a critical case study of the state of local political information environments, a best-case scenario compared to, say, a municipality with no distinct sense of community, no local media, and a one-sided local political situation. It is also a community studied during the election campaign itself, presumably a period of heightened attention to local public affairs. Our starting point was the administrative definition of Næstved as a municipality with clearly demarcated geographical borders, a definite population, and a formal political structure nested within the wider Danish political system (leaving it an open question to what extent people living in the area identified with Næstved and saw themselves as part of one or more local communities there).

This gives us a case community with about 82,000 inhabitants, half of them living in the central town after which the municipality is named. The area is covered by a range of different news media. First, Næstved is home to a local newspaper, *Sjællandske*, where a newsroom of seven journalists produce content for a daily print edition and its website, and work with four more journalists working for the same publisher, who produce a separate weekly paper (*Ugebladet Næstved*) and news for a local commercial radio channel (at the time, it also ran a 24/7 regional rolling news channel available online and on cable television, since closed). The paper also covers two smaller, adjacent municipalities, but Næstved is its main focus, centre of operations, and main circulation area. Second, people in the municipality live within a larger area serviced by two different licence-fee-funded regional public service broadcasters, one based around television (TV2Øst, with 17 journalists) and one based around radio (DR Sjælland, with 19 journalists), both with websites too. These two public service broadcasters both cater for a regional audience of about 600,000 citizens and cover 12 municipalities (their broadcast areas overlap but are not completely identical), stretching about 200 km from north to south and covering more than 6,000 km². Third, people in Næstved have access to three other weekly freesheets published by other companies, one distributed to all households in the whole municipality (*Næstved Bladet*) and two oriented specifically towards some of the smaller villages (*Fuglebjerg Posten* and *Glumsø Ugeblad*), as well as a local community radio station run by volunteers (Næstved Lokalradio). Fourth, people have access to various forms of stakeholder media ranging from the professionally run and continually updated municipal government website to the rather more unevenly maintained websites of the local political parties and the (sometimes eagerly updated) social media profiles of local politicians. Fifth, of course, people in Næstved have access to a range of national Danish news media as well as international offerings including various forms of social media. Finally, they have access to each other, to conversation with families and friends, as well as personal contact with local politicians. (It is worth noting that people in Næstved do not have access to any online-only local news media, any established local bloggers – apart from one infrequently blogging city council member – or any lively bulletin boards focused on local affairs.) The local media system is thus generously supplied by many kinds of media. In this respect, Næstved reflects the situation in much of the rest of Denmark. Local newspaper markets consolidated into local monopolies in most towns in the 1950s and 1960s. (The disappearance of the politically diverse party press and the emergence of local monopoly catch-all papers raised plurality concerns, but to some extent the decline of external pluralism was countered by increased internal pluralism in the surviving titles.) Regional public service broadcasting was established first on radio in the 1960s and later on television in the late 1980s. The rise of digital media from the 1990s onwards has seen Danes become avid internet and social media users – with some of the highest levels of use in the world – but has, despite several attempts, not seen the emergence of any significant and sustainable online-only local media so far. The availability of a wide range of media in the community is important to underline because, even in this media-rich context, the importance of the local newspaper stands out.

As part of our larger research project on local political communication and municipal democracy in a time of media change, we used a combination of methods to map the flow of information in Næstved. First, we conducted a telephone-based survey of Næstved's population with 1,450 representative respondents and a range of questions about media use, forms of civic and political engagement, and relative satisfaction with the state of local politics and municipal affairs. Second, we collected all editorial content produced by the main local media (the newspaper *Sjællandske*, the two regional public service broadcasters TV2Øst and DR Sjælland, and the various smaller local media) as well as all information posted on websites and social media by all candidates for city council and by the municipal government for a three-week period leading up to the 19 November 2013 municipal elections. A total of 6,540 units were collected and coded. Of these, 5,298 were editorial units produced by the main local and regional media (the rest were mostly website and Facebook postings from candidates running for city council). Third, we completed ten one-on-one semi-structured telephone interviews with individual citizens sampled on the basis of socio-economic status and self-reported engagement in local affairs and five focus groups sampled to ensure a diverse group from a range of different locales within the municipality to produce data on different people's own experience of their engagement with local politics and public affairs in Næstved. We also did extensive fieldwork in the municipality and conducted interviews with local politicians, journalists, and citizen activists.

Sources of and producers of information about local politics

In this part of the chapter, I use our survey data, content analysis, and interviews to address the two core questions raised here about the local political information environment. First, what are the various *sources* of information people say are most important for how they follow local politics? Second, what kind of information is actually *produced* and made available by these sources? It is on the basis of this analysis that I will advance the argument that the local newspaper, despite its diminished reach and resources, actually plays an increasingly important role as a 'keystone medium' in the local political information environment, qualifying as (a) the main provider of distinct and important kinds of information and (b) as enabling other media to cover these aspects in the community.

Sources of information

First, in our survey, we asked people to rate a range of possible sources of information in terms of how important they considered them for how they stayed informed about local politics. We included a range of possible means of accessing information about local affairs and establishing 'public connections' (Couldry et al., 2010). We operated with four broad kinds of sources:

(1) national news media sources;
(2) local news media sources;
(3) online-only sources; and
(4) offline interpersonal sources.

In terms of national news media, we included just one question asking whether the respondent used any kind of national media, whether one of the main broadcasters or main newspapers, whether offline or online. In terms of local news media, we asked about the main local brands, including questions about the local newspaper (*Sjællandske*), each of the two regional public service broadcasters (TV2Øst and DR Sjælland), and the weekly freesheets available in the municipality. In each case, we asked about brand, not platform, so reading the newspaper online or accessing a regional broadcaster via mobile is recorded the same as a reading in print or listening via FM. In terms of online-only media, as there are no hyperlocals, citizen journalism websites, or active bulletin boards, we asked only about whether people used the websites or social network profiles of local parties or politicians, whether they used the social networking site Facebook, or the microblogging service Twitter as a source of information about local politics. Finally, we asked about a range of possible interpersonal sources of information about local politics, including conversation with family and friends, personal contact with politicians, personal contact with party members or campaign volunteers, or town hall meetings. Table 2.1 presents the responses from our representative sample, including summarising results for the percentage of people who rate at least one of the options in each category 'important' or 'very important' for how they stay informed about local politics.[4]

Table 2.1 Relative importance of ways of staying informed about local politics

	'Important' + 'Very important'
(1) National news media sources (one or more)	54%
(2) Local news media sources (one or more)	80%
– Local newspaper	32%
– Regional public service TV	55%
– Regional public service radio	30%
– Weekly freesheets	45%
(3) Online-only sources (one or more)	19%
– Political websites and/or SNS profiles	15%
– Social networking sites (Facebook)	11%
– Microblogging service (Twitter)	2%
(4) Offline interpersonal sources (one or more)	70%
– Conversation with family and friends	61%
– Personal contact with politicians	29%
– Personal contact with party/campaign volunteers	20%
– Town hall meetings	12%
No source rated 'Important'/'Very important'	8%

Data from telephone survey of Næstved ($N = 1450$), question wording 'How important would you say the following are for how you follow local politics (if you follow local politics)?'

Our data confirm that local news media overall remain the single most widely used kind of source of information about local politics. 80% of the respondents find at least one of the local or regional news media important or very important. Regional public service television (55%) and local weekly freesheets (45%) are the most widely used kinds of local news media. Offline interpersonal communication (70%), especially conversation with family and friends (61%), is the second most widely used source of information about local politics. National news media make a surprisingly strong showing, given their dearth of actual local content (54%). Online-only sources, on the other hand, are only used by a minority (19%). This is in a sense surprising. Most Danes live highly digitally connected lives, and almost all local politicians have a website and/or a social networking site profile. But only 15% find political websites important or very important sources of information about politics, and though social media are widely used for social purposes, only 11% report that Facebook is an important or very important source of information about politics (2% for Twitter). This is not because politicians are not on Facebook. It is because people do not really seem to 'like' most politicians on Facebook (as shown elsewhere, e.g. Nielsen and Vaccari, 2013). In interviews and focus groups, people would sometimes talk about having discussed politics with friends of theirs on Facebook, and some follow local and regional media, who all operate Facebook pages. But no one interviewed individually or in focus groups followed a local politician. Twitter was even less popular. Not only did very few citizens report accessing information this way, there was very little information to access. Just 40 Tweets appear under the hashtag #Naestvedpol; 31 of these come from just two candidates for city council (neither of whom were elected).

Our survey produces a picture of a relatively connected local citizenry and a community where most people use multiple sources of information to follow local politics. Only 8% do not consider *any* of the above-mentioned sources of information important or very important for how they stay informed about local politics. The survey shows Næstved as a community shot through with national media, used not only to understand national and international issues, but also considered by many a source of information about local affairs. It presents a community where regional public service television, local weekly freesheets, and conversation with families and friends are the most widely relied upon sources of information about public affairs. Only a third of the respondents consider the local newspaper an important or very important source of information about local politics – about the same number that report that personal contact with local politicians is important to them. Only 13 respondents, less than 1% of the 1,450 who participated in the survey, name *only* the local newspaper as an important source of information about local politics. When considering the sources of information available and actually used in the community, the local newspaper is not so much a mainstream medium as it is a medium of choice for a minority of the older, more affluent, and more well-educated citizens. In interviews and focus groups, these people praise it for its coverage of local affairs and describe its function in terms reminiscent of how journalism studies scholars might describe it, as an important source of information, as a way of being exposed to different points of view, as a part of what ties people together in the community, etc. But younger, less affluent, less well-educated citizens rarely read it. In what would probably have been a traumatic experience for the editor of the paper had he heard it, one young man interviewed, who grew up in the area, did not even know that there *was* a local newspaper in Næstved (though *Sjællandske* is the heir to a line of local titles that have covered the community since 1866). Local politicians, community activists, and of course more than anyone else the journalists and editors working on the paper itself are aware that its reach – despite its multi-media operations across print, digital, radio, and cable television – is not what it used to be.

Producers of information

But if we turn from considering the *sources* of information available and used to the *producers* of information about local politics, the local newspaper and its role in the local information environment appears in a different light. In this part of the analysis, I rely primarily on the extensive array of content we collected and coded from 29 October to 19 November 2013. This dataset includes 6,540 published units, including 5,298 editorial units produced and published by the local and regional news media across print, web, radio, and television broadcast, as well as 1,181 units published by local politicians on their Facebook profiles or websites and 61 units published by the municipal government on its Facebook profile or website. It has not been possible to collect comprehensive data on interpersonal conversations about politics on Facebook, nor to systematically map conversations with friends and families or personal contacts with politicians, party members, and the like. We did do extensive fieldwork during the election campaign and our interviews and focus groups spoke to these sources of information, but they will be bracketed here in favour of a closer look at what kind of information is actually produced by the most important sources of information about local politics – the local news media.

Consider first the information produced by the local news media. All content was coded for geographic focus (Næstved municipality, another municipality, regional focus, national focus, international focus, other) and for whether it dealt with local politics (operationalised as mentioning either local politicians, government authorities, or clearly and explicitly bringing up questions concerning collectively binding decisions). Of the 5,298 editorial units collected from the local news media, 1,769 focused on Næstved. (The rest had other geographical focus or dealt with issues not tied to geography, showing clearly how the local is only part of what local and regional media cover.) Of the 1,769 editorial units focused on Næstved, 535 dealt with politics in one way or another, for a total of 10% of all the editorial content available. Figure 2.1 presents our data in terms of the number of editorial units focused on Næstved and dealing with politics sorted by the news organisation that has produced it. (The percentage in parentheses is the proportion of the total news coverage of local politics produced by the organisation in question.)

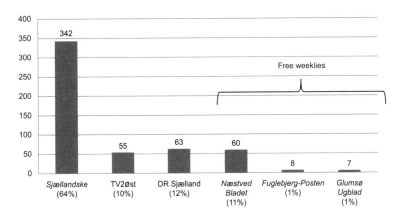

Figure 2.1   Coverage of local politics by media organisation (29 October–19 November 2013)

As can be seen, 342 out of 535 units dealing with local politics – 64% – come from the local newspaper, published across its print daily, its website, its weekly freesheet, its commercial radio station, and the 24/7 local breaking-news cable channel it still ran at the time. Across these platforms, *Sjællandske* published 2,860 editorial units over these three weeks – more than half of all the editorial content collected – 953 units focused on Næstved geographically (33%), and 342 of these (36%) focused on local politics in Næstved municipality. Though the local newspaper is not particularly widely regarded as an important *source* of information about local politics, much of what it publishes is about local politics, and it *produces* a very large proportion of the news coverage of Næstved's local politics. The central position it occupies is perhaps most strikingly illustrated by attending one of the monthly open city council meetings, where the editor of the local newspaper is almost always the only journalist in attendance, sitting at his own desk behind the horseshoe where the council members are seated, flanked by one or more members of the municipal government's communication staff. In interviews with local politicians and municipal government civil servants, everyone is aware of the key role played by the local newspaper. One council member acknowledges that *Sjællandske* does not have as many readers as they used to, but also underlines 'they completely dominate' coverage of local politics. This is the first dimension of the local newspaper as a keystone medium in the local political information environment. It is the *primary provider* of a distinct and important kind of information in the community, namely relatively independent, ongoing, and diverse coverage of local politics.

But the sheer volume of news about local politics produced by the local newspaper and local politicians' awareness of its role are not the only indicators of its wider ecological importance. Closer examination of the content produced by other local and regional media in the community suggests that *Sjællandske* is important not only as a producer of news, but also as a supplier of leads to other media (the kind of role in the news food chain that Lund and his collaborators argue especially broadsheet newspapers and news agencies play nationally). A detailed qualitative analysis of every other source of news available in the community is beyond the scope of this chapter, but consider one particularly important and illustrative counterpoint: the regional licence-fee-funded public service television broadcasters TV2Øst, the single most widely relied upon local media source of information in Næstved.[5]

In its mission statement, the station highlights its commitment to covering the region and to putting 'everyday life at the centre' of their content. It produces multiple daily television news bulletins, and also maintains a website and a Facebook profile with more than 25,000 followers. During the election season, the channel complemented the ordinary array of news programmes with a daily political debate programme and dedicated extra editorial resources to covering local politics. Despite this, genuinely *local* news coverage on the channel remains superficial, episodic, and limited (as is the case with local television news in other countries, e.g. Fowler et al., 2007).

Across all these platforms, the regional public service broadcaster produced 55 editorial units focusing on local politics in Næstved from

29 October to 19 November (21 days). Fifteen of these stories were broadcast during the 19.30 regional news bulletin, by far the most popular news programme from TV2Øst. Most days saw at least one story on the municipality at some point during the day, but five days saw no coverage of local politics in Næstved (31 October; 3, 7, 8, 16 November). Of these 55 pieces, ten are different versions gradually expanding coverage of the same basic story over the course of multiple television newscasts during the day, or stories posted on the station's website or Facebook profile simply repeating something already covered on television. Twenty-two editorial units focus wholly on the political process itself, on the fact that there is an election, when it is, how you vote, news segments announcing forthcoming town hall meetings, the broadcaster's own plans for covering the election, and reporting on various campaigns initiated by national and local government authorities in an attempt to raise turnout. The remaining 23 editorial units covering local politics in Næstved produced by TV2Øst in the course of these three weeks report on different substantial political issues in the community. Three individual stories account for 16 of the units published: five stories about decision by the city council to cancel the planned closure of a unit of care homes for people with dementia (5 November), five stories about a city council decision to try to use zoning laws to prevent a Dutch biker gang from acquiring a property in the municipality (6 November), and six stories about the handling of a controversial decision by the city council to erect three large windmills in a corner of the municipality (14–15 November). Many people in Næstved consider TV2Øst an important or very important source of information about local politics. These three stories represent most of what they were told about substantial issues in the run-up to the election. (There was no coverage of issues like, for example, the municipality's budget, the school system, or local zoning laws, all covered extensively in the local newspaper.)

Interestingly, all three of these issues were covered in front-page stories of the print edition of the local newspaper *before* the regional public service broadcaster took them up. The story about the care homes was on the front page of *Sjællandske* on 5 November. TV2Øst covered the story in its 12.30, 19.30, and 22.20 regional news bulletins on television, mentioned it in the evening political debate programme, and posted a story about the issue on its website at 16.48 on the same day. The story was attributed to *Sjællandske* from the outset. The story about the biker gang started with a city council decision on the evening of 5 November. The local newspaper was the only news medium to have a journalist present at the council meeting, and covered the story on the front page of the print edition on 6 November, following up with no less than six more stories inside the paper. Again, TV2Øst covered the story in its 12.30, 19.30, and 22.20 regional news bulletins on television, touched on it in the evening political debate programme, and posted a story about the issue on its website at 19.09 on the same day. The story about the three windmills stretched over two days; it was first covered on the front page of the print edition of the local newspaper on 14 November, and followed up with a new front-page story on 15 November (four days before the election) announcing that many local politicians had refused to tell the paper where they stood on the issue. On the first day of the story, TV2Øst only mentioned the issue briefly in the 22.30 political debate programme, but on the second day, the story was covered on the website with a story posted at 07.17 directly referring to the local newspaper's coverage and it was followed up throughout the day with a story in the 12.30 bulletin and with additional stories on the website and the station's Facebook page.

TV2Øst did much to disseminate information originally reported by the local newspaper to a much larger audience, and also in a few cases moved the story by doing additional reporting. The station also broadcast the only televised debate between the leading candidates for city council. But it produced very little original reporting, and only touched on very few of the multiple issues discussed elsewhere in the course of the campaign – in the local newspaper, on Facebook by politicians, and at town hall meetings with the citizens who show up to listen to and question the candidates. This is not unique to TV2Øst. The picture is much the same at the regional licence-fee-funded public service radio broadcasters DR Sjælland, which also produces news for a regional audience across a number of radio news bulletins in the course of the day in addition to maintaining a website and a Facebook profile. Here, one journalist answers candidly about how one covers local politics in Næstved when working for a regional broadcaster: 'I read Sjællandske [the local newspaper].' The editor-in-chiefs of the two public service broadcasters both explained their situation in essentially the same terms when interviewed: they have a limited number of journalists producing a great deal of content for several platforms catering to a large and geographically dispersed regional audience. Sjællandske operates a newsroom with a total of more than ten journalists covering three municipalities with a combined population of 160,000, whereas the two public service broadcasters with less than 20 journalists each cover 12 municipalities with almost 600,000 inhabitants. This means that resources are scarce and concentrated on genuinely regional issues – which they feel newspapers in the region, with their local focus, tend to ignore – and that local affairs are covered mostly through the lens of exceptional events that will interest not only the inhabitants of one particular municipality in the region, but also people who live hundreds of kilometres away. Day-to-day local politics, even when dealing with substantially important issues concerning thousands of people, large sums of money, or decisions of principle, are rarely thought to be of such interest. And when they are, the coverage frequently relies heavily on stories originally broken in *Sjællandske*. This is the second dimension of the local newspaper as a keystone medium in the local political information environment. It *enables other media* to cover local politics as they can monitor its coverage and follow up on select stories without having to maintain an ongoing presence in the community.

In sum, the local newspaper in Næstved is not a mainstream medium. Most citizens do not read it regularly, and only a relatively small number name it an important or very important source of political information. People rely much more on regional public service television, free weeklies, and personal conversation. But the local newspaper is nonetheless a keystone medium in the local political information environment as the primary provider of a specific and important kind of information (news about local politics) and as a medium that enables other media to cover this aspect of the community. In contrast to other studies that have highlighted the central role of newspapers as news producers in local media ecosystems (e.g. Project for Excellence in Journalism, 2010), it is *not* the case that the news produced by *Sjællandske* is quickly picked up and recirculated by other regional or local news media on- or offline. To the contrary, most of the many stories about local politics produced by the local newspaper never appear anywhere else. Most local political coverage in Næstved appears once and in one place only, seen, if at all, by the readers of the local newspaper. Because we know from years of research that the very fact that news is made public – even when its audience is limited – helps keep local government and local politicians responsive to their constituents, this news production is important for the local political information environment and for local democracy even when few read it and no one else follows up on it. The local newspaper structures the local political information environment and has an impact far beyond its own audience.

Local newspapers as keystone media – and what comes after?

On the basis of a close study of what sources of information people rely on to follow local politics and what kind of information is actually produced and made available by these sources in a specific case community, I have argued that the local newspaper, though diminished in terms of reach and resources, occupies a critical role in the local political information environment. It is what I have defined as a *keystone medium*, the primary provider of a specific and important kind of information – news about local politics – and a medium that enables other media's coverage of this area. It is true in Næstved as in the local Swedish communities studied by Ekström et al. (2006) that the local newspaper's coverage is hardly hard-hitting investigative watchdog journalism. But it is the only kind of relatively independent, ongoing, and diverse news about local politics available in the community. This is important even though the newspaper has a limited and shrinking audience because the publication and diffusion of this information shape the local political information environment and the local media ecosystem.

The central importance of the local newspaper in the critical case of Næstved has broader implications as the community in focus is one that is served by a range of different national, regional, and local media including public service broadcasters, free weeklies, and various digital media. Despite the abundance of other media available to people in Næstved, including no less than two comparatively well-funded regional public service broadcasters, the newspaper still occupies a crucial position in the local media ecosystem. In countries where there are local newspapers (most of the Western world), but where public service media are not as strong as in Denmark, the newspapers are likely to be even more important locally than in the case community in focus here.

Local newspapers in Denmark are stronger than in many other countries in Western Europe. (In some countries, a municipality of 80,000 will not sustain a local newspaper.) But they are unlikely to remain strong. Print circulation is declining, newspaper advertising shrinking, and digital growth is not compensating for the revenues lost. Like almost all other newspapers, local Danish newspapers like *Sjællandske* have cut their newsroom in recent years, and even with the title's wide range of print, digital, and broadcast activities, the road ahead is a challenging one and one that is almost certain to involve further cost-cutting. There are few signs indicating that other media will be in a position to increase their investment in local news as newspapers cut theirs. Public service broadcasters are likely to have at best the same resources available. Free weeklies are suffering from declining advertising revenues. Online-only local news media are almost completely absent from the Danish market and there are currently few reasons to believe that they would be sustainable as businesses unless they find revenues well beyond digital advertising.

What would the local political information environment in Næstved look like without the local newspaper? Today, *Sjællandske* pays the salary of the only reporter who regularly attends city council meetings in Næstved, produces two-thirds of all news about local politics available in the community, and enables other, regional, media, who reach a wider audience to cover the community (even if in a more superficial, episodic, and limited fashion). Many people probably would not even notice if the newspaper substantially cut its coverage or even stopped it altogether, as only a minority read it regularly. It is not a mainstream medium in the community. But the overall political information environment in Næstved would look very different without its voluminous production, as the amount of information *available* about local politics and public affairs would significantly decrease. (Local politicians, keenly attuned both to the limited audiences of the newspaper and its role as the only producer of regular coverage, would certainly notice the difference.) The regional public service broadcasters – no longer able to rely on the newspaper's constant coverage of the community – would have a much harder time monitoring events in Næstved and deciding when to allocate scarce editorial resources to covering events in the municipality. The very structure of the local political information environment would change with the disappearance of a keystone medium and the community would lose its only major source of relatively independent, ongoing, and diverse coverage of local politics.

Many citizens would not feel this directly, as they do not consider the local newspaper a particularly important source of information about local politics. But they would live with the *ecological* consequences as the media that they *do* rely on for information – regional public service media, weekly community freesheets – would have to make do without the steady stream of local news coverage produced by the local newspaper. The future this points towards is one in which there would certainly still be a multitude of media available to citizens locally, and where one outlet less may not look like much of a change. But it is a future in which the further diminution and possibly ultimately the disappearance of already diminished local newspapers will have severe ecological consequences due to the keystone role of newspapers in local political information environments.

Notes

1   This is the case throughout Denmark where online-only local news media are few and far between.

2   According to Edward O. Wilson (1999), keystone species are those that have a disproportionate impact on their ecosystems, that is by affecting the survival and abundance of many other species. From a conservation perspective, Wilson notes, removing them entails a significant shift in the ecological community.

3   This research project was funded by a grant from the Center for Power, Media, and Communication at Roskilde University. Laurids Hovgaard was an exemplary research assistant on the project and was responsible for both collection and coding of content.

4   3 or 4 on a scale from 'not very important' (1) to 'very important' (4).

5   Free community weeklies are the second most widely used local news medium. Of the four titles available in the municipality, only one, *Næstved Bladet*, contains more than a few articles about local public affairs. Most of the articles in the title in question are paid advertorials announcing local council business, and not independently reported news.

Bibliography

Aalberg, Toril, and James Curran (eds). 2012. *How Media Inform Democracy: A Comparative Approach.* Routledge New Developments in Communication and Society. New York: Routledge.

Aalberg, Toril, Peter van Aelst, and James Curran. 2010. 'Media Systems and the Political Information Environment: A Cross-National Comparison', *International Journal of Press/Politics*, 15(3): 255–71. doi:10.1177/1940161210367422.

Anderson, C. W. 2013. *Rebuilding the News: Metropolitan Journalism in the Digital Age.* Philadelphia: Temple University Press.

Berelson, Bernard, Paul F. Lazarsfeld, and William N. McPhee. 1954. *Voting: A Study of Opinion Formation in a Presidential Campaign.* Chicago: University of Chicago Press.

Cook, Timothy E. 1998. *Governing with the News: The News Media as a Political Institution*. Chicago: University of Chicago Press.

Couldry, Nick, Sonia M. Livingstone, and Tim Markham. 2010. *Media Consumption and Public Engagement: Beyond the Presumption of Attention*. Basingstoke: Palgrave Macmillan.

Curran, James, Shanto Iyengar, Anker Brink Lund, and Inka Salovaara-Moring. 2009. 'Media System, Public Knowledge and Democracy', *European Journal of Communication*, 24(1): 5–26. doi:10.1177/0267323108098943.

Ekström, Mats, Bengt Johansson, and Larsåke Larsson. 2006. 'Journalism and Local Politics', *Journalism Studies*, 7(2): 292–311. doi:10.1080/14616700500533627.

Esser, Frank, et al. 2012. 'Political Information Opportunities in Europe: A Longitudinal and Comparative Study of Thirteen Television Systems', *International Journal of Press/Politics*, 17(3): 247–74. doi:10.1177/1940161212442956.

Fowler, Erika Franklin, et al. 2007. 'Does Local News Measure up?', *Stanford Law and Policy Review*, 18: 411.

Franklin, Bob (ed.) 2006. *Local Journalism and Local Media: Making the Local News*. London and New York: Routledge.

Friedland, Lewis, et al. 2012. *Review of the Literature Regarding Critical Information Needs of the American Public*. Washington, DC: FCC.

Katz, Elihu, and Paul Felix Lazarsfeld. 2006. *Personal Influence: The Part Played by People in the Flow of Mass Communications*. 2nd edn. New Brunswick, NJ: Transaction.

Lazarsfeld, Paul Felix, Bernard Berelson, and Hazel Gaudet. 1968. *The People's Choice: How the Voter Makes up His Mind in a Presidential Campaign*. New York: Columbia University Press.

Lund, Anker Brink (ed.) 2000. *Først med det sidste, en nyhedsuge i Danmark*. Århus: Ajour.

Lund, Anker Brink, Ida Willig, and Mark Blach-Ørsten. 2009. *Hvor kommer nyhederne fra?, den journalistiske fødekæde i Danmark før og nu*. Århus: Ajour.

Nielsen, Rasmus Kleis, and Cristian Vaccari. 2013. 'Do People "Like" Politicians on Facebook? Not Really. Large-Scale Direct Candidate-to-Voter Online Communication as an Outlier Phenomenon', *International Journal of Communication*, 7: 24.

O'Neill, Deirdre, and Catherine O'Connor. 2008. 'The Passive Journalist', *Journalism Practice*, 2(3): 487–500. doi:10.1080/17512780802281248.

Park, Robert E. 1938. 'Reflections on Communication and Culture', *American Journal of Sociology*, 44(2): 187–205. doi:10.2307/2768727.

71

Park, Robert E. 1974. *The Collected Papers of Robert Ezra Park*, ed. C. Hughes Everett. New York: Arno Press.

Project for Excellence in Journalism. 2010. 'How News Happens'. http://www. journalism.org/analysis_report/how_news_happens.

Ryfe, David. 2012. *Can Journalism Survive?* Cambridge: Polity.

Wilson, Edward O. 1999. *The Diversity of Life*. New York: W. V. Norton.

3

How News Travels: A Comparative Study of Local Media Ecosystems in Leeds (UK) and Philadelphia (US)

C. W. Anderson, Stephen Coleman, and Nancy Thumim

Introduction

News travels. Through word of mouth, online networks, printing presses and the blasting waves of broadcasting, stories circulate; places are characterised; first and later drafts of history are written; what 'everyone knows' comes to be either accepted as truth or the object of suspicious doubt. News defines for people who and where they are; it reflects and distorts, illuminates and confuses, links and disconnects.

Much scholarly attention has been paid over the years to the political and moral effects of news diffusion. At its worst, news serves to mystify and distract – to divert people from an understanding of causes by overwhelming them with a drama of unexplained effects. At its best, news exposes people to more than they had expected to find; it makes vivid the lives of others and meaningful perspectives that might otherwise seem strange or unspeakable. How local communities imagine themselves and are imagined by outsiders is determined to a great extent by how their everyday experiences of place and sociability are narrated by the media. This chapter is less concerned with exploring these political and moral effects than in understanding the dynamics and diffusion of local news circulation. In short, regardless of their effects, we are interested in *how* local news stories travel; how some move fast and far, while others remain marginal or forgotten; how technologies of narrative diffusion shape the cartography of potential news diffusion; and how combinations of structural opportunity and creative agency might be changing the scope for local actors to tell and circulate the stories that define their communities.

Our focus in this chapter is upon local media ecologies – or ecosystems. This contrasts with two other approaches to the study of local journalism. One is to take a particular city as an environment to be studied, asking questions about how accurately local news *captures* what is going on in the city. The other is to take a select cluster of local news organisations and explore how they go about *covering* the city. We believe that these approaches – and the italicised metaphors used to describe them – fail to acknowledge the close interdependence that exists between what constitutes a community and how it is communicated. In taking a media ecology approach to local news, we argue that the story and its telling – the place and its depiction – are inextricably entangled. Following Dewey's (1916: 5) assertion that 'There is more than a verbal tie between the words common, community, and communication', the aim of both of the empirical studies reported here is to understand the ecological interrelationships between shared environments (common), people's connectedness within them (community) and the mediation of this mutual reality (communication). By adopting an ecological perspective we acknowledge that cities as places are not simply uncovered or exposed through communication, but are products of communication; the urban space as context is made present through the contextualising work of communication. In saying this, we are not claiming that cities are somehow inventions or fictions, engendered by strategies of communication, but that only through what are often competing and contradictory communications do communities emerge as meaningful places rather than dots on a map.

Two studies of local news lie at the heart of this chapter. One of them was conducted by Anderson and took place in Philadelphia, PA. The research was conducted, in fits and starts, between 2006 until 2012 as part of the project that resulted in *Rebuilding the News* (Anderson, 2013). The second study was of Leeds, in the United Kingdom, and was carried out by the Leeds Media Ecology team led by Coleman and took place in Leeds, West Yorkshire, between 2010 and 2013, with an intensive period of tracking local news circulation in September 2011.[1] We present findings from the two distinct projects, in turn, exploring both what we have learned about Philadelphia and Leeds specifically and what we have learned about how news travels through the ecology of the city, more generally. We conclude by addressing four key issues which these two studies, taken together, raise for the study of local journalism early in the twenty-first century:

(1) the manner in which much online news can be seen as 'interpersonal conversation' made transcribable and indexable;
(2) the desire of news organisations to focus on what they called 'real people' and the way that so-called citizen journalism may be appropriated by news organisations under the banner of 'authentic narratives';
(3) the continued importance of legacy media institutions in both Leeds and Philadelphia; and
(4) the continued existence of 'information ecosystem blockages' in digital ecosystemic space.

It should be immediately obvious that these studies were launched and completed independently; they were never a part of any formal comparative research. Nevertheless, they are united by their embrace of the research goals discussed above: to understand the social and technological processes through which cities construct themselves in and through their news making, and the ways that the practices of that construction are changing in the digital age.

Chronological differences in the initiation and duration of the two research projects are obvious when we turn to Anderson's work in Philadelphia. Although *Rebuilding the News* was published in early 2013, the project began as early as 2006 and really hit its stride in 2008 – a good five years before the work was eventually published. The differences between 2008 and 2013 are too numerous to list, but they include the fact that in the former the newspaper crisis was only in its opening year, Twitter had yet to achieve widespread adoption, and 'blogging' was still considered a (relatively) new activity, particularly for journalists. Anderson's book is based on more than 300 hours of newsroom-specific fieldwork, along with more than 60 semi-structured interviews with journalists, editors, activists, bloggers, and media executives. Anderson took research trips to Philadelphia in 2006 and 2007, spent much of 2008 and 2009 in newsrooms for days or even weeks at a time, and conducted follow-up site visits in 2010–12.

While Anderson used quantitative analytical methods in order to facilitate his qualitative, ethnographic work, the focus of the Leeds study was on in-depth, qualitative richness rather than the visualisation of patterns across big data, although the qualitative approach was supplemented by some basic quantitative material via a survey of Leeds citizens and a content analysis of a 'week in the news'. In short, over two years (2010–12) the study deployed four methods: in-depth interviews with stakeholders/mediators, content analysis of a week in the news, focus groups with members of the public, and a survey of members of the public. Both Anderson and the Leeds team embraced, from the start, the idea of 'small data' (e.g. Couldry et al., 2013). Thus, a range of methods were used in order to explore *how* news travels in the media ecology and *what* happens *as it travels*. We turn to a brief discussion of this small-data approach in the conclusion.

There are major differences in the goals and methods of the two studies – but despite that, they are usefully framed in a comparative context for one simple and powerful reason: they are the only two completed research projects to date that attempt to understand how local journalism happens by looking at the *entire ensemble* of journalistic organisations in a particular geographic area rather than a few select traditional media organisations. One further similarity in the Leeds and Philadelphia studies is worth noting in this introductory section. At the heart of both studies is a constructionist approach to understanding both urban spaces and the news that flows across these spaces. This constructionism is obviously an operational mindset even if it is not strictly a methodology per se. But it is important to note that, influenced by theoreticians as diverse as Pierre Bourdieu (who called upon scholars to explore the 'construction of the pre-constructed object', 1992: 229) and Bruno Latour, both studies aim to ask a set of more open-ended questions about what local news is, about the types of practice that make it up, and about what role and value these practices might have than much traditional media sociology to date.

Before turning to a discussion of the findings we will briefly introduce the two cities, Philadelphia and Leeds, as places where news is made, where news is experienced, and where news travels – or does not.

Leeds is a large, ethnically diverse city in the county of West Yorkshire in the north of England and is the third largest city in the UK (depending on where the boundaries of the city are drawn). In 2011, when the ecology study began, Leeds was in the midst of accommodating itself to its post-industrial condition. The city was built on the wool and worsted industries, and later, by engineering. However, by 2008 Leeds had three times more people working in the business and finance sector than in manufacturing. By the end of the first decade of the twenty-first century, Leeds seemed to be fairly successful in adapting to the economic priorities espoused by all three major political parties in the UK. And yet the immediate backdrop to our study of the media ecology of the city and the news within it was economic crisis and urban riots. As Stillwell and Shepherd (2004: 128) noted in their study of social inequality in Leeds, even during the boom years

> A substantial proportion of the local population [...] remained excluded from the opportunities that economic growth and prosperity [...] brought. Levels of unemployment, poverty, health, crime, educational performance and environmental quality vary widely between localities across the city, with problems being particularly acute in some inner city areas.

Leeds escaped full-scale rioting in 2011 (which some commentators attributed to successful collaboration between the police, youth services, and local community leaders). Nevertheless, as we shall see in what follows, in the minds of Leeds' residents, fear of urban disorder and assumptions about its cause were far from absent; and different fears and assumptions prevailed in different parts of the city. Our study asked how these perceptions come to be formed, mediated, shared (or not), and revised within an urban media ecology.

Philadelphia is the fifth largest city in the United States and unusual, in terms of media, insofar as it remains a two-newspaper town whose tabloid (the *Daily News*), broadsheet (the *Inquirer*), and major news website (Philly.com) are all owned by a single company. When Anderson began his fieldwork, the two newspapers and their website had just been sold by Knight-Ridder, beginning what would become an odyssey in which the media properties would have six owners in nearly as many years. Most recently, the papers have been owned by a consortium of local political operatives and real-estate developers, leading to fears that the papers might become politicised in ways that would compromise their independence. (These developments occurred after the end of the period of fieldwork discussed here, however.)

Philadelphia is fairly typical of large north-eastern American cities insofar as it has tried to compensate for a declining industrial base by marketing itself as a tourist destination (a number of Revolutionary War-era events occurred in Philadelphia, including the drafting and signing of the US Declaration of Independence) and by taking advantage of the current wave of gentrification inside urban downtowns with their shops, restaurants, and youth-oriented amenities. Nevertheless, and again like most urban areas, Philadelphia remains a 'majority-minority' city, with 41% of the city white, 43% African-American, and 12% Hispanic. While racial tensions have flared up periodically in the city (particularly in the 1970s, when a townhouse serving as the headquarters for an African-American political organisation was firebombed by the city's mayor) there have been no events there comparable to the 2011 riots in the United Kingdom, though the city was the site of political protest in 2000 during the Republican National Convention held there.

Beyond the specifics of these cities in and of themselves, we think they are united by some additional factors that makes them worthy of comparison: both are large post-industrial areas that have distinct urban characters and yet are resolutely *not* so-called 'world cities', like, for example, the metropolises of London or New York. This is analytically important for understanding the specific localism of urban media ecosystems away from cities which are more connected to global information flows (Anderson, 2013). It is easier to grasp and differentiate what constitutes local city news in Leeds and Philadelphia than it is in New York City, for instance, and while these distinctions between local and global are not unproblematic, they do make a useful analytical heuristic for the purposes of the present chapter, and they facilitate a comparative perspective – a comparison to which we will now turn.

Findings in Philadelphia

The scope of the Philadelphia study was more circumscribed than the research conducted in Leeds; nevertheless, even within its basic framework of news diffusion analysis, *Rebuilding the News* touched on a diverse number of topics. Its historical chapters revealed the contours of an earlier, pre-digital Philadelphia media ecosystem and traced how digitisation affected the contours of that ecosystem. It also showed how local news organisations were far more open to experimentation with news-reporting processes than the usual caricature of them as slow-moving dinosaurs might lead us to believe. The book analysed how technological innovation moves through different news organisations, as well as the processes by which different storytelling tools are adopted in a variety of institutional settings. It unpacked the relationship between the traditional and the so-called 'alternative' press in Philadelphia, and the way these relationships affected patterns of news diffusion. It spent a good deal of time trying to uncover why newsroom collaborations – seemingly such a promising management strategy in an era of resource cutbacks and digital connectivity – failed so often. And it acknowledged the deep sociological importance of the city's traditional journalistic institutions, as well as the paradoxical fact that this very cultural importance rendered them less well equipped to adapt to the new digital media era.

The Philadelphia study reached several important conclusions with regard to the way news diffuses in twenty-first-century news ecosystems, findings primarily centred on the tension between patterns of information diffusion and the structural blockages within these emerging digital pathways. The extensive study of news work in Philadelphia concludes that the usual formula of 'journalists report, the networked 5th estate comments' is far too simplistic a model to explain how local journalism diffuses in the early twenty-first century. Rather, news in Philadelphia was often broken by quasi-journalists on the margins of the ecosystem, fully reported out by traditional media, and finally commented on and synthesised by non-traditional media workers like local and national bloggers (Anderson, 2009). This news was often reported on and analysed *again*, however, by the institutions that broke the news in the first place, organisations operating on a different time cycle than the more established press and thus using their relative temporal freedom to revisit stories the traditional newspapers had forgotten or considered no longer new. What is more, *Rebuilding the News* makes it clear that news in the digital age does not 'diffuse' like an algae bloom, a virus, or a genetic meme. Rather, quasi-journalists and political actors (whom the book labels 'fact entrepreneurs') move news, often in highly strategic ways. The patterns are spelled out in the book's case study of the Francisville Four, which details, in a step-by-step fashion, the way a single local news story in Philadelphia originated, spread across the communication channels of the city, and eventually died away. Along the way the study paid as much attention to institutional priorities that blocked the further elaboration of news stories as it did to the way that news moved, as we can see in this brief excerpt from the researcher's field notes:

> *Editorial meeting. After all the work, the Francisville Four story is off the front page and it looks like follow up on the story is through. Not censorship or anything [like that] but simply the fact that Philadelphia's #1 tabloid couple 'Bonnie and Clyde' [the nicknames of a pair of particularly attractive scam artists operating in Philadelphia in the summer of 2008] have had developments in their case. New news in other words. (Ethnographic notebook, 2 July 2008)*

79

Not only does news diffuse across a local media ecosystem – technologies and particular journalistic practices diffuse across that ecosystem as well. Research for *Rebuilding the News* found that new journalistic practices, formats, and communicative technologies usually got their start at the margins of the Philadelphia media world and then worked their way towards the centre. But having reached that centre, they were often transformed in order to more easily align with the dominant cultures and work routines of traditional news institutions. One particular example of this is the (by now quite old) practice of blogging. Chapter 2 of *Rebuilding the News* chronicles how blogging began as a project of small-scale and opinionated *information synthesis* rather than the generation of new information from scratch. Blogging was about aggregation, in other words, rather than so-called 'original reporting'. But once Philadelphia newspapers finally adopted blogging, as both a practice and a platform, workers there usually repurposed it into a platform through which journalists could break news more quickly rather than synthesise already extant information. While newspapers both in Philadelphia and elsewhere have finally, many years later, adopted more traditional forms of blogging and aggregation, that process was sharply curtailed and delayed by the obsession with original reporting at many of the traditional local news outlets.

The Philadelphia study also uncovered a particularly interesting aspect of the motivation of traditional journalists for including so-called 'citizen journalistic' content in their news reports: they see this content not as the work of a journalistic competitor, but as the activity of sources who happen to be so-called 'real people' and thus particularly authentic. Anderson calls this process one of 'categorical misrecognition' in which journalists see other journalists as 'sources', activists see journalists as 'targets', and bloggers see traditional media as 'conversation partners'. The importance of ordinary people in news production, and the way this emphasis relates to circulation dynamics in media ecosystems, will become even clearer when we turn to the research in Leeds.

Having cast the net far and wide in the study of local news production and diffusion in Philadelphia, did Anderson learn about the role played by the traditional media in particular? Does studying a local media ecosystem, and chronicling the growth of that ecosystem, mean that we can dispense with the institutional press, on either an empirical or a normative level? Far from it. Indeed, one of the useful aspects of examining a media ecosystem as a whole is that it gives us an understanding of traditional journalism that goes beyond platitudes – which is often what journalists' claims of their own importance amount to.

The early pages of *Rebuilding the News* make it clear that cities have always been composed of media ecosystems – they have never been the preserve of a few centralised newspapers and TV stations, even at the height of the monopoly era in metropolitan news production. Digital technology did not create a Philadelphia media ecosystem out of thin air – there have always been local pirate radio stations, alternative newsweeklies, and even television stations like PEG. What digital technology *does* do, however, is increase the number, visibility, interactivity, and textual transparency of these fragmented media outlets. Media ecosystems aren't new, but what *is* new is the fact that the existence of that ecosystem is so obvious, so searchable, and so navigable. This creates the possibility – but not the certainty, as we will see – that the different local journalistic players might more consciously coordinate with each other and leverage the diverse resources of this newer, 'self-aware' ecosystem (Anderson, 2009; Anderson, 2013: 34–52). Nevertheless, one of the key findings – perhaps *the* key finding – of the Philadelphia study was the continued importance of legacy media institutions in Philadelphia, despite the new entrants and despite the newly networked nature of news production. As Anderson notes in one of his ethnographic field notebooks:

Continually amazed by the amount of journalistic production occuring at the Inquirer and DN [Daily News] when compared to the other parts of the media ecosystem I studied. Even in their diminished state (and I noted yesterday the shockingly large number of empty desks at the Inky), the amount of work happening here is just incredible. You can't walk in and not be impressed by the industrial process. (Field Notes, 14 June 2008)

Looking holistically at the radically diminished economic capital of Philadelphia's legacy press and the digital textuality of the emerging online ecosystem, Anderson initially hypothesised that the period between 2006 and 2010 would see a growing number of collaborations between different Philadelphia news organisations. On a formal level, different news outlets would begin to share personnel and other resources; more informally, they would begin to link to other news organisations to supplement coverage they could no longer provide alone. In Jeff Jarvis' words, more journalistic institutions would 'do what they did best and link to the rest'. However, this turned out to *not* be the case, either formally or informally. Deliberate collaborations amongst members of the media ecosystem in Philadelphia were often hampered by the overwhelming focus of resources on the traditional tasks of reporting the news as well as the rather haphazard work practices of many alternate organisations that were more open (in principle) to collaboration. In other words, legacy media outlets could not be bothered to collaborate when there was so much news to be reported (which they saw as their primary task), nor could they find a way to rationalise the highly informal production systems of most emerging news organisations in order to make such collaboration possible.

One of the key studies usually cited to back up the self-important claims of traditional journalists is the Project for Excellence in Journalism study of Baltimore (2010). This study revealed, in the words of its authors, 'that much of the "news" people receive contains no original reporting. Fully eight out of ten stories studied simply repeated or repackaged previously published information. And of the stories that did contain new information nearly all, 95%, came from traditional media – most of them newspapers. These stories then tended to set the narrative agenda for most other media outlets' (Pew Center, 2010). Anderson's Philadelphia research, conducted around the same time as the Baltimore content analysis and in a similar city, confirmed these findings in a deeply granular way. In other words, the evidence for the centrality of traditional news organisations can be uncovered ethnographically as well as in numerous other ways. Local newspapers, *Rebuilding the News* concludes, remain the dominant producers of most reported information in a local community or city. To watch a local newsroom at work, even in their diminished state, is to witness an industrial process of original information production that simply dwarfs that of all other ecosystemic players. And the ability of emerging organisations to pick up the slack is often hampered by the fact that they lack the resources and structures of actual institutions. To the degree they report the news at all, they usually tend to do so in a haphazard, unstructured, or highly focused fashion.

In sum, the Philadelphia research uncovered a few key findings, among them the continued importance of legacy media institutions for the production of news and the continued existence of 'information ecosystem blockages' in digital ecosystemic space, often attributable to organisational imperatives. Two additional findings – the way that so-called citizen journalism may be appropriated by news organisations under the banner of 'authentic narratives' and the way that a wide variety of news production can be seen as the 'interpersonal conversation' made transcribable and indexable – will be elaborated further as we turn to the findings of our second study, conducted in Leeds.

Findings in Leeds

While Anderson drew on his ethnographic immersion in order to focus on the emergence and diffusion of a few key stories in Philadelphia, the Leeds research team relied on a variety of methods, including content analysis of news stories, a representative survey of news consumers, a series of semi-structured interviews with news producers, and focus groups. The content analysis paralleled Anderson's analysis of news diffusion, demonstrating that in Leeds, too, stories unfurled across the media ecosystem in particular ways, and some nodes (particularly traditional media outlets) were more central than others.

The content analysis of a week across media forms and genres allowed the Leeds team to track the travel of such stories as they interweave within the news ecology. The form of media made for very different roles in the production, circulation, and practice of news and, moreover, there were important differences across the mainstream news providers' treatment of the local. Not only did different local news forms provide quite different 'takes' on what constituted local news, but generic styles of presenting such news varied markedly. We cannot present here anything like a comprehensive account of our content analysis findings, except to say that they often pointed to a frustrating duplication of stories across several media platforms and channels, often derived from single institutional sources. Prevalent notions of what constituted local news and how it should be presented were only rarely interrupted by more creative or investigative modes of news presentation. Unlike the Baltimore study and the Philadelphia ethnography, there were no significant examples of any major news stories emerging online in Leeds.

A representative sample of the Leeds population provides rich data on the audience for local news as well as the facts of its production. Analysis of the survey suggests that frequency of local news consumption in Leeds is quite substantial and in the case of the most popular news medium, television, was almost as great as national viewing. Approximately three-quarters of the respondents agreed with the proposition that local news was as important as national news – even among those individuals who thought that the quality of local news had worsened over the previous five years. And when asked which qualities they would expect to find in local or national news coverage of the same story, the former was rated more highly for relevance, accuracy, trustworthiness, interest, and not being sensational; though found liable to be more superficial. Individuals who described themselves as 'very interested' in politics were somewhat less critical of national news by some of the above criteria; they too tended to be positive about the provision of local news. Most respondents rated BBC local television and radio as the most trustworthy source of news. BBC's daily *Look North* (local news programme) was regarded as better at representing 'the city really well' (64% of respondents) than the main local newspaper *Yorkshire Evening Post* (34%), or the daily news programme on the commercial channel, ITV (34%). When it came to the question of which news provider stands up 'well for you and people like you', 45% of respondents opted for the BBC's *Look North* compared with 31% for the *Yorkshire Evening Post*, and 26% for ITV's *Calendar*. Here we note that the city's main public service news provider is what we call an *ecological pivot*: a central node of both information provision and information verification that is particularly trusted by local residents.

Unstructured, but broadly comparable interviews were conducted with leading personnel of the mainstream local news media in Leeds (*Look North*, *Calendar*, Radio Leeds, and the *Yorkshire Evening Post*). These covered the informants' perspectives on their outlets and their own work in respect of such topics as: recent developments in their outlets' situations; the outlets' overall roles and purposes; most satisfying types of stories to present (and least); local story priorities and preferences; types of 'voices' (or actors) preferred and to be avoided in the output if possible; perceptions of and relations to their audiences; uses of social media; and any lines of self-criticism. A startling finding from the interviews with mainstream media personnel was the explicit decision to feature 'real people' as much as possible in the news:

> *There can be too much reliance on that white, middle-class voice when it comes to explaining stories and not enough real people and the more real people we can find, the better. There has been a growing emphasis on real people and hearing real people's voices and real people's experiences and I think it's becoming even more important now. Real people are almost making the media themselves. I think in my early days it would have been more about the suits and more about official voices. (Assistant Editor, BBC Radio Leeds)*

And this phrase 'real people' was repeated with striking frequency by interviewees from across the mainstream news providers; seemingly offered up as evidence of their striving to provide authentic, trustworthy stories to a public who had access to a wide set of sources for stories and information across the contemporary media ecology:

We don't want the suits, we would rather hear from real people who are affected. (Deputy News Editor, BBC Look North)

I don't want too many suits on the programme; I think you need [them] but it's hugely important that we reflect the views of normal people. (News Editor, ITV Calendar)

[We] got real people talking about the issues in a way they wouldn't get the chance to anywhere else. So within minutes of it being announced that five, or possibly three, care homes were going to be closed by the council, we had very angry families of residents talking about what it would mean. Actually, hearing those voices and giving them a place to vent, was the most important thing yesterday and not necessarily getting the facts right 100%. (Assistant News Editor, BBC Radio Leeds)

This emphasis on using the voice of 'real people' makes absolutely clear that mainstream news providers are convinced that the public does not trust political and other elites as sources of news. And this finding chimes with both our focus group discussions with members of the public (discussed below) and our interviews with individual alternative media producers.

While few survey respondents went online as their first source for local news, over half designated the internet as the source to which they would turn if they wanted *more* information about something happening in the city. Almost half the entire sample agreed with the statement that the local media do not 'do enough to hold powerful people to account', as against only 15% who disagreed. Perhaps one of the most significant ecological findings was that local news provides material for conversation and discussion among individuals after they had been exposed to media content:

It depends what [the story] was! Lots of informal network on Facebook group pages for small local groups. (Comment from survey respondent)

While survey respondents reported talking about national and international news with other people somewhat more frequently than they did local news stories, such talk tended to correlate with a prior interest in politics. In the case of talk about local news, there was no such correlation, suggesting that local news providers actually managed to stimulate discussion amongst groups who would not see themselves as natural political or news junkies – and this conversation carried on in offline and online spaces.

The analysis of eight focus groups provided valuable insights into how people make news, make sense of news, relate it to their own lives, and fit it into their everyday routines. One of the more intriguing findings from these interviews is that for many people word of mouth grapevines are crucial both to the acquisition of local information and to the ways in which they make connections in their communities.

> *Local information I would say 90% comes from school when dropping off or picking up. Either actually speaking to people or just overhearing. (Female Focus Group 3)*

> *Yes, it's quite a close knit village – it's word of mouth really. (Female Focus Group 2)*

For most of our focus group participants 'local' meant 'my street' or 'my neighbourhood'; it almost never meant the city of Leeds as reported in the 'local paper', the *Yorkshire Evening Post*, and certainly not the vast regions of Yorkshire and beyond covered by TV news programmes such as the BBC's *Look North* or ITV's *Calendar*. And 'news' meant, at once, both local information and storytelling – understood by our respondents as potentially clashing functions:

> *No, she works in a local shop so she chats to everybody and passes it on. She is very informative. (Male Focus Group 2)*

> *Well I've got local mates that are in various bits and bats, ex-coppers that seem to know everything before its even happened. (Male Focus Group 6)*

Analysis of media coverage of a series of major cuts in council expenditure suggested that public engagement has several contested meanings, ranging from a one-way flow of information from government to citizens to the creation of empowered citizens who are not only listened to through consultation, but also empowered as partners in decision-making. This uncertainty about the meaning of public engagement leaves both local government communication strategists and journalists somewhat confused about their roles in relation to local civic participation.

Picking up this question of the role of news vis-à-vis the civic sphere, we asked: what is the role of local media in bridging distances of 'race', ethnicity, and class? Focus group participants stated that they had no sense of local media performing this bridging role; even when they try to it is received as cliché. In the case of Leeds' Chapeltown Carnival – reportedly the oldest West Indian carnival in the UK, mainstream news providers' annual photographs picturing happy carnival goers are received as a cover for what really goes on 'down there in Chapeltown'.

> F: *It's never really appealed to me to go, and it's not that far away.*

> M: *I think it's because you know exactly what goes on there; it's not all singing and dancing. (Exchange, Focus Group 2)*

Indeed, there were mixed views in the focus groups as to whether bridging distance is even something that the media *should* be doing. Media workers absolutely see this as a part of their role, and community activists agree. Members of the public expressed a range of views on this subject of the role of the media in fostering diverse perspectives. Moreover, personal experience and its lack combine to make word of mouth news that is both trusted and at the same time unreliable. Where people's actual interaction with people of other 'race', ethnicity, and class groups is minimal, storytelling fosters dissatisfaction and division; for instance, several of our focus group participants complained that Chapeltown receives a disproportionate amount of public funding:

> *It's an absolutely fantastic event having been and the sense of community and everything is amazing. There is a frustration about the amount of money that is spent down there but ... (Focus Group 1, Female interviewee)*

> *We call Chapeltown elastic; if there's a shooting in Moortown they'll say Chapeltown. If resources come to Chapeltown it'll go somewhere else. And we know that factually and we see it. Chapeltown is used as a tool to gain mass resources. Whether the work gets done there for*

young people or for adults in them areas is another thing in itself.
(Interview with Lutel James, Chapeltown Youth Development Centre)

What does seem to be (largely) agreed on by our range of interviewees is that local news media representation contributes to an *idea* of Chapeltown (and its annual carnival) which, at the very least, does not break down distances of race, ethnicity, and class and, at worst, fosters them. Here then, the Leeds Media Ecology study confirmed that local news is at once practice (e.g. Bourdieu, 1977, 1992; Couldry, 2004) and story; both relied upon and yet distrusted information, travelling through the media ecology of a city, yes, but – much like the news diffusion in Philadelphia – encountering blockages of troubling kinds:

I played pro-football for ten years full-time. The biggest question I used to get asked all the time is 'What's it like living down there?' I says 'It's not a zoo, it's an area.' But I understood some of their perceptions because all they see factually is the media coverage, so the media coverage informed them and that's why they came up with a view that there must be loads going on down there negative. Not one time did they bring reference to anything positive.
(Lutel James, Chapeltown Youth Development Centre)

You only come to us when you want to talk about extremism, you only want to talk to us when there is an incident at the Chapeltown carnival. So I think yes, that is significant because, for me, the diversity has to be embedded in who you talk to about things that are of importance and relevance to a wider audience. That's work in progress.
(Rozina Breen, BBC Radio Leeds)

F: I think they need to recruit more ethnic minority people, definitely.

M: I would say it's OK saying they are multicultural without showing it – they should show it as a multicultural society in Leeds [...] They have got to show it in the programme that Leeds is a multicultural society. When you can see it on the programmes you can say they are doing something. Even if they slot a small time for ethnic minorities or show a multicultural society, it's a starting point. Up to now they haven't done that. If they do this that will be a good start.
(Exchange, Focus Group 4)

Conclusion: the media ecology of the city, implications for understanding local journalism

We want to conclude this chapter by exploring overlaps in the findings of the two, distinct, projects that shed light on the production and circulation of news in the contemporary city. First, we consider the usefulness of 'small data' (Couldry et al., 2013) for understanding news in the media ecology of the city. Secondly, we suggest that, while Anderson discovered early reporting around the edges of news stories and the Leeds team did not, these distinctions may reconcile themselves at the level of *interpersonal conversation*. Therefore we suggest a crucial and central role for interpersonal communication in the construction and subsequent movement of news through the media ecology of the city. Third, we speculate that, taken together, the two studies provide insights into the beliefs of media producers and the perceived role of the audience or news consumer – particularly the desire of news organisations to focus on what they called 'real people' and the way that so-called citizen journalism may be appropriated by news organisations under the banner of 'authentic narratives'. Fourth, we consider briefly the way our studies demonstrate the continued importance of legacy media institutions in both Leeds and Philadelphia. Finally, we discuss how the Leeds study adds an important cultural component to Anderson's analysis of 'information ecosystem blockages' in Philadelphia.

What can we learn about local journalism through an ecological or ecosystem approach? The small-data approach central to both the Philadelphia and Leeds studies methods for exploring that ecology clearly works to deliver a rich set of pictures of what news is; how this varies; how news travels and does not and how the answers to these questions are in flux in the contemporary digital culture. In reflecting upon the contrasts and significant similarities between these two studies, we are convinced that, despite the increasingly grand claims of 'big data' studies, there is much to be gained from the analysis of small data – and of big-data collections, such as the two we conducted, being treated as composites of small data that are best understood through qualitative disaggregation. The Leeds study relied on empirical social science techniques, with particular attention paid to the individual experiences of citizens reading, exchanging, and producing the news. Anderson's work turned nodes on a social network map into real people, institutions, and activists, all with a variety of motivations to share, produce, and consume information.

Both studies focused significantly upon the role of interpersonal communication in the flow of local news. Anderson's focus was in the agency of nodes within what are all too often depicted as faceless online networks. His study shows how the making and diffusion of news depends upon personal actions, often connecting with degrees of 'savviness' on the part of entrepreneurial citizens. Beyond that his study highlights how, within digital space, the line between person-to-person communication (or small group to small group communication) often shades imperceptibly into *journalistic* communication. In the Francisville Four study, for instance, Anderson shows how initial reports about the eviction of four political activists from their neighbourhood home by police was originally seen as 'news' by the activists themselves and as 'personal communication' by news providers. These examples can be multiplied throughout the chapter. The more qualitative aspects of the Leeds study, on the other hand, also drew attention to the crucial function of civic influencers: people who spread the messages of local news as part of their everyday interactions. Much of the news diffusion tracked by Anderson can indeed be seen as a materialisation, through digital technology, of the kind of ordinary conversation discussed in the Leeds study – the kind that has always occurred around items of news, this time rendered permanent and searchable via the World Wide Web.

Both studies highlighted a strong media interest in somehow capturing the percieved authenticity of these local voices; of inflecting the formality of news with the accents of 'real people', while at the same time subjecting these real voices to a gauntlet of journalistic oversight and professional scrutiny. While Anderson did not study the audience in consumption mode, both studies speak to the particular role of the 'people formerly known as the audience' (Rosen, 2006) in relation to the production and circulation of news in the contemporary media ecology of the two cities in question. Indeed we suggest that one key outcome of both studies is precisely to highlight the theoretical limitations of the category 'audience' and the related clearcut separation between producers and audience. As noted in the analysis of the Philadelphia findings, news organisations often incorporated 'citizen produced content', not because they were convinced of its newsworthiness or the fact that it fulfilled journalistic obligations, but simply because it provided those organisations with original sources of information that carried with them the whiff of 'authenticity'. And news producers in Leeds, likewise, provided some further evidence of the strength of this desire by continually appealing to the importance of 'ordinary folks'. The role of so-called citizen journalism, in other words, may be more to provide traditional media outlets with authentic content than to rewrite the rules of news production as such.

This ties into a key finding of both projects, one increasingly reiterated in digital journalism studies of various kinds, but one perhaps still under-appreciated – the continued importance of centralised, bureaucratic, legacy media organisations within a fragmentary media landscape. The Philadelphia and Leeds studies come at this question from opposite angles, and together their findings make the point even sharper. In Philadelphia, as Anderson argues, the vast majority of 'original reporting' was still carried out by the legacy news organisations of the *Inquirer* and the *Daily News*. While non-professional journalism was important, in the grand scheme of analysis it amounted to only a fraction of the total amount of news in the city. And in Leeds, while the researchers did not conduct a census of original reporting, they did discover that citizens still trusted the established news outlets, like BBC North, far more than they did the other local players.

When we turn our gaze to an entire local media ecosystem, finally, we can see that there are still 'blockages' of various kinds in these theoretically frictionless digital networks. The Philadelphia study, with its social network analysis and ethnographic immersion, points to structural and institutional blockages. But the Leeds study makes an important addition to Anderson's somewhat antiseptic analysis, reminding us that local news in the digital age does not inevitably (even with increased participation from a variety of digital contributors) break down distances of race, ethnicity, and class but can actually foster these attitudes. In other words, the information cul-de-sacs in Leeds and Philadelphia do not simply stem from the long-tail shape of the ecosystem, nor simply from institutional priorities, but can also be attributed to very real cultural codes embedded in the ideologies of much important media content. The media ecosystem is not a utopia of freely flowing knowledge, even in the digital age – in part due to digital structure, but in part also due to attitudes and cultural lenses that have always existed within news organisations and other cultural producers.

While Chapter 1 with its analysis of Seattle in the US and Toulouse in France has primarily focused on the differences in cross-national local news production, this chapter instead found a number of similarities within the emerging urban news ecosystem in both Leeds and Philadelphia. The fact that local news institutions here as in the Danish case analysed in Chapter 2 are both important and trusted even as they become only one of many information producers on the web, the fact that much content generated online has always existed in the form of 'citizen talk' but is now digitally traceable in a new way, the fact that news both moves because people make it move and is often blocked because of cultural, structural, and organisational factors – these findings are not new, per se, but the fact that they emerge from a comparative context adds weight to a body of literature that sees the digital transformation of local news production as resulting in neither complete stasis nor utopian revolution, but rather in a complex mix of change and inertia.

Note

1   The members of the Leeds team are Christopher Birchall, Jay G. Blumler, Stephen Coleman, Giles Moss, Katy Parry, Judith Stamper, and Nancy Thumim, all from the Institute of Communications Studies, University of Leeds.

Bibliography

Anderson, C. W. 2009. 'Journalistic Networks and the Diffusion of Local News: The Short, Happy News Life of the Francisville Four', *Political Communication*, 27(3): 289–309.

Anderson, C. W. 2013. *Rebuilding the News: Metropolitan Journalism in the Digital Age*. Philadelphia: Temple University Press.

Bourdieu, P. 1977. *Outline of a Theory of Practice*. Cambridge: Cambridge University Press.

Bourdieu, P. 1992. *The Logic of Practice*. New edn. Cambridge: Polity Press.

Couldry, N. 2004. 'Theorising Media as Practice', *Theorising Media and Practice*: 35–54.

Couldry, N., H. Stephansen, A. Fotopoulou, and R. Macdonald. 2013. 'Digital Citizenship? Narrative Exchange and the Changing Terms of Civic Culture', *Citizenship Studies*, 18(6–7): 615–29.

Darnton, R. 2000. 'An Early Information Society: News and the Media in Eighteenth-Century Paris', *American Historical Review*, 105(1): 1–35.

Dewey, J. 1916. *Democracy and Education*, ed. J. A. Boydston and P. Baysinger. Carbondale, IL: Southern Illinois University Press, 1985.

Howard, Philip. 2002. 'Network Ethnography and the Hypermedia Organization: New Media, New Organizations, New Methods', *New Media and Society*, 4(4): 550–74.

Latour, B. 2005. *Reassembling the Social*. Oxford: Oxford University Press.

Law, J. 1994. *Organizing Modernity*. Oxford: Blackwell.

Marres, N., and R. Rogers. 2005. *Recipe for Tracing the Fate of Issues and their Publics on the Web*. http://eprints.gold.ac.uk/6548/1/Marres_05_Rogers_recipe_copy.pdf.

Park, R. E. 1925. 'The City: Suggestions for the Investigation of Human Behavior in the City Environment', *American Journal of Sociology*, 20(5): 577–612.

Park, R. E. 1938. 'Reflections on Communication and Culture', *American Journal of Sociology*, 44(2): 187–205.

Project for Excellence in Journalism. 2010. *How News Happens: A Study of the News Ecosystem of One American City*. www.journalism.org/2010/01/11/how-news-happens.

Rantanen, T. 2009. *When News was New*. Malden, MA: Blackwell Publishing.

Rosen, Jay. 2006. 'The People Formerly Known as the Audience', *PressThink*. http://archive.pressthink.org/2006/06/27/ppl_frmr.html.

Stillwell, J. C. H. and P. Shepherd. 2004. 'The "Haves" and "Have-nots": Contrasting Social Geographies', in R. Unsworth and J. C. H. Stillwell (eds), *Twenty-first Century Leeds: Geographies of a Regional City*. Leeds: Leeds University Press, 127–46.

Part II

Local Journalism and its Interlocutors

Local news is usefully seen as the product of a set of relational practices that involve far more than professional journalists and conventional media organisations (whether old legacy media or new start-ups) and also include self-interested sources like politicians, government officials, businesses, community groups, and sometimes individual citizens. If the notion of local media ecosystems highlights the environment in which news moves, the idea of local journalism as a set of relational practices involving various interlocutors highlights how news is produced, disseminated, and perceived, by whom, where, and why within an ecosystem, and invites us to consider who else but journalists are involved in these processes. One view tends towards the more holistic and structural, the other towards individual agents and their sometimes ephemeral and occasional practical relations.

Journalists and the media organisations they work for remain central to the production and circulation of local news. But it is important to recognise that they also explicitly and implicitly work to *present* themselves as central to the production and circulation of credible information in the community; that they, consciously and unconsciously, stage their own symbolic role. We should not simply accept this self-presentation at face value. Broader analysis of local news as the result of a set of relational practices brings in a wider range of perspectives from the activists, civil servants, PR professionals, and the ordinary people who are also involved, sometimes as sources and co-producers of local news, sometimes simply as audiences (or not even as audiences). Journalists may present themselves as gatekeepers who exercise editorial control over the flow of news in the community. But leading politicians and senior bureaucrats may well feel they have considerable influence over what is covered (and what is not), just as some community activist groups seem confident in their ability to set a media agenda, challenge and change seemingly dominant narratives, through the news or by other means. Similarly, individual citizens may not share journalism and media organisations' sense of self.

Seeing local journalism in the context of its various interlocutors and the practical relations it is part of connects with a long tradition of warning against 'journalism-centric' and 'media-centric' (Schlesinger, 1990) approaches to understanding news production and circulation, and embraces work underlining the importance of a wide range of sources in co-producing the news (Cook, 1998), especially local government, politicians, and businesses and their PR work (Lewis et al., 2008) as well as perhaps community activists of various sorts (Anderson, 2010). It builds on a recent tradition interested specifically in the practical dimensions of how news is produced, circulated, and understood by actors on the ground in the local ecosystem (Anderson, 2013; Domingo and Le Cam, 2014; Firmstone and Coleman, 2014).

The potential of seeing local news in terms of both local journalists and their interlocutors (including a wide range of different actors such as co-producers, rivals, and users) is demonstrated here by three chapters focusing on a variety of actors and their relations with and perceptions of local journalism. In Chapter 4, Florence Le Cam and David Domingo examine the role of local politicians, community activists, and community media as co-producers of local news in a case study from Brussels in Belgium, paying particular attention to the ways in which each type of actor works to define their own role in local news production processes. In Chapter 5, Julie Firmstone and Stephen Coleman analyse how city council officials, journalists, and citizen journalists in Leeds in the UK define the role of local legacy media and new digital media in the local communicative space, in particular in terms of public engagement. In Chapter 6, Bengt Engan presents a study focusing on how two very different groups of Norwegians – local politicians and young people who live in the same communities – see the relevance and credibility of local journalism from their own separate vantage points.

These chapters show how a broader view of local journalism as a set of relational practices involving many different interlocutors in turn helps us understand the concrete processes through which local news is produced, contested, circumvented, and how it is perceived by people in the local community.

References

Anderson, C. W. 2010. 'Journalistic Networks and the Diffusion of Local News: The Brief, Happy News Life of the "Francisville Four"', *Political Communication*, 27(3): 289–309. doi:10.1080/10584609.2010.496710.

Anderson, C. W. 2013. *Rebuilding the News: Metropolitan Journalism in the Digital Age*. Philadelphia: Temple University Press.

Cook, Timothy E. 1998. *Governing with the News: The News Media as a Political Institution*. Chicago: University of Chicago Press.

Domingo, David, and Florence Le Cam. 2014. 'Journalism in Dispersion', *Digital Journalism*, 2(3): 1–12. doi:10.1080/21670811.2014.897832.

Firmstone, Julie, and Stephen Coleman. 2014. 'The Changing Role of the Local News Media in Enabling Citizens to Engage in Local Democracies', *Journalism Practice*, 8(5): 1–11. doi:10.1080/17512786.2014.895516.

Lewis, Justin, Andrew Williams, and Bob Franklin. 2008. 'A Compromised Fourth Estate? UK News Journalism, Public Relations and News Sources', *Journalism Studies*, 9(1): 1–20. doi:10.1080/14616700701767974.

Schlesinger, Philip. 1990. 'Rethinking the Sociology of Journalism: Source Strategies and the Limits of Media-Centrism', in M. Ferguson (ed.) *Public Communication: The New Imperatives*. London: SAGE, 61–83.

4

The Plurality of Journalistic Identities in Local Controversies

Florence Le Cam and David Domingo

Introduction

Journalists have for decades claimed jurisdiction over the production and circulation of news (Delporte, 1995; Schudson and Anderson, 2008) and, consequently, have monopolised the symbolic role of the actors who *do* journalism. In the last decade, some French researchers have tried to understand – inspired by the work of Michel Foucault – the *'dispersion'* of journalism (Ringoot and Utard, 2005) by proposing that journalism is the product of the diversity of definitions that a plurality of actors in a society propose in their daily interactions to narrate current events. Therefore, journalism cannot be reduced to those whom a process of institutionalisation has consolidated as professional journalists. It has to be extended and seen as involving a much broader diversity of actors (Ringoot and Ruellan, 2007: 73–4). This chapter explores this proposition in order to find a way to trace this potential *dispersion of journalism* in a local context, and to understand the plurality of journalistic identities coexisting in the same geographical area. We would like to move from the already fruitful description of the variety of actors involved in producing journalism today to an analysis of their relationships, their strategies, and the outcome of these dynamics (Domingo and Le Cam, 2014). If we take as our point of departure the idea that any social actor can potentially perform journalistic practices, researchers are then finally able to retrace without any preconceptions power relationships, negotiations of what qualifies as news, and the documents produced and circulated. The main objectives of such a research programme would be to analyse (a) the dispersion of professional identity and the efforts of imaginary boundary building and (b) the dispersion of news production and the construction of narratives.

Local journalism provides the best scenario for tracing this multiplicity of news producers, their interactions, and their strategies to ensure their own position in the journalistic 'ecosystem' (e.g. Anderson, 2013). Local news circulates between actors who know each other: local media are well-known in the territory; relations between politicians, public relations professionals, journalists, and citizens can take place in observable time and spaces (Frisque, 2010; Gans, 1980; Gieber, 1964; Harrison, 2006; Le Guern and Leroux, 2000; Ollivier-Yaniv, 2001; Schudson, 2003).

In order to analyse these relationships, we needed to find a specific moment in time and space in which dispersed discourses about a topic highlight the different positions of the actors, rendering understandable and traceable discourses and practices. Controversies (Callon, 1981; Jobert, 1992) are especially useful for tracing the dispersion of journalism, as the different social actors involved are more visible than in other circumstances. For any social event, there are two main overlapping categories of actors: those involved in the event, and those engaging in producing the narrative about the event. In many cases actors involved are active producers of narratives, but not necessarily. And although professional journalists are usually just producing narratives, they may end up being involved. For the researcher, it is important to identify both, in order to have a comprehensive account of the diversity of actors.

But choosing a controversy is a delicate process. Our attention has been drawn to an event that occurred in May 2012, mixing radical Islamism, multiculturalism, and a pre-electoral context in a local municipality called Molenbeek, in Brussels (Belgium). This case, explained in the first part of the chapter, helped us to reconstruct the practices and discourses of all the actors involved in the production of the news narrative about the controversy: journalists from mainstream media or from the Muslim community, politicians, policemen, bloggers, etc. We were intrigued by the news production and circulation practices of these actors outside the boundaries of normative definitions of journalism, and how they (re)define journalism as a social practice beyond the identity and practices of professionals.

This chapter explores how the actors who participated in the construction of the news narrative think of themselves, and construct their own position in the media landscape. It builds on an earlier analysis where we mapped the actors who achieved visibility in the mainstream media during the controversy and thus gained a preliminary picture of the core of those involved in producing the narrative in the news (Domingo and Le Cam, 2014). We found that every local actor we met develops (personal or collective) strategies to ensure his position and to construct his identity. They all use a specific discourse of domination in the construction of the narrative. In doing so, in this local place, at the time of the controversy, every actor was convinced that he played a major role in shaping the news narrative. In fact, they were all also contributing to a collective discourse about the plurality of journalistic identity. This chapter first explains the local controversy chosen, its nature, and the methodologies applied to trace it; then it explores how the actors try to control the narrative and how they participate to make the news; afterwards it analyses how actors think as if they were journalists themselves. Finally the chapter concludes with some proposals to consider journalism as a social practice in dispersion.

Tracing a local controversy

Defined as 'at the same time a large village and a small metropolis', Brussels offers

> a panoply of languages, cultures and social codes [that] rub against each other. It very clearly demonstrates the notion that urban culture is generated by the encounter and the interaction between different and independently functioning social, economic and cultural systems. Indeed, Brussels is a pre-eminently polytopic city, a collection of disparate places where a lot of things happen simultaneously in so many different ways. (Sterken, 2004: 93)

Brussels is the capital of Belgium, and the largest municipality of the Brussels-Capital Region, which comprises 19 municipalities, like Anderlecht, Etterbeek, or Molenbeek.

The media landscape in the city is mostly bilingual, representing the two main cultural communities in the country: French-speaking and Flemish-speaking. At the same time, Brussels' multiculturality is also reflected in a plethora of other journalistic projects: many migrant communities and European actors have their own news outlets. Local and national newspapers, radio, or TV can reach the same audiences

101

in the city. An inhabitant of Brussels can hypothetically read a national newspaper in French, listen to the radio in Flemish, and watch Maghreb TV on the web at the end of the day. In Brussels, community journalism does not represent a big part of the news production. Some radio, web TV, and newspapers do exist, defined by a target audience with cultural similarities (language, origin, religion), and are designed by and for this particular group.

For the purpose of this chapter, we could not reach all the actors in so many different languages. For convenience, we chose to analyse the French-speaking media sector of the city (which includes some of the Muslim community media), and to focus on a local event in the Brussels-Capital Region. The controversy discussed in this chapter – the research programme of which it is part will, eventually, focus on several cases – occurred on 31 May 2012. In the morning, a woman in niqab was questioned by Brussels police in the street. In Belgium, this piece of clothing that just leaves the eyes uncovered has been forbidden by law in public spaces since 2010. She refused to show her face, and an altercation followed with the policemen. She was brought to the police station in Molenbeek (a multicultural municipality with a vibrant Muslim community). In a few hours, information started to circulate through text messaging, Twitter, and Facebook, instigated by a Salafist group called Sharia4Belgium (as we would understand the day after). Protests erupted at the end of the day and caused disturbances in the city for at least two days. Politicians, especially the mayor, the Interior Minister, and the police, tried to manage the event, as did Sharia4Belgium. On 1 June, the group convened a press conference in which its leader and the woman in niqab gave their version of events and called for revenge. Every actor knew that the topic was very touchy, mixing radical extremism, multiculturalism, and an electoral context (local elections were to be held in October 2012). We called this incident the Molenbeek case.

As we explained in the first step of the study (Domingo and Le Cam, 2014), we analysed the mainstream media coverage during the first six days following the incident between the police and the woman in niqab and we interviewed the journalists who produced the news stories. The main aim of this phase was to map the actors who achieved visibility in the mainstream media, to have a partial picture of the core of those involved in producing the narrative of the controversy, and to understand the relationships the professional journalists have with their sources.

From our sample, based only on mainstream media content, it would seem that professional journalists have a crucial role in producing the news narrative, giving more space and prominence to some sources over others. These first results could tempt us to conclude that institutions that traditionally have been stable and privileged sources for journalists are central in this controversy and impose their discourse as the core of the news narrative. Journalists in mainstream media defend a hegemonic position in the construction of an event's news narrative by dismissing alternative voices in favour of the trusted institutional ones and by not recognising the role of community media. These results tally with that of other research, and refer to the efficiency of news sources (Gans, 1980), and the symbiotic relationships (Gieber, 1964) or the interdependence (Legavre, 2011) between journalists and sources. Local journalists have even been called 'passive journalists' (O'Neill and O'Connor, 2008) and referred to as 'mere processors of one-sided information or bland copy dictated by sources'. Nevertheless, these preliminary conclusions were focused on the use of sources: which of them appear, which of them are silenced. We were tracing the nature of sources and the circulation of news to try to understand the actors involved in the narrative. Beyond the sources that were explicitly quoted in the articles, during the research interviews, professional journalists shared the *invisible* and *alternative* sources which they regularly interacted with, but seldom appeared represented in their stories: Muslim community media, NGOs, and activist groups.

From this starting point, we then focused on the practices of non-professional journalistic actors, gathering the content they were producing without the mediation of mainstream media, on websites, community radios, and social media. We interviewed the spokesperson of the police in Brussels West (S1), the mayor of Molenbeek (S2), the director of the Centre pour l'égalité des chances, the Centre for Equality, an independent public organisation against racism (S3), two editors in chief, one from a monthly community magazine, *Le Maroxellois* (C1), another from a local community radio station, Radio Al Manar (C2), as well as a freelance journalist and blogger (J8). Our aim in this new step was to reconstruct the practices and discourses of these actors involved in the production of the news narrative about the controversy: they use journalistic practices (genres, angles, sources) to produce their own proposals of the news narrative through interactions with professional journalists and also produce their own narratives through radio broadcasts, magazines, web TV, institutional websites, blogs, and social media. These actors represent other forms of news making that may reach different publics than the mainstream media and play a crucial role in the formation of a plural public opinion.

The analysis has thus gradually moved away from the study of the circulation of news and the construction of the narrative and on to explore the discourses about the journalistic identity of those who contributed to the news narrative. In order to understand the dispersion in our local case, we gradually constructed the hypothesis that every actor we met (1) was arguing about the fundamental role he or she played in the narrative, (2) was developing discursive strategies to ensure this position, and (3) in part constructed his or her identity in regard to journalism. In doing so, all actors involved voiced a discourse of domination with themselves positioned above others: sources thought they dominated journalists by carefully planning their interactions, professional journalists felt that they dominated the narrative over alternative media, alternative media considered they had an advantage over mainstream media because of the knowledge they had of their community, etc. And this expression of domination seems to be a strategy to build up some sort of journalistic identity, not in the sense that they think they *are* journalists, but in that they construct a specific role they play *in* journalism. The next paragraphs will expand on this hypothesis, by focusing on how the official sources, Muslim community journalism, and other actors talked about the circulation of news.

Making the news, controlling the narrative

During our research interviews, every actor involved in the controversy articulated a discourse which gave them a central role in the construction of the narrative. Not only did they explain how they tried to control the narrative, but they also detailed their strategies to construct their dominant positions. Their strategies reveal the way they manage interactions, how they construct a figure, a representation of themselves towards others – especially with spokespersons who centralise the flow of news – and how they all use silence when necessary in order to maintain their position or the way they want others to understand the narrative.

The initial key sources for mainstream media in the Molenbeek case (the police, the prosecutors' office, the mayor of the municipality) systematically attempt to control the discourses and the timings of the newsgathering process by channelling their relationships through centralised spokespersons and by structuring the interactions in daily rituals. In the police headquarters, the morning starts with an internal meeting where a 'filter' of events of the previous day is prepared to share with the press, with an emphasis on 'spectacular' ones (S1). The list is sent to the prosecutors' office, who checks with the judges what stories can be released, and they are then forwarded to the emails of journalists of the crime beat. Two press conferences are held by the prosecutors' spokesperson at 11 a.m. and 2 p.m., and a journalist of the national news agency Belga is always there. The next day, the internal meeting at the police headquarters includes a press clipping of the articles reporting on their activities, and the spokesperson may call those journalists who have misrepresented the information he provided. This effort to centralise and structure their interactions does not deter 'good journalists' (S1) from consulting other sources, including policemen, but the police spokesman insisted to his people that they should always defer to him, that there should be just one voice for the institution. On the political side, at the local level discourses were also mainly concentrated on the mayor of Molenbeek. Other local politicians preferred to stay away from the media focus in such a delicate issue in the multicultural municipality.

This centralisation is a strategy to reduce the dispersion of discourses, a way to order the circulation of news. But this centralisation seems to be a recent development among these institutional sources. At least, our respondents recalled that this has not always been their communication strategy: there has been a historical evolution from dispersed practices (corridor work of the journalists, informal contacts with judges) to concentrated ones, from institutional silence as the main strategy to regular communication as the way to guarantee the domination over the news narratives constructed by the journalists. Nowadays, the official sources do not only provide press releases or interviews, but also pictures, and the spokesperson of the police is available for the journalists at any time: he recalls being interviewed live on television in front of his own home over the weekend. There is a paternalistic attitude towards the media in this eagerness to provide them with information in a constant and structured way: 'If they did not have the information from an official source, they would just write stupid things in the newspapers' (S1). Official sources tend to portray it as an asymmetric relationship, with them imposing the power of their credibility over the journalists, whom they assume would take anything they say as the truth.

Official spokespersons usually have a team of communications professionals working for them to make processes run efficiently. But the centralisation makes the relationships with the media personal: the police spokesman and the mayor himself were the ones responding to the journalists during the controversy, not the members of their public relations team. This individualisation of the voices shows how sources can become nodes in the process of circulation. Our discourse analysis of news stories (Domingo and Le Cam, 2014) has illustrated the limited diversity of actors appearing on mainstream media coverage; one of the reasons could be this centralisation and the personal incarnation of institutions through individuals.

Sharia4Belgium, the Salafist group involved in publicising the controversy, reproduced many of the strategies of these institutional sources, which helps explain their success in getting their discourse represented in the news, even if it was framed by other discourses that condemned its radicalism. Compared to other non-official sources, our interviewees agreed with the journalists that Sharia4Belgium was very efficient in their communication strategies. 'Their leader knows very well how the media works' (C1). A secondary source (S3) to the news coverage interpreted that the woman in niqab was most likely trying to reactivate the debate about the law passed in 2011, and that her close connection with Sharia4Belgium suggests that this was an incident consciously staged to attract media attention. The activist group also tried to centralise their discourse through their spokesperson, who was the only one appearing openly, speaking for the woman and for the group. He had given his phone number to many journalists, and was eager to answer their calls and to send them announcements via SMS. He controlled his public appearances, and was also using YouTube to directly address the supporters of the movement.

The respondents who belonged to the Muslim community developed their own discourse about the Molenbeek case: the incident is not representative of the attitudes of the entire community. They insist in reducing the significance of the case, trying to isolate it from other events that are part of the daily life of Molenbeek. Sharia4Belgium make 'a lot of noise' but 'only represent themselves' (C1), they insist: Muslims in Brussels are not activists of this sort. They criticise the mainstream media for giving too much attention to Sharia4Belgium and making generalisations that harmed the image of the community, instead of interviewing the people who work with the community every day, who do positive things for the community. The sole professional journalist producing news in French for the local Muslim community radio argues that the Molenbeek case was too tempting for journalists who want to sell newspapers. These discourses can help us to understand the coverage community media gave of the event, which was much less intense than that of mainstream media. The community magazine actually silenced the case: it devoted an issue to the phenomenon of extremism in Belgium, but did not discuss specifically the Molenbeek incident. The magazine has a 'pedagogical' tone, based more on interviews with key voices in the community than on reporting on events.

The freelance journalist, acting as a local blogger as well, also did not think it was worth devoting energy to reporting on this controversy. He is known for having produced and diffused online (on YouTube and his own blog) the first video reportage about Sharia4Belgium a few months before the controversy our case study focuses on, and is a recurring reference in the discourse of traditional journalists. In producing the video, he was following his interest in discovering for the public unknown social actors which may have a future impact in public opinion, people with 'media potential' (J8). He did not follow the Molenbeek case, because the radical group was already a 'media star' by then, and he prefers not to cover well-known people. This could be interpreted as a personal strategy to position himself professionally as a reference for mainstream media, who may identify him as the expert in specific topics such as multiculturalism in Brussels. In that sense, discovering unknown social actors is also a way to dominate the flow of news, to accumulate power in the local media arena.

The Centre for Equality, the anti-racism NGO, only participated in the news narrative in a reactive way, when approached by the journalists regarding the possibility of banning Sharia4Belgium. They refrained from giving press releases because of their previous negative experience of being misquoted and ignored by the media a year before when they defended the need for a thorough public debate about the proposed law to ban clothing that covers the face. They mainly silenced the case to control their own discourse and the consequences of a negative mediatisation.

Silence does not occur only during interactions with professional journalists; it is also a strategy used in other communication activities. Many institutions have created official magazines to communicate with the citizens (Le Bart, 2000), and more recently websites have been added to these institutional journalism publications. But neither the police, the municipality, nor the Centre for Equality used their own media outlets to report, explain, or just communicate about the case. They silenced the

Molenbeek incident, preferring to focus on other topics that fostered a positive image of their institutions. The mayor argued that the municipal magazine of Molenbeek has to go to everybody, and in that sense is limited to 'information in a strict sense' (schools, cultural activities, holidays). A conscious decision was made to avoid polyphony and cacophony.

Thinking as a journalist

All actors are very aware of the process of news production: the temporality of newsgathering and publication, the need for a reliable flow of information, the practice of 'off the record', the fact that many journalists are freelancers and paid by the piece. Actors anticipate interactions with and reactions of others. They develop a well-informed discourse about the process of producing local news and to some extent internalise what they perceive to be the news values and production routines of local media in order to better manage how they appear in the news (similar to what has been found with social movements, e.g. Gitlin, 1980: Sobieraj, 2011). For example, institutional sources punish with silence the journalists that do not follow their rules, and with disciplinary action the members of the institution that leak information without following the official channels. These practices consolidate a self-representation of their dominant position. However, despite this self-image of powerful sources, actors also admitted that news making is in fact a process of interdependency (Legavre, 1992, 2011), where sources strive to get a positive image of themselves in the media coverage by being very strategic in what they share with journalists and what they silence, but where they never have complete control over what the journalists end up reporting. 'The bad things, [journalists] will know by themselves' (S1). Sources and journalists need each other and build a relationship based on a fragile mix of trust and distrust (Legavre, 2011).

The expectations of sources regarding professional journalists are quite intuitive. The communication practices of the spokespersons develop from personal experience, from their process of socialisation with the newsgathering process. They had to discover for themselves what the most effective attitude is. Even if some of them had had some training, they refer to their expertise as something cumulative, based on practice: 'I am part of the old generation. I have never been organised concerning public relations. I am an improviser concerning relations with the press. I have long been a star for TV programmes because I am very reactive' (S2). They know and they anticipate what can become a good story for the media. They immediately identified the Molenbeek case as something that would make the front pages of the newspapers. Being quick to react to journalists' questions requires that one is constantly up to date with what is happening in their jurisdiction, especially now that social media spreads rumours so quickly. Despite the fact that among our interviewees journalists seldom mentioned using social media as a source systematically, sources were very concerned about the risk that Facebook or Twitter posed to their control over the timing in releasing information. They admitted not knowing how to deal with these communication methods, despite being very interested in adding them to their set of tools to circulate their discourses (S1, S2, S3).

The dynamics of the news coverage in the first days of the Molenbeek case were partly defined by these existing structures and practices, but also influenced by very specific circumstances that disrupted the usual rituals. The information about the detention in Molenbeek quickly was relayed to the spokespersons a few hours after it happened. The mayor warned the police about possible protests as he was confronted by some young men when walking in the neighbourhood. They reacted quickly to the first calls for details from journalists covering local issues. The police spokesman knows these reporters very well, but the political implications of the connection between the Molenbeek incident and Sharia4Belgium quickly brought onto the scene other journalists who specialised in national politics. This made the spokesman much more careful in how much information he released about the incident, 'because I did not have a link of confidence with them' (S1). That first evening most of the information exchange with the journalists was done on the spot, as events were developing (S2). Roles were very naturally divided between the different sources, with the police discussing the details of the detention and the action taken against the protests, and the politicians dealing with the condemnation of radicalism. To reassure the police, and due to the process of coverage, the initial story (the accusation of police violence made in Molenbeek and Sharia4Belgium) was not followed up by national journalists, who were framing the story from the angle of political debates about integration. Even if sources seem very careful when dealing with multiculturalism, conscious that it is a delicate topic, they mostly agree that media tend towards coverage that privileges polarised positions, erasing from the discussion voices that ask for dialogue. The coverage of the Molenbeek case was interpreted as predictable by several interviewees (S2, S3, C2), in the context of previous news narratives that stigmatised Molenbeek as the home of Islamist radicals and public insecurity. 'Media think that their publics are polarised, and that they should accommodate their views, but I am convinced that it is their coverage that polarises public opinion' (S3). They are also quite aware that, sometimes, the commercial interests of the media push journalists towards a coverage that tends to ignore positive events: 'If you try to explain that things are going better than we think, this is not fascinating for journalists as we know them today' (S2).

In contrast with these expectations regarding the mainstream media, community journalism has usually been depicted as news producers fighting against simplistic and scandal-prone coverage, or, at least, developing a discourse about a failure by mainstream journalism to meet the diverse needs of the community (Meadows et al., 2009). But, surprisingly, the two community journalists used their knowledge of journalism to present themselves in a very traditional way. The editor in chief of the community radio programme built his own credibility by referring to a very normative discourse on journalism: the basic rules, neutrality, objectivity. He explained that he wants to 'normalise' the community radio programme, reach out to the wider public, and presented himself as a traditional journalist. He claimed that the radio programme cannot be the spokesman of the community, and argued that promoting neutrality in their coverage is the best way to calm the tensions within the community (C2). This journalist had to deal with the coverage of local and international news, and could not devote much time to the Molenbeek case, even if it made the headlines in the hourly bulletin for a few days. He wanted to be objective, trying to broadcast 'only the facts' with 'the most simplicity possible'. The lack of resources in the radio newsroom at that time forced him to cover the event from his desk, searching for information on the websites of traditional media, reproducing their angles, which did not seem problematic as he shared similar journalistic values. Every half hour, they alternated two radio bulletins, one in French, the other one in Arabic. Sometimes the two journalists, one for each language, were translating their news for each other; sometimes they were working separately. They were trying to be complementary. Besides the newscasts, the Molenbeek case was covered in the other programmes of the station, debates and talk shows. The community journalist distinguishes his work from the approach of those programmes, which are much more engaged in an activist attitude.

The editor in chief of *Maroxellois* (C1) presents the magazine as a mirror of the Moroccan community and a tool for it to present itself to the rest of the city. He considers himself as an actor of the community, as a citizen who wants to defend and protect the image of the community, distinguishing the magazine from mainstream media. But at the same time, he resorts to traditional rules of the process of news production: the magazine has an informal network of 'neighbourhood correspondents' who provide information that the five members of the association producing the magazine then verify and report on. They are acting like other journalists: trying to contrast discourses, verifying facts, and then building a narrative. They do not want to be seen as activists, but rather as serious actors who produce news (on events or through debates). The editor adheres to a normative definition of journalism, downplaying the differences between the magazine and mainstream media. He never mentioned difficulties in reaching official and institutional sources. He acknowledged that they could not be considered a mainstream publication, but he proudly boasted about his links with the key local sources: he could call them and have exclusive news relayed.

Institutional sources themselves have diverging points of view regarding their relationship with community journalists. The police spokesperson is not always comfortable with MaghrebTV or other community media as they challenge his position. He thinks that he always has to defend himself as he feels under attack when he is invited by these media. Despite this, he considers that he needs to keep in touch with them as they talk to his neighbourhood; they help him reach out to the Muslim community. The mayor of Molenbeek expressed having good relationships with the local community radio station. He felt confident about being accessible to them, because the stories he would share with the editor in chief were taken into account in the news bulletin. The community media's attitude of docility or aggressiveness towards their sources shapes their relationships.

Conclusion: playing with – and inside – journalism

Journalism as a social practice is the result of the identities and actions of multiple actors. In the Molenbeek case, personal conversations had a central role in events, becoming a key journalistic practice that orthodox analyses of news production would surely have overlooked. The mayor of

Molenbeek first heard about the case by chance: he was passing in front of the police station and was addressed by young people. During the events, his strategy was to communicate with the people, the police, and the media face to face. He also met a delegation of imams from the local mosques in order to relay his position to the Muslim community through them, without the intermediation of mainstream media that are mostly distrusted in the neighbourhood. The mayor considers this offline social network as fundamental. The editor in chief of the monthly magazine confirms that in the Muslim community most of the information circulates in the cafés, in conversation. 'If you go to a café, you will get to know everything that is happening in Brussels, you do not need to listen to the radio' (C1). He gets many story ideas for his magazine or his blog this way. This orality in a way takes us back in time, to the early forms of journalism and the troubadours or the African *griots* (Colson et al., 2013). The oral circulation of news was also, in the Molenbeek case, a way to express a cultural identity, a way to play with journalism with other codes.

Journalism, as a social practice, is historically defined. The Molenbeek case is relevant to trace current trends in the production and circulation of news narratives. Our analysis, however, did not encompass all the discourses produced around the controversy: traditional media, community journalism, and institutional sources do not distribute all the information about local events. Diverse tools or practices are relevant to understand how information spreads, and how local news ends up reaching citizens: SMS, social media, word of mouth, and meetings are among the strategies that surfaced during the Molenbeek case. SMSs were sent by Sharia4Belgium to call for protests, videos on YouTube were broadcast, personal Facebook profiles helped to spread the news ... Policemen have smartphones and personal Facebook accounts and they may post pictures and comments from crime scenes that disrupt the centralised discourse attempted by the spokesman. This is against the rules, but they sometimes do it 'innocently' (S1). This 'viral circulation' is much harder to follow in a qualitative study. But the discourses of our actors are very relevant on this topic. For the journalist of the community radio station, the first news of the incident spread through social media. He is critical about the potential consequences, though: 'Social media can cause the news, but do not necessarily give the news' (C2). All the sources admitted that they have neglected this aspect of circulation of news. The director of the Centre for Equality admits that they should have created interactive spaces and used social media to convey their discourse about migration and integration.

But they did not have the skills or resources to do so. The mayor thinks that, at the time of the Molenbeek case, he was too conservative: he neglected social media. According to him, a very dynamic minority can change public opinion. The Molenbeek case seems to reveal an abyss between citizens and institutions concerning the appropriation of social media.

All in all, journalism as a social practice is what a wide variety of social actors think it is. In the Molenbeek case, every actor developed personal or collective ways of thinking and acting in journalism. Everyone involved constructed a discourse of control, using centralisation of speeches to make sure their voices would be heard. They thought in terms of domination over the others, always stressing their role and position in the process of news production. In doing so, they engaged in producing journalism, multiplying the actors involved in it, extending the practices of journalism beyond the professionals. Schudson (2003) proposed calling 'parajournalists' all those actors facing professional journalists: public relations firms, public officers, political staff, etc. The Molenbeek case leads us to think that, instead of being 'parajournalists', these actors construct, in their own way, a plurality of 'journalistic identities'. A large variety of local actors, in some specific cases, not only want to play a role in the production of news, but also to have an impact in journalism, to participate in the definition and the practices of journalism. They stage-manage a hybrid identity that includes a journalistic identity, an identity fashioned to appear as part of a journalistic narrative. They spend so much energy anticipating, understanding, avoiding some of the newsgathering strategies, acting in the process of local production of information, that without claiming a professional journalistic identity, they definitely participate in the dispersion of journalism, acting as news producers, thinking as news workers.

Bibliography

Anderson, C. W. 2013. *Rebuilding the News: Metropolitan Journalism in the Digital Age*. Philadelphia: Temple University Press.

Callon, Michel. 1981. 'Pour une sociologie des controverses technologiques', *Fundamenta Scientiae*, 2(3–4): 381–99.

Colson, Vinciane, Juliette De Maeyer, and Florence Le Cam. 2013. *Du Pigeon voyageur à Twitter: histoires matérielles du journalisme*. Brussels: Espace de Libertés.

Delporte, Christian. 1995. *Histoire du journalisme et des journalistes en France: Du XVIIe siècle à nos jours*. Paris: Presses Universitaires de France.

Domingo, David, and Florence Le Cam. 2014. 'Journalism in Dispersion: Exploring the Blurring Boundaries of Newsmaking through a Controversy', *Digital Journalism*. doi:10.1080/21670811.2014.897832.

Frisque, Cégolène. 2010. 'Des espaces médiatiques et politiques locaux?', *Revue Française de Science Politique*, 60(5): 951–73.

Gans, Herbert J. 1980. *Deciding What's News: A Study of CBS Evening News, NBC Nightly News, Newsweek and Time*. London: Constable.

Gieber, Walter. 1964. '"News is what newspaper men make it"', in A. Dexter Lewis and David Manning White (eds), *People Society and Mass Communication*. London: Free Press of Glencoe, 289–97.

Gitlin, Todd. 1980. *The Whole World is Watching*. Berkeley, CA: University of California Press.

Harrison, Shirley. 2006. 'Local Government Public Relations and the Local Press', in Bob Franklin (ed.), *Local Journalism and Local Media: Making the Local News*. London: Routledge, 175–88.

Jobert, Bruno. 1992. 'Représentations sociales, controverses et débats dans la conduite des politiques publiques', *Revue Française de Science Politique*, 42(2): 219–34.

Le Bart, Christian. 2000. 'Les Bulletins municipaux: Une contribution ambigüe à la démocratie locale', *Hermès*, 26–7: 175–84.

Legavre, Jean-Baptiste. 1992. 'Off the record: Mode d'emploi d'un instrument de coordination', *Politix*, 5(19): 135–57.

Legavre, Jean-Baptiste. 2011. 'Entre conflit et cooperation: Les journalistes et les communicants comme "associés-rivaux"', *Communication et langages*, 169: 105–23.

Le Guern, Philippe, and Pierre Leroux. 2000. 'Les Limites de l'espace public médiatisé: L'exemple d'une télévision locale', *Hermès*, 26–7: 159–73.

Meadows, Michael, et al. 2009. 'Making Good Sense: Transformative Processes in Community Journalism', *Journalism*, 10(2): 155–70.

O'Neill, Deirdre, and Catherine O'Connor. 2008. 'The Passive Journalist', *Journalism Practice*, 2(3): 487–500. doi:10.1080/17512780802281248.

Ollivier-Yaniv, Caroline. 2001. 'L'Indépendance des journalistes à l'épreuve du politique et de la communication: Le localier, le chargé de communication et l'élu local', *Quaderni*, 45(1): 87–104.

Ringoot, Roselyne, and Denis Ruellan. 2007. 'Journalism as Permanent and Collective Invention', *Brazilian Journalism Research*, 3(2): 67–76.

Ringoot, Roselyne, and Jean-Michel Utard. 2005. *Le journalisme en invention: Nouvelles pratiques, nouveaux acteurs.* Rennes: Presses Universitaires de Rennes.

Schudson, Michael. 2003. *The Sociology of News.* New York: Norton.

Schudson, Michael, and C. W. Anderson. 2008. 'Objectivity, Professionalism and Truth Seeking in Journalism', in Karin Wahl-Jorgensen and Thomas Hanitzsch (eds), *The Handbook of Journalism Studies.* New York: Routledge, 88–101.

Sobieraj, Sarah. 2011. *Soundbitten.* New York: New York University Press.

Sterken, Sven. 2004. *Brussels, City in Plural: Some Thoughts Concerning the Image of the Belgian Capital.* Leuven: KU Leuven. https://lirias.kuleuven.be/bitstream/123456789/430810/1/Argos_sven-EN.pdf.

5

Rethinking Local Communicative Spaces: Implications of Digital Media and Citizen Journalism for the Role of Local Journalism in Engaging Citizens

Julie Firmstone and Stephen Coleman

Introduction

There is concern in the UK about the current and future role of the local news media in informing and educating citizens about local democratic processes and issues. The landscape of the local media is undergoing a multitude of changes. Changes in cross-media ownership rules have encouraged media companies to increase their market share and to expand across delivery platforms; hyperlocal news sites are emerging; a recent government-led initiative has created 19 local TV licences; and local newspapers are struggling to retain readerships or shutting down completely. Coupled with ongoing debates about the inadequacy of the local media in fulfilling their role as informers, opinion leaders, and watchdogs, these developments create potential challenges to the established value of local mainstream journalism in mediating between local authorities and the public. It is not just that local media are in a state of flux, but that their normative role of serving citizenship is also changing (Blumler and Coleman, 2013). The need to do more than simply 'get a message across' or provide information during elections is compelling local authorities to explore ways of communicating directly with citizens and engaging them in local issues without journalists as intermediaries (Aspden and Birch, 2005; Lowndes et al., 2001; Michels and De Graaf, 2010). Strategies designed to promote public engagement are now commonplace among local authorities and have become particularly relevant in the context of economic austerity, when citizens and communities are under increasing pressure to provide and/or manage their own services. Citizenship is no longer conceived in terms of reactive or passive service consumption. As governments have increasingly employed the rhetoric of 'active citizenship' and 'the Big Society', both citizens and local media have found themselves under pressure to adopt new roles in relation to the democratic polity.

The emergence of digital media has amplified opportunities for citizens to participate in local democracies, both as consumers of increasingly diverse sources of information relating to local issues and in newly configured production roles via social networks. These changes in the context of local journalism raise questions not usually addressed in journalism studies, which have tended to adopt a media-centric perspective. Potential new roles of citizenship and journalism are evolving in a communication ecology in which traditional divides between governing institutions, journalistic intermediaries, and citizens are no longer as centralised, linear or manageable as they used to be. In local communication ecologies the flow of messages, memes, and images exceeds the industrial production–distribution–reception model and takes a much more uncoordinated, though still interdependent, form. Whilst there is a widespread sense on all sides that such change is happening, there is much less certainty about how the dynamics of local communications ecologies function in reality, and perhaps most importantly, the implications this may have for the democratic value traditionally attributed to the local mass media. In order to evaluate the changing value of journalism in relation to local democracy, we need to better understand the relational dynamics of a wide range of interested parties in the production and consumption of local news.

The research presented in this chapter contributes to this understanding by examining practices of public engagement as a tangible feature of contemporary local democracy. It draws on theories relating to the normative roles of the news media in order to evaluate the value of local journalism as a contributor to democratic public engagement. Through a case study of the UK's third largest city, Leeds, we evaluate the implications for the roles and values fulfilled by local journalism of three emergent characteristics of the relationship between the news media, citizens, and governing institutions. These characteristics are:

(1) strategies designed by local authorities with a view to engaging citizens in matters relating to local governance;

(2) heightened opportunities for citizens to use digital media in order to become producers and disseminators of local news; and

(3) the potential of digital media to allow local government to communicate directly with citizens without journalists as intermediaries.

We suggest that these characteristics should be regarded as ideal conditions, not unlike Weber's (1952) 'ideal type'. That is to say, they derive from accounts of how democratic relationships could or should work. We can refer to such ideal conditions as measures to explore and evaluate empirical reality. By identifying elements which contribute to an ideal condition, we might come to see how aspects of the ideal are dependent on a range of structural opportunities and constraints. For example, the *ideal* of representative political institutions using digital media to speak with citizens directly is often predicated on the scope for interactivity afforded by such technologies and the possibility of this generating a permanent conversation characterised by vertical and horizontal communication flows between citizens, governing institutions, and other interested parties. The *ideal* of citizen journalism imagines citizens producing a different type of local news from the mainstream media, based upon citizens' ease of access to and familiarity with local information. Thus citizen journalists would produce an alternative source of news, characterised by the wisdom of local knowledge, that would compensate for the insufficiencies in local news coverage left by the decline of the local mainstream media. Each of these projected situations would have implications for the role of the mainstream news media in a local communication ecology, perhaps diminishing their value to governing institutions and citizens in setting political agendas and facilitating democratic debate. We consider the value of local journalism in terms of the normative functions commonly attributed to news, which suggest that journalists should inform and educate citizens about local issues, be representative of the opinions and voice of citizens, hold governing bodies and organisations to account on behalf of citizens (the watchdog role), and proactively campaign on matters of public interest (Barnett, 2009; McNair, 2009).

Following a description of the research method, this chapter is set out in four sections. First, we define public engagement and discuss how various actors in a local communication ecology regard the roles of digital media and local journalism in facilitating democratic engagement. Next, we construct a typology of citizen journalism, considering the various roles that citizens can assume in the creation and circulation of local news. This typology is used to evaluate the structural reality of the way that different forms of citizen journalism contribute to engagement. Third, we consider the implications for the role of the mainstream local news media of one local council's current use of digital media to communicate directly with citizens. The chapter concludes by evaluating the implications of our findings for the value of mainstream local journalism in engaging citizens in local democracy.

Method

Our case study centres on one local council in the UK. Whilst we think that this case is indicative of opportunities and constraints in similar cities, we do not claim that it offers a complete picture of relationships between citizens, local journalists, and governing bodies across the UK or globally. Rather, we aim to provide some empirically grounded reflections on the changing role of local journalism in contemporary local democracy.

We focus on the large post-industrial city of Leeds (also discussed in Chapter 3), situated in the north of England in the county of West Yorkshire. The city has a fast-growing, ethnically and culturally diverse population of 751,500 (as of the 2011 census) and is the third largest city in both England and the United Kingdom. Leeds City Council (LCC) is responsible for providing all statutory local authority services, including education, housing, planning, transport, and social services. Although each of the three main political parties in England (Labour, Liberal Democrat, and Conservative) is represented on the council, LCC has historically been governed by a Labour majority, with the party being elected into power in each election between 1980 and 2004 and again in 2010 and 2014. In spite of its recent economic success as a financial and commercial centre, the 'Indices of Deprivation' for 2010 revealed high levels of poverty in parts of Leeds and there is evidence of a large digital divide. The mainstream local broadcast media in the district comprise two regional television news programmes (BBC's *Look North* and ITV's *Calendar*), BBC Radio Leeds, and several independent radio stations with limited news output. The BBC also has an online news service based in the region. The most popular daily newspapers are the *Yorkshire Evening Post* (*YEP*, focused on the locale covered by LCC), its sister publication the *Yorkshire Post* (covering the region), and two local papers in the outlying towns of Morley and Wetherby. Like in most UK cities, the hyperlocal news, citizen journalism, and blog sector in Leeds has grown in recent years. It ranges from arts and culture orientated sites and hyperlocal news sites to online versions of magazines advertising local services.

Three different semi-structured interview schedules were designed to investigate public engagement from the perspective of actors fulfilling a variety of roles in the engagement process: council-based actors involved in engaging the public on behalf of the council; actors who fulfil a role in engaging citizens in local issues through the media, digital and mainstream (journalists and citizen journalists); actors who are neither part of the media nor the council but have experience of public engagement exercises (local NGOs). Twenty-three face to face interviews were conducted, recorded, and transcribed in the summer of 2012.[1] During the hour-long interviews all actors were asked the same questions, with the wording of some questions tailored to their role. Interviewees were selected to represent the three functions described above. The 12 council interviewees included elected politicians (councillors) (3), council engagement strategists (2), members of the council communications team (3), heads of directorates (2), front-line council workers (2), and, as the lowest tier of local government, parish councils (2) (see Table 5.2). Outside of the council the sample focused on media actors from the mainstream local news media and new digitally based forms of citizen-led news media. We selected for interview four journalists who report on local politics, one from BBC TV, one from BBC Online, and two from the *YEP*. Our interest in citizen-led media was limited to those sites whose content contributes to debates about local democracy. This led us to select interviewees from two hyperlocal sites, Beyond Guardian Leeds and South Leeds Life, as well as the author of a well-known civic-orientated local blog. In addition, we interviewed two locally based NGOs. Interview questions were designed according to a constructivist approach. Thus, in addition to asking explicitly about perceptions of the local media's role in engaging the public in local issues we attempted to detect how actors understood the role of different media from broader questions about public engagement. Actors were also asked to give practical examples of contributions of the news media to engagement, and to think about how this has changed and may change in the future. The following discussion is based on a detailed reading of the transcripts from which a set of common themes were identified.

The relationship between public engagement and modes of communication

Before turning to an evaluation of the ways in which local journalism contributes to public engagement, it is important to consider what this term means to the various actors involved in local democracy. Although public engagement is increasingly expected and required of local authorities, we found significant variations in the ways that the term is understood, both by actors within local government and the local media. As we have written elsewhere, it is clear that the construction of the concept of public engagement is highly contested, reflecting a range of normative approaches to democracy that might not be compatible with one another (Coleman and Firmstone, 2014). To capture this, we have developed a simple typology to describe three contested conceptions of engaging the public. Depending on which of these conceptions is being used at a particular moment, actors will envisage different criteria of success and thus have differing expectations of the role of communication in realising them.

A first definition of public engagement, according to our typology, is mainly *informational*, entailing a one-way process of disseminating useful knowledge to citizens. By ensuring that citizens understand the role and actions of the council, interviewees considered that expectations could be managed with a view to facilitating a positive relationship between the council and the public. Thinking of engagement as a linear process of information dissemination mainly entails a monological use of digital technologies by the council, with interactivity limited to users' capacity to navigate their way to personally relevant data. The role of local media in facilitating informational engagement is as a medium for the provision of civically relevant information.

A second definition of public engagement is more active, with the objective of enabling citizens to have a *conversation* with the council about local issues. The aim here is to enable citizens to contribute their views to policy processes from which they had been hitherto excluded. The most obvious form of this is through consultations where the public is encouraged to feel that they are able to 'have a say', with the expectation that they will be listened to. Crucially, for consultative engagement to be considered successful, it is important that the public understand how they have been listened to, and in what ways, if any, their contributions have been acted upon. Feedback, or at least some form of dialogical communication, is therefore a key characteristic of successful consultative engagement. This calls for the inventive use of dialogical communication paths that can encourage not only one-to-many messaging by the council, but many-to-one and many-to-many.

The third and least common conception (and practice) considers engagement as a partnership between governing institutions and citizens, through which the latter are *empowered* as partners in decision-making. This requires the council to do more than just listen. It requires citizens to take responsibility for their input into decision-making and to have a considerable degree of control over technologies of interaction – for it would be rather meaningless to speak of 'partnership' if only institutionally embedded partners are able to manage either the decision-making process or channels of communication through which policies are formed and debated.

In the latter two, more active forms of engagement, the local media could add value by not only providing critical information about policy options, but helping to publicise opportunities for participation, providing channels for feedback and negotiation, and comparing and contrasting the diverse sources of opinion, experience, and expertise gathered from individuals and communities, as well as governing institutions. This need not place the local media in a position of merely advertising the council's attempts to generate public engagement. They would continue to have a critical role, but one that also acknowledges the existence and consequence of new democratic pathways.

The relationship between citizen journalism and public engagement

The term 'citizen journalism' is defined in many different, sometimes contradictory, ways (see Robinson and Deshano, 2011; Williams et al., 2011, for useful summaries of citizen journalism). Whether described as participatory journalism, user-generated content, hyperlocal news, or citizen journalism, the only point that scholars seem to agree upon is that digital media have changed the nature of the relationship between consumers of news (the audience) and those who traditionally produced news, information, and critical commentary (journalists). Given the pace of change in the technologies affording non-professional journalists a vocal role in the media ecology, such role instability is unsurprising. However, in order to consider the relationship between the multiplicity of non-professional journalist identities and mainstream journalism, and the resultant implications for the value of mainstream journalism in local democracies, it is necessary to untangle the various definitions and interpretations of citizen journalism. Accordingly, we have developed a typology of citizen journalism based on our interviewees' perceptions and understandings of the roles citizens can now play in news production (see Table 5.1).

Table 5.1 Typology of citizen journalism

When citizens contribute to the news media as (usually) collectively organised producers of information and opinion independent of mainstream news media through hyperlocal news sites and (usually) individually organised civic-orientated blogs, we call them *CJ producers*.
When individual citizens contribute to mainstream and citizen journalist produced news media as active and deliberate sources of information through the provision of unsolicited content, be that photographs/video or text, we call them *CJ contributors*.
When individual citizens' participation in Twitter, Facebook, or other social media is used as a news source by mainstream journalists, we call them *CJ sources*.
When individual citizens engage in a participatory role in local news and opinion through the online forums and social media of mainstream news media, we call them *CJ participants*.

These differing types of citizen journalism are distinguished by whether they are organised collectively or individually, and whether their content requires a host media (CJ contributors, CJ sources, CJ participants) or is independently mediated (CJ producers). They are also differentiated by the contributions they make to the ideal of citizen journalism. Goode suggests that 'citizen journalism feeds the democratic imagination largely because it fosters an unprecedented potential, at least, for news and journalism to become part of a conversation' (2009: 8). However, the contribution of citizen journalism to this conversation or, more precisely, to public engagement in local issues, is determined by a number of elements which determine how far citizen journalism can contribute to the realisation of a more engaged local democracy. These elements include the extent to which citizen journalism

(i) empowers citizens by bolstering their participatory role in setting the news media's agenda;

(ii) establishes valued and trusted channels through which local authorities are prepared to communicate with citizens;

(iii) establishes citizen journalism in a 'replacement' role to fill the gaps left by the decline in local mainstream media (Metzgar et al., 2011; Ofcom, 2012); and

(iv) encourages active citizenship by facilitating dialogical communication between local authorities and citizens.

In what ways did any of these elements of citizen journalism contribute to public engagement in our case study?

Participating in setting the agenda

In principle, citizen journalism could play a part in reshaping the local media agenda. Mainstream local news organisations could incorporate contributions from citizen journalists as a new element of news production. This might involve either mainstream journalists including CJ content in their own stories or CJ producers becoming established within the local communication ecology in their own right. However, we found that, although the journalists we interviewed did not consider CJ producers as competitors, they had not nurtured working relationships with hyperlocal news sites and blogs and did not see CJ producers as a regular or reliable source in newsgathering. Journalists also raised concerns about the validity of using other forms of citizen journalism (CJ contributors, sources, and participants) in professionally produced news. They were concerned that information and news available from individual citizens may be at odds with their obligation to produce news according to the professional norms of objectivity and impartiality. Several journalists pointed to the need for caution in using material produced by citizens, including information given by individuals on Twitter, due to the often biased motives of the producers who were perceived to be pursuing their own agendas rather than public-interest values. These perceptions echo findings from other studies which have suggested that mainstream journalists' caution about the value of much content produced by citizen journalists serves to heighten the role of mainstream journalists as 'gatekeepers' (Hujanen, 2012; Lewis et al., 2010). Another way for mainstream journalists to represent the views of citizen journalists in news could be by hosting 'conversations' in which citizens can comment on the news as it seems to them. When describing the ability of audiences to reflect on news stories via comment boxes and social media, journalists were silent about their own participation in this. The fact that audience participation in news is not seen as an interactive or dialogical process suggests that journalists do not see engaging with the audience as part of their professional role. A superficial analysis of comments from the audience on news pages suggests that they are rarely responded to by journalists or by key local actors, such as councils. At best, they are horizontal conversations between the audience, and at worst they are 'one-off' comments thrown into a black hole which is unlikely to convince anyone that their voices are being heard. This suggests that journalists have a perception of their role in public engagement which is limited to being a source of information, and although they consider themselves to represent the public interest this does not involve engaging directly with the public. This supports claims by Paulussen et al. (2007) that mainstream media have been slow to embrace the possibilities for interaction and the hosting of citizen-generated conversations. It also seems to replicate journalists' reactions in the past to non-digital forms of audience engagement, such as letters to the editor. Wahl-Jorgensen (2007) suggests that most journalists do not embrace engagement with their audiences, who are often dismissed as 'cranks' when they voice their opinions. The lack of a visible dialogue between journalists and citizens perpetuates the distance that classical studies of journalism suggest exists between those who have the power to construct the news and the 'other' who remains in a passive role as consumer.

Establishing a valued role in the media ecology

If individual citizen journalists only very rarely contribute to the mainstream news agenda, are collectively organised citizen journalists any more effective? Might such CJ producers be regarded by the council as having a significant position in the communication ecology and thereby able to be used as a new channel through which to engage with citizens? Our research showed that CJ producers are not perceived by the council as alternatives, future substitutes, or even additional outlets to the mainstream media. Council officials, elected representatives, and spokespeople from local third-sector organisations were not widely aware of the local CJ producers operating within their area. Although the changing nature of the local news media landscape was recognised by those involved in communications and engagement at the council, relationships with CJ producers had not been established and were not being pursued. Overall, the contribution of CJ producers to public engagement was perceived as at best a way to access niche audiences. For example,

> I think it's potential at the moment and I think most of it reaches a very niche market. (Engagement strategist, senior)

Although one of the disbanded hyperlocal news sites had piqued the interest of several interviewees and was perceived as providing some new connections with citizens, the current activities of CJ producers were not perceived to be of any significant value to the council in terms of reputational management or informational engagement. For example:

> That [Guardian Leeds – now closed] was really good actually because daily it would really tap into what was happening in Leeds that day and we'd get a lot of people contributing to it. It was much more interactive than anything that had gone before. (Communications team, press)

The press team and representatives of hyperlocal news sites corroborated each other's descriptions of a distant, arguably non-existent, relationship, characterised by a lack of dialogical contact.

> They publish their own views but they don't actually come to us for comments or interaction on stuff. We'd certainly help them out if they did but they've never really felt the need to. (Communications team, press)

There had been no conversations between the council and local citizen producers about public engagement. One of the hyperlocal news sites did not think the council 'cared' about their role in public engagement, and only knew that the council was aware of their existence from analysing their web traffic and identifying some users as being from the council:

> From the council's point of view, I don't think we even signify [in public engagement]. (Hyperlocal journalist B)

Comments from the council's press team revealed scepticism about considering CJ producers' activities as journalism. Perhaps unfairly, there was an expectation that, despite the non-professional and community-based (non-profit-making) nature of CJ producers, they should adhere to professional journalistic norms and values such as objectivity and transparency when contacting sources. For example:

> I'm tending to find there seems to be a slipping of standards where, because it's open to anybody now, people don't really understand how they need to be honest and ethical, although actually I do find a lot of student journalists also are a little bit questionable like that. It's not just citizen journalists. (Communications team, press)

The expectation for citizens to conduct their communications with the press office according to norms and values associated with professional journalism is an indication of the need for councils to think about how to 'de-mediatise' their communications or, in other words, how they communicate with citizens without the journalists as intermediaries.

Filling the local journalism gap

A third element of the ideal type of citizen journalism is that it would 'fill the gaps' left by the often commercial, partisan, or resource-starved mainstream local media. Based on interviewees' perceptions of the perceived deficiencies of mainstream local news in Leeds, this would require CJ producers to take a more locally orientated approach to news than the regionally organised television media; represent the voice of citizens in certain areas of the city that are perceived to be under- or misrepresented by mainstream news; and attempt to hold the governing institutions to account by resuming regular attendance at official council meetings, which has been abandoned by many mainstream news organisations in recent years. By exploring the motivations and practices of CJ producers, we found that hyperlocal news sites and local bloggers are not necessarily attempting to replace or compete with existing mainstream journalism, do not identify themselves as journalists, have very few ties with mainstream journalism, and often have clear civically orientated motivations (Firmstone and Coleman, 2014). CJ producers, although often referred to as citizen journalists or hyperlocal journalists, do not all consider themselves to be producing news according to professional journalistic conventions and/or values. For example:

> All we're doing is taking news that has been created by other people and aggregating it. That is in the process of changing this year, we're going to

start [...] going out and finding stories rather than passively regurgitating it, but for the time being we are a news aggregation service, we're not journalists. (Hyperlocal journalist B)

Whilst some would like to move towards a more journalistic function in the future, such as acting as a watchdog and reporting on council meetings, most recognised that their skillsets and business models prevent them from operating as news media organisations in the traditional sense:

Well, we had some fairly limited objectives when we set up, one of which was a sort of village noticeboard, making sure that people could find out what was going on. And part of it was about counteracting what we saw as a bias against South Leeds in the mainstream press and providing good news stories [... and] help people have a voice. (Hyperlocal journalist A)

Our case study suggests that citizen-produced news media in Leeds are being formed to represent a small minority of the population whose views and interests are neglected or misrepresented by mainstream local media. In many ways, such hyperlocal news sites and civic-orientated blogs are more akin to interest groups, run by volunteer citizens (not paid professionals), in the interests of a specific group of people, with the aim of helping their audiences 'have a voice'. Indeed, mainstream journalists see this knowledge as one of the strengths of CJ producers and one of the ways citizen-produced media can be more valuable than mainstream journalism. For example:

Obviously they [bloggers/hyperlocal new sites] are able on some specific campaigns to be, I won't say better than the BBC, but they're able to – like on planning arguments – really get involved with the council and hold them to account, particularly on very small things; or not small things but important to them, important in specific areas. (BBC journalist, online)

Whilst this may suggest that CJ producers are fulfilling a democratically valuable campaigning or watchdog role, we should look more closely at the methods, motivations, and professional values of citizen journalists before concluding that they are pursuing such roles according to the same role orientations, norms, and values as professional journalists.

129

Facilitating dialogical communication

A fourth ideal condition of citizen journalism would be to facilitate a style of dialogical communication between local authorities and citizens that allows the consultative and co-productive aspects of public engagement to be realised. Digital media such as Facebook, Twitter, and discussion forums create the possibility of a permanent conversation between a variety of local actors and citizens through horizontally and vertically structured communication. Such a conversation would afford local authorities three ways of encouraging public engagement in local issues. First, there is an opportunity for direct communication with citizens through websites and social media. Second, digital media have the potential for councils to foster two-way relationships with citizens which would enable the essential conditions for consultative engagement – a dialogue between those in power and those they are supposed to represent. Third, the public-facing nature of digital media enables councils to analyse communication about local issues as a source of public opinion, even when councils are not directly involved in the communication. This latter surveillant function might take the form of sentiment analysis or the mapping of social networks.

Limitations of digital media

Given the potential of digital media to allow governing institutions to 'cut out the middle man' – journalists – and communicate directly with engaged citizens, we were interested to discover how committed Leeds council was to pursuing this approach. Council actors were certainly aware of the potential for digital media to contribute to an interactive and dialogical relationship with the public, but pointed to three important constraints. First, they had some difficulty developing a coherent strategy that could nurture interactive relationships with citizens via digital media. Secondly, they expressed concern that the digital divide would exacerbate existing social inequalities and believed that the mainstream local media are still likely to reach the kind of mass public consistent with democratic communication, at least for the foreseeable future. Thirdly, they lacked the resources and skills needed to manage online public engagement and interpret the vast range of opinions and sentiments expressed by citizens online. The combination of these factors resulted in limited and incoherent use of digital media and suggests that the mainstream media continue to be valued as the dominant means of communicating with citizens.

Leeds City Council has yet to establish a coherent strategy for direct communication with citizens through digital media (Firmstone and Coleman, 2015). Current use is highly fragmented and does not offer a viable alternative to communication through the mainstream media, even at the basic level of informational engagement. The motives for using digital platforms such as the council website and social media (two Twitter feeds and a Facebook page) have not involved any consistent attempt to exploit the dialogical potential of digital media and have therefore failed to contribute to consultative engagement. The absence of a clear strategy for digital media is linked to the uncertainty among those people fulfilling different engagement functions within the council about what public engagement means. The diverse range of uses of digital media by council actors include a mix of one-way information dissemination for reputational management by the press office; attempts to offer service provision and ensure customer satisfaction by the council's website team; and a variety of uncoordinated uses by different council departments. For example, the council website (which functions separately from the press office, despite being part of the same communications team) is used principally for service-related transactions and information provision communication – that is, paying for school dinners online and providing information on dates for refuse collection. The website team runs one of the council's two branded Twitter feeds, but only uses them for service-related information management. Another Twitter account is run by the press office where it is principally viewed as a way of publicising press releases, although they are slowly beginning to address the potential to communicate directly with citizens through this platform. However, they are aware that this requires them to develop a new set of communication skills which they have not yet fully understood. Until now the council press office has been locked into a mediatised form of communication, with journalists as the key targets of their messages. They are gradually adapting to what we have called a *civic de-mediatisation strategy* (Firmstone and Coleman, 2015) which requires messages to be tailored to a new logic whereby information is packaged in ways that appeal directly to the sensitivities of the public.

Concerns about the digital divide are used to justify strategic inertia around digital engagement. In order not to overlook the digitally disenfranchised, the mainstream media continue to be valued as democratic channels. Like many cities in the UK, Leeds has a diverse population, with significant sections rarely or never accessing the internet and lacking the skills needed to exploit the potential for digital engagement. Digital technologies clearly provide opportunities for the council to communicate directly with communities who are online, such as the thriving Leeds-based Twitter forums which focus upon local arts and culture. But the vast majority of people in Leeds do not access local news online:

> *Well there's a massive digital divide in Leeds [...] a report was done a couple of years ago on digital disenfranchisement in Leeds and there's whole postcodes that really don't care and there needs to be more engagement in those communities. (Hyperlocal journalist B)*

Thus, perceptions of the advantages of digital media were offset by overriding concerns about the difficulties of engaging the 'hard to reach' – which, in our interviews, seemed to include most of the city's population.

Even putting concerns about the digital divide to one side, interviewees commonly perceived mainstream media as the most trusted source of local news for citizens and therefore the most promising space for engaging with the public. This view was voiced by almost all interviewees, with comments suggesting that the local news media still have a greater ability to get information across to citizens than the council do themselves:

> *I would think if you take the media as a whole [...] a lot of the contact that an ordinary person has is reading about what the council has done. So I think we play a very big part because some of the other stuff that the council do directly themselves probably isn't read as much or seen as much. (Journalist, BBC Online)*

This view is supported by audience research which continues to rank mainstream local news media as the most common source of information about local issues, with television remaining by far the most important source of local news (Hargreaves and Thomas, 2002; Ofcom, 2013). Whilst people access local news from many sources, including online versions of newspapers and the internet in general, 46% cited television as the most important source of local news to them in Ofcom's 2013 survey.

Overall, then, council actors were aware that citizens' voices are increasingly conspicuous in digital media and some understood that this could provide valuable new ways for councils to interact and engage with citizens in dialogical forms of engagement. However, our case study suggests that the council does not yet have the skills, resources, or will to exploit digital media in this way. At best, the council is monitoring social media to gather information that may help in its reputational management, and in some isolated cases with service delivery. Interviewees suggested that this is mainly restricted to council-based Twitter and Facebook feeds, with no one mentioning monitoring the activities of CJ participants in digital versions of local media (mainstream or CJ-produced) or other non-council-hosted social media sources. From the perspective of our typology of public engagement, it would seem that citizen journalism is acknowledged as a contributor to an expanded space of information pluralism, but that it thus far lacks the reach or legitimacy to serve as a meaningful consultative or co-productive decision-making channel. As such, the council's approach to citizen journalism can be summed up as reactive and cautious. Citizen journalists as sources, contributors, and particularly as participants provide the council with a source of public opinion that can be analysed, but does not require any active engagement on the council's part. Without developing a mechanism to react to this type of engagement, citizen journalists will remain unaware that the council is listening to them. In the case of those citizen journalists who do not necessarily intentionally engage with local issues (CJ contributors and CJ sources), this is perhaps not expected. However, existing media forums (CJ participants) present a potentially viable platform for councils to engage with citizens who have signalled an interest in an issue by posting a comment and could be a valuable way of convincing citizens that councils are listening to them. Whilst the democratic potential of citizens' participation through digital media has been heralded, such participation does not necessarily lead to meaningful or successful engagement without some form of dialogue. Put simply, the following quote can only be true if someone is listening:

> *Anybody who's got a mobile phone can now comment on any story via Twitter or Facebook and so it is democracy in action on the largest scale ever really because everybody who previously had an opinion but didn't necessarily express it can now do it. (Reporter, YEP)*

Conclusion

Discussions of the role of media in local democracy tend to paint a bleak picture of readers abandoning newspapers, television news struggling to cover wider and wider regional remits, and newsgathering operations of local independent radio becoming more regional as they are merged with local sister stations (Aldridge, 2007; Franklin, 1998, 2006). There are particular anxieties about local newspapers, with Franklin concluding that 'Local newspapers are increasingly a business success but a journalistic failure' (Franklin, 2006: 4). Whilst these concerns are well founded, and indeed exacerbated by current economic pressures, our case study suggests that it would be unwise to assume that the normative democratic value of mainstream local media in relation to public engagement is any less important than it used to be, or that it is being displaced by citizen-driven digital media. While it is alluring to assume that the communication ecology within which local democracy operates is being reconfigured around the participatory potential of digital media, thereby diminishing the value of mainstream media, our evaluation of the structural opportunities and constraints which shape the local communication ecology in Leeds suggests that this is not (yet) happening. Mainstream local news remains the dominant and most trusted way of councils communicating with citizens. Digital media have certainly broadened the communication ecology, but a combination of a lack of understanding of new forms of media, limited resources to implement a digital strategy, and conservative perceptions of the media preferences and skills of the public serve to maintain the value of mainstream news media above that of digital media. Actors within the council perceived that the mainstream local media had an important historical relationship with local citizens which has established them as trusted voices in the communicative space of the city:

> I think the local newspaper, although its circulation has shrunk a lot, it still gets a lot of interest and it has a website and there's a lot of interaction there and they are still seen as an authoritative voice of Leeds and therefore it's important for us to work with them. (Communications team, senior)

Mainstream news organisations were trusted brands partly because their motivations, values, and limitations were widely recognised and understood by the political class. Journalists' roles in representing the public, acting as trusted sources of public information, and campaigning on local issues were seen as underpinning their contribution to public engagement. In comparison, there was uncertainty about the motives, legitimacy, and credentials of citizen-produced journalism. Interviewees clearly identified with professional journalists as operating according to a recognised code of conduct, according to professional ethics which serve as some sort of guarantee that they will facilitate fair and impartial communication with citizens. Whilst no one suggested that citizen journalists are unscrupulous, a lack of familiarity and understanding of their purpose in the communication ecology limited the value ascribed to them in relation to public engagement. This suggests that further research should investigate the motivations, routines, and practices of citizen journalists to establish their contribution to democratic debate.

In one sense, it is reassuring to see that those responsible for public engagement are not blinded by the rhetoric of transformation and empowerment that surrounds discussions of the potential of digital media to increase participation. Our interviewees highlighted the realities of the digital divide and the enduring preference of the public to access local news via mainstream journalism as important reasons why the participatory potential of digital media does not necessarily translate into increased instances of active citizenship. There were also indications that citizens not only still turn to mainstream news media for information, but also assign news organisations a continuing powerful voice as trusted mediators on behalf of the public. For example:

> *They [readers] look to us in terms of engagement to help them to engage because they do feel if it's in the paper the council take more note than [if it's said by] them alone [...] I don't know how many times I've had people say, 'Get it in the paper, they [the council] won't listen to us but they'll listen to you.' (Veteran journalist, YEP)*

This quotation and other findings caution against attributing a greater opportunity for individual political efficacy to the participatory potential of digital media.

Our typology of citizen journalism differentiates between participation in news production by collective and individual citizens. The analysis suggests that the voices of citizens acting as individuals have not yet been enhanced by their participation as citizen journalists or commentators. Digital media do not necessarily heighten individual citizens' access to the news media as sources, participants, or contributors. Due to the current structural characteristics of the council's media use, neither one-way nor dialogical uses of digital media systematically engage with individuals. There are also few indications that current opportunities afforded by digital media for citizens to participate in the construction of news, either as CJ sources, CJ participants, or CJ contributors, have eroded traditional barriers between media professionals and citizens. This further reinforces the notion that we should be cautious in assuming that the existence of technological capability will necessarily result in a transformation of citizenship or an increase in individual efficacy. More research is needed into audiences and their democratic engagement with representative institutions via digital media. There is a need for audience research into how citizens themselves feel about where they get their information from, what role they want different media to play, and what role they themselves want to play in the production of such information. How do citizens perceive their contribution to the communications ecology through citizen journalism and other participatory digital media – do they feel listened to, empowered? Such research must inevitably take on board continuing challenges of unequal access to digital media as well as pervasive problems surrounding attempts to incorporate citizens' experience and expertise in the most efficient and transparent fashion.

Most importantly, we conclude that all of the relevant actors discussed above – council, mainstream local media, citizen journalists, communities – are operating within a diverse and dynamic communication ecology. The days of evaluating local news and opinion circulation in linear terms of monological transmission are fast disappearing. The pressing need is for all actors to think about their democratic roles in the context of an interdependent communication ecology that transcends the institutional control of any one of them. Finally, given the valuable role attributed to mainstream journalism in our study, it is reassuring that, despite the challenges they face in fulfilling a democratic role in society, some of them remain committed to doing so:

> We are the eyes and ears of the public, of the tax payer, and it's our job to represent the facts of what the council is doing to better life for them. [...] My job as a journalist should be to get facts out there and to try and increase people's understanding of things that they might not otherwise understand. (Reporter, YEP)

Table 5.2 List of interviews conducted July–September 2012

3 × Elected Representatives (Councillors – Conservative, Labour, Liberal Democrat)

2 × Council Executives (Engagement team)

2 × Directorates (Youth/Leisure)

2 × Frontline Council workers (Youth/Leisure)

3 × Communications Team (Head of Communications, Head of Press Office, Head of Website)

2 × Parish Councils (one with an online presence, one without)

2 × NGOs/Interest groups (Youth)

4 × Mainstream local mass media (TV – BBC, Online – BBC, Press – *YEP* × 2)

3 × Non-mainstream media (2 × hyperlocal sites, 1 × blogger)

Note: All interviewees were given anonymity.

Note

1   Funding for these interviews was gratefully received from the EPSRC Digital Economy Communities and Culture Network.

Bibliography

Aldridge, M. 2007. *Understanding the Local Media*. Maidenhead: Open University Press.

Aspden, J., and D. Birch. 2005. *New Localism: Citizen Engagement, Neighbourhoods and Public Services. Evidence from Local Government*. London: Office of the Deputy Prime Minister.

Barnett, S. 2009. *Journalism, Democracy and the Public Interest: Rethinking Media Pluralism for the Digital Age*. Working Paper. Oxford: Reuters Institute for the Study of Journalism.

Blumler, J. G. and S. Coleman. 2013. 'Paradigms of Civic Communication', *International Journal of Communication*, 7(1): 173–87.

Coleman, S., and J. Firmstone. 2014. 'Contested Meanings of Public Engagement: Exploring Discourse and Practice within a British City Council', *Media, Culture and Society*, 36(6): 826–44.

Firmstone, J., and S. Coleman. 2014. 'The Changing Role of the Local News Media in Enabling Citizens to Engage in Local Democracies', *Journalism Practice*, 8(5): 596–606.

Firmstone, J., and S. Coleman. 2015. 'Public Engagement in Local Government: The Voice and Influence of Citizens in Online Communicative Spaces', *Information, Communication and Society*, 18(8).

Franklin, B. 1998. *Making the Local News: Local Journalism in Context.* 1st edn. London: Routledge.

Franklin, B. 2004. *Packaging Politics: Political Communications in Britain's Media Democracy.* 2nd rev. edn. London: Bloomsbury Academic.

Franklin, B. 2006. *Local Journalism and Local Media: Making the Local News.* 2nd edn. London: Routledge.

Goode, Luke. 2009. 'Social News, Citizen Journalism and Democracy'. *New Media Society*, 11(8): 1287–305. doi:10.1177/1461444809341393.

Hargreaves, I., and J. Thomas. 2002. *New News, Old News.* London: ITC and BSC Research Publication.

Hujanen, J. 2012. 'At the Crossroads of Participation and Objectivity: Reinventing Citizen Engagement in the SBS Newsroom', *New Media and Society*, 15(6): 947–62.

Lewis, S. C., K. Kaufhold, and D. L. Lasorsa. 2010. 'Thinking about Citizen Journalism', *Journalism Practice*, 4(2): 163–79.

Lowndes, V., L. Pratchett, and G. Stoker. 2001. 'Trends in Public Participation: Part 1. Local Government Perspectives', *Public Administration*, 79(1): 205–22.

Mcleod, J., D. A. Scheufele, and P. Moy. 1999. 'Community, Communication, and Participation: The Role of Mass Media and Interpersonal Discussion in Local Political Participation', *Political Communication*, 16(3): 315–36.

McNair, B. 2009. 'Journalism and Democracy', in K. Wahl-Jorgensen (ed.), *The Handbook of Journalism Studies.* London: Routledge, 237–49.

Metzgar, E. T., D. D. Kurpius, and K. M. Rowley. 2011. 'Defining Hyperlocal Media: Proposing a Framework for Discussion', *New Media and Society*, 13(5): 772–87.

Michels, A., and L. De Graaf. 2010. 'Examining Citizen Participation: Local Participatory Policy Making and Democracy', *Local Government Studies*, 36(4): 477–91.

Ofcom. 2012. *Public Service Broadcasting Annual Report 2012.* http://stakeholders.ofcom.org.uk/broadcasting/reviews-investigations/public-service-broadcasting/annrep/psb12.

Ofcom. 2013. *Communications Market Report 2013.* http://stakeholders.ofcom.org.uk/binaries/research/cmr/cmr13/2013_UK_CMR.pdf.

Paulussen, Steve, et al. 2007. 'Doing it Together: Citizen Participation in the Professional News Making Process', *Observatorio Journal,* 1(3): 131–54.

Robinson, S., and C. Deshano. 2011. 'Citizen Journalists and Their Third Places', *Journalism Studies*, 12(5): 642–57.

Singer, J. 2010. 'Quality Control: Perceived Effects of User-Generated Content on Newsroom Norms, Values and Routines', *Journalism Practice*, 4(2): 127–42.

Thurman, N., J.-C. Pascal, and P. Bradshaw. 2012. 'Can Big Media Do Big Society? A Critical Case Study of Commercial, Convergent Hyperlocal News', *International Journal of Media and Cultural Politics*, 8(2): 269–85.

Wahl-Jorgensen, K. 2007. *Journalists and the Public: Newsroom Culture, Letters to the Editor and Democracy.* New York: Hampton Press.

Weber, Max. 1952. 'The Essentials of Bureaucratic Organisation: An Ideal Type Construction', in R. Merton (ed.), *Reader in Bureaucracy.* New York, NY: The Free Press, 18–27.

Williams, A., C. Wardle, and K. Wahl-Jorgensen. 2011. 'Have They Got News for Us?', *Journalism Practice*, 5(1): 85–99.

Williams, A., et al. 2013. *The Value of Hyperlocal News to Democracy.* Paper presented at the Future of Journalism Conference, Cardiff University, September.

6

Perceived Relevance of and Trust in Local Media

Bengt Engan

Introduction

The term 'local newspaper' suggests that (1) the editorial anchoring is *local*, and (2) the authoritative, edited *news media* product is genuinely important, meaningful, and relevant to those situated in a specific geographic area within a nation. Based on this assumption and a series of interviews with a sample of (potential) users of local media, specifically young people and local politicians, this chapter discusses how three newspapers in different municipalities in the northern part of Norway work as 'local' 'newspapers': *Bladet Vesterålen* in Sortland, *Avisa Nordland* in Bodø, and *Helgelands Blad* in Alstahaug (circulation 7,400, 19,900, and 4,800, respectively). To the extent that they, like other media, seem to fulfil this role, I will further assume that they do so because they provide certain sociocultural *values* to their communities in terms of journalistic content that contributes towards building identity, stimulating economic development and promoting general vitality and optimism. 'Values' refers to media content that in some way appears as significant and beneficial to the public – or rather: the product *is given* a value by the users because they consider it to be significant (Picard, 1989: 35). The local news industry therefore may provide such sociocultural values if it actually helps people to orient themselves within their everyday social and physical environment, thereby enabling them to make conscious choices and facilitate people's understanding of their own and their community's position in a national and global context, to name just a few major functions. Based on the informants' reflections on the relevance of local media, I discuss *innovation* in local media somewhat indirectly. What user experiences and assessments imply that innovative initiatives are necessary if local newspapers are to be perceived as relevant and important in the years to come?

With a population of only 5 million scattered throughout a territory considerably larger than the UK, local and regional distinctiveness and identity have traditionally been essential to Norwegian culture and politics. Local administration and politics take place in as many as 428 municipalities, half of them with less than 5,000 inhabitants (Statistics Norway, 2013). The vast majority of the 229 Norwegian newspapers are local, which presumably reflects the readers' orientation towards their more or less immediate surroundings. At the same time, it should be noted that Norway has long been at the forefront of building digital infrastructure and helping to facilitate the widespread use of digital informational devices of all kinds. The general wealth has also contributed to a rapid penetration of a digital lifestyle and thereby an increasingly international orientation, not least among younger people, but also in the population as a whole. Hence, globalisation as a general phenomenon may pose some challenges to the local as a major social, cultural, and political anchoring point.

Thus far, revenues from subscriptions, single-copy sales, and advertising, combined with government support,[1] have made the newspaper industry in Norway as a whole a thriving and diverse 'self-sustaining system' (Omdal, 2012: 29; Mathisen, 2010). However, this applies in particular to the local press, as national papers have been facing a significant decline in circulation over the past two decades. But even for the local news media, the arrows are now pointing downwards, and only a small minority of them still enjoy circulation increases from year to year. The three newspaper enterprises in this study also experienced circulation losses over the past year, and even though this is not dramatic so far, it confirms that nothing can be taken for granted with respect to these newspapers' economic capacity in the years to come. This at least holds true so long as their revenues rely heavily on the income from print circulation. To some extent, fewer newspaper buyers are offset by the fact that local news is increasingly being read online. Nevertheless, this represents an insignificant part (1–5%) of the basic revenues for local newspapers. Consequently, they are still totally dependent on revenues from the print edition to maintain their business (Høst, 2013: 48).

The discussion in this chapter is based on interview data from 30 young people aged 17–20 years, and 15 local politicians from different parties in the three municipalities under study. The idea behind this choice of informants was that two groups being so different according to age, social position, and resources may represent an interesting span in relation to how local media are perceived and actually used. Young people are important because their preferences, assessments, and reflections may indicate certain aspects of a general lifestyle-related orientation, what role media of various types have in their everyday lives, and how the local newspaper fits into all of this. As for the politicians, they are of vital interest as sources for journalists, and thus are key players in the social contract of journalism, which in the end is an indispensable reason for maintaining journalism as a profession and a social institution.

The interviews took place from November 2012 until January 2013. They were semi-structured and mostly carried out in focus groups, primarily because this method is often regarded as being suitable for encouraging participants to discuss, rather than just answering questions, hence providing more nuanced statements that enable the researcher to 'obtain interpretations with socio-cultural relevance' (Gentikow, 2005: 86). The main purpose of the interviews was to examine the informants' relationship with the local paper, and what impact the media seem to have. More than just mapping the extent of media use, the study attempts to shed light on the reasons informants have for their use of these media (or lack thereof), whether in a print or online edition.

Young onliners

The young people who participated in the study were randomly selected from classes in high school, and the sample had a roughly equal gender distribution, with a slight majority of girls. The interviews reveal some (minor) differences with respect to attitudes and values, lifestyles, and media preferences. However, the material does not give any impression of systematic differences between the three cities/areas, and certain findings are clearly dominant.

First of all, and not surprisingly, the youngsters are avid media users, and the main tools for communication and the consumption of media content are smartphones and laptop computers. Social media are central; virtually all the informants use Facebook – and to some extent Twitter – regularly, and all day long. Photo-sharing services such as Instagram and Snapchat have also become an important part of everyday life. Facebook seems to be the pivot point for many types of information access and exchange, from making deals with friends and general chat to recommendations via links, including those leading to news media:

> [U2, Bo]² *I use Facebook all the time. Get important information about the sport I'm doing there. Everything is there, everything is stored there. Even things I do at school I upload to Facebook.*

> [U8, Al] *Many of the conversations we have at school and elsewhere are about what we have been aware of while using Facebook.*

> [U1, Sl] *After getting my iPhone it's much easier to check Facebook on it than on the PC. I simply get quite addicted to Facebook …*

> [U2, Sl] *I check Snapchat, Instagram, and Facebook on my mobile phone as soon as I wake up in the morning …*

Only a small minority of the young informants routinely monitor local news, and to the extent that they actually do so, they clearly prefer online editions of local newspapers. Those who have access to the local news in a print format at home are primarily seeking it to find something newsworthy within special interest areas, mainly within sports and culture. The young informants do not seem to pay much attention to the general, local journalistic content. When they do seek news they do it in a targeted way, because they were given a hint about something via social media. It seems that many see this channel as the place where they get information, even if they end up reading an online news article. A typical statement is:

> [U5, Al] *It is Facebook that provides information on what happens, you know …*

Younger people obviously do not acquire local printed news themselves, and they also generally seem to have a rather distant relationship with their local newspaper. If their family happens to subscribe to the newspaper, or buy it regularly in single copy, a few of the youngsters claim they read selected portions of the paper, that is, within a field that specifically interests them, but this is also a clear condition for them to have any dealings with their local media, at least in print.

When asked about what kind of news is of the most interest (to the extent that news engages at all) local news is most often considered trivial and quite uninteresting:

[U5, Bo] *I followed some of the presidential election in the United States. I think it was exciting. The local is not what I follow the most – strangely enough [...] it is perhaps what I should follow the most, since it is about my neighbourhood [...] I guess it's because there's not much dramatic news here in Bodø, not like murder, rape and the stuff happening in Oslo.*

[U6, Sl] *There is a lot of uninteresting news in the local papers and NRK Nordland [the regional branch of the government-owned broadcast company ...] there's a lot of silly stories ...*

Quite a number of the young interviewees are keen to regularly follow the news, but the ones who are most interested in news actually seem to prefer *international* news. The reason they give is that conflicts and the often spectacular content in news from abroad are more interesting than news from their own home town, which is regarded as 'small' and insignificant. Although presidential elections, wars, or natural disasters on a different continent are not perceived as crucially important for their own lives and their future, these types of news stories contain general issues and elements of drama that make them attractive. Local news in particular is indirectly conveyed via social media, with links and recommendations ('likes'). When asked about what local news they may be interested in, the informants typically mention accidents and other dramatic events, but a key criterion is whether there are any personal acquaintances involved in what has occurred:

[U16, Bo] *I am most interested in hearing about accidents and stuff around here, because someone I know may be affected. I am not that interested in [local] politics, because not many political issues here really concern me.*

A key issue for newspaper companies with a declining circulation is whether young people in the future will do as they used to – subscribe to a print edition as part of establishing themselves as adults. This is obviously difficult to predict with any certainty, although the circulation figures in *Avisa Nordland* suggest that this does not happen any more, or at least it happens to a much lesser extent than previously thought; each year that passes now means that the average age of newspaper subscribers increases by approximately one year.[3] In other words, new young subscription customers do not replace the old ones who leave (mostly from natural causes). If young adults in the future are likely to subscribe to a print newspaper, one crucial reason for doing so may be that in their earlier life they have learned to associate a newspaper with being an adult, in that it has been part of the family's window to the local public news. As circulation figures from the three papers indicate, one cannot take for granted that the parents of today's youngsters actually subscribe to a newspaper, or purchase it regularly in single copy.

Proximity

As previously mentioned, the definition of a local newspaper is based on the fact that it is rooted in a fairly well-defined geographical unit, that is, usually one or a few municipalities. Geographical proximity is therefore a key condition for any raw journalistic material, be it a phenomenon, a topic, or an event. Olav Njaastad (2004) argues that the very concept of proximity is the key journalistic news criterion, regarded as an overarching principle with a number of different dimensions. Njaastad partially uses the term as a metaphor, by referring to 'closeness' in time, consequences, culture, and emotions, as well as geography. There will often be an overlap between several such proximity qualities of a phenomenon, thus making it even more journalistically relevant. The success of local newspapers is explained by the geographical anchoring as the major principle, which has enabled the reader to comprehend the journalistic content, in addition to accepting that it may have a direct impact on him/her. The content has also been linked to values in a local culture that are immediately intelligible.

But even though certain values and attitudes, interests and preferences provide directions for each individual in his/her *life-world*, this is by no means something that is fully based on geographical affiliation. Njaastad's extended concept of proximity may therefore prove to be relevant as something more than just a criterion of journalistic relevance. Economic relations, political structures, and cultural impulses are largely separated in our globalised era from local physical, material, time-and-space determined contexts, not least because of the flow of mediated information. In other words, communication no longer necessarily takes place within a *local* framework of references and common interpretations. When the young interviewees in my material state that they spend a lot of time doing online gaming with unknown people living elsewhere in the world, or that they prefer consulting the website of Manchester United football club regularly instead of reading about their favourite team in Norwegian media, it indicates that the internet makes it possible to transcend the space dimension in young people's lives in a rather profound way. Their way of living everyday lives has hence become much more uniform across geographical distances than in the past, both because of the standardisation of interaction implied by technologies (and the patterns of behaviour thereby prescribed) and because social relationships simply exist to a greater extent because they are mediated. We should also note what sociologist Anthony Giddens characterises as a central feature of modernity, namely the 'disembedding' of processes and relations that in pre-modern times were rooted in a local context. This term refers to 'the "lifting out" of social relations from local contexts and their rearticulation across indefinite tracts of time-space' (Giddens, 1991: 18).

The importance of *local* is also under pressure because our notion of time and place has changed its character; mediation makes something happening far away become present and seen as a reality, here and now. The functional *what* thus becomes more important than the territorial *where*. Moreover, social media such as Facebook and Instagram seem to be extremely suitable for establishing and maintaining close, albeit virtual, relationships. Some of what is being conveyed in this way is probably in the grey area between private and public exposure, but nearly all of the young informants in this study expressed that these channels are primarily used to continuously update the 'status' of family members and close friends. It therefore seems that the local community – be it the village, town, or municipality – as a social foundation for the young ones may turn into a sociocultural space – or even a void – between the very close and private, and the larger world.

Traditionally, we tend to envisage a clear distinction between a local, regional, national, and global 'level'. However, the media (and in particular the internet) create a continuum of contexts, like ripples in the water, that people without much effort may move between. It is difficult to predict whether young adults will inevitably orient themselves towards the local community as they become established and included in new contexts of employment and private life. Moreover, if they do so, it is far from certain that local news media will continue as the major channels for maintaining the local public as a communicative practice. A lot will probably depend on whether local media are still able to identify and address the specificity of the local, and if this appears to be relevant, as has traditionally been the case.

Selecting and deselecting

The young informants seem to have a fairly structured daily schedule, with school and homework, employment in the evenings and weekends, with sports and other organised leisure activities filling most of their time from early morning until night. As they have access to an abundance of mediated information, they need to select and deselect. The web and radio/TV offer fundamentally different user experiences, and for the vast majority of my interviewees the latter do not seem to appeal very much:

[U17, Bo] I think online reading is very straightforward. You can skim read down the page and see what is most important, without having to delve into anything.

[U13, Bo] I'm very impatient, and I hate to sit and watch an entire programme broadcast just to get the news I'm interested in. I like to just enter what I want to read, and ignore all the other stuff ...

The majority of the young ones state that the programme structure of TV suits them rather badly, and this especially applies to journalistic content. At the same time, they are of course very familiar with contemporary visual media culture – not only as consumers, but also as producers and distributors of their own images and videos, as Eiri Elvestad and Anne Vogt (2010) also point out in a thorough review of research on child and adolescent use of newspapers. My interview material suggests that girls in particular seem to be the most enthusiastic users of photo-sharing services such as Instagram and Snapchat. Like the messages on Facebook, it is all about sharing experiences and moments with a variety of other, more or less well-known people.

In the formidable amount of information that surrounds each and every one of us, recommendations from people one knows or has something in common with are an important resource. As Clay Shirky (2013) has pointed out, an increasing number of readers nowadays tend to reach news articles not via the front page in online media, but rather through external sources. Online news is still presented as editorial packages of various content, but this traditional newspaper concept is basically being torn apart by a more selective and fragmented reading practice. For example, the online edition of the *New York Times* essentially continues the concept of a news*paper* as a package of content, with a mix in which all readers are supposed to find at least something of interest. We should not draw a comparison between a major US newspaper and Norwegian local newspapers too far, but one aspect of reader behaviour may turn out to be quite similar. Young people tend to continuously pick and choose media content, except when (if) they grapple with their local newspaper, and encounter a news package that someone else has edited and adapted. Indeed, unlike the linear presentation in radio and TV, a news package provides the reader with an opportunity to obtain a quick overview of current issues. But the margins of what young people accept or prefer might also become smaller, simply because there are so many other options providing information and entertainment outside the local media. We should not forget that in our mediatised culture, time is also perceived as a scarce resource by young people. Picard (1989: 35) stresses that a value is not something that exists in a product or service, but something that the user chooses to impart to the product. Once again, the active selection is key.

In other words, a clear majority of the young informants do not seem to have any great need for the printed newspaper as an authoritative review of the last day's events. Online publishing of local news is obviously attractive, at least for now, because of the content being free. Still, online journalism is at the mercy of a media context, the internet, which basically does not have anything to do with journalism. When all the world's information and entertainment are immediately (and freely) available on the same platform as the local newspaper, reading local news more than ever requires the user to actively select it. The statements from the young informants indicate that in their everyday life such a choice is not a matter of course.

Power and trust

Politicians and the press have an almost symbiotic relationship, both for practical-strategic and ideological reasons. The basic idea is that political power can only be conducted in a legitimate way as long as interests are made visible, and opinions and positions are played out in a public sphere, at the 'marketplace of utterances' (Sjøvaag, 2010).

Like other journalistic media, local newspapers get their official legitimacy from the social contract of the press. This means that the papers are supposed to serve as a controlling authority between those who govern and those who are being governed. The contract provides the press with privileges, power, and responsibility, and is based on a relationship of trust. Politicians and other persons and entities with legitimate power must, like any media user, expect the press to present political issues and decision-making as truthfully and in as balanced a way as possible. The press therefore has a responsibility to offer the public information that promotes involvement and participation, and gives citizens the best possible foundation for making autonomous assessments and rational choices.

For practical reasons, and due to the complexity of a modern society, each citizen's basic democratic right to supervise those in power is delegated to journalists. This can be regarded as another example of *disembedding* (Giddens, 1991), in which an expert system, that is, the journalistic media and journalism as a profession, has acquired certain social relations, namely those between political authorities and citizens, and made them subject to professional practice. In order to work properly, this relationship must be based on trust, which according to Giddens is central to understanding how a modern society is kept coherent.

The Danish media scholar Stig Hjarvard (2011) discusses the relationship between a general *mediatisation* of society and culture, and the emergence of media institutions in Western societies. After the termination of the formal ties to political parties in particular, the press has obtained a clearer status as a separate social institution. Like other institutions, the media are controlled by more or less explicit rules and principles, some general (such as laws and freedom of speech as a right), and some internal and more specific (such as the Code of Practice). A sanctioning authority (i.e. the Independent Press Standards Organisation), as well as practices guided by overall principles and objectives regarding publishing, further implies that the media should be considered a social institution. Hjarvard (2011: 47) also refers to Bourdieu's concept of *fields* – 'social areas characterized by a certain autonomy and internal structure'. The point here is that what goes on in such a field is determined in part by its own logic, and in part under the influence of other fields. A field therefore consists of two *poles*, one 'autonomous' and the other 'heteronomous'. Hjarvard argues that the institutionalisation of the press can be understood as a significant empowering of the autonomous pole. Equally important is that this has led to a weakening of autonomous poles in other social fields. Examples of this include how the political system is influenced by the media logic and how premises such as general elections are nowadays staged as media events, with governmental departments relying on PR consultants to handle the media. A major reason why a strong autonomy in the media tends to weaken the autonomy of other institutions is a distinctive feature of the media, namely that they are crucial to the flow of information in society, thus making the link *between* social institutions such as politics, market, family, public and private enterprises, etc. A common set of experiences is formed, which requires other institutions to adapt to the media's own logic, reflected both institutionally and technologically, and by expression.

This means that to the extent that the local press operates according to the general principles of the social contract of the press, it has a strong autonomous pole. On the other hand, if the major purpose of media is to serve the local community and its institutions (by consistent positive publicity and uncritical approaches to local phenomena and issues), the strongest pole in the newspaper as an institution will be the heteronomous one. The local papers may work as 'glue' or a 'magnifying glass', as a building/ positive versus a critical/revealing (Mathisen, 2010: 36) agent, which denotes a state of tension based on the level of institutional autonomy.

This autonomous status of media is also crucial when Paul Bjerke (2011: 42) emphasises why journalism should be regarded as a profession. Editors and journalists have actually managed to achieve an outstanding position as managers of 'the social communication'. In this sense, the journalistic profession is a structure in which certain economic, political, and ethical prerogatives have been delegated from an authority level to a certain group of people. These privileges are based on the notion that journalism is free and independent, and that it is simply an imperative part of democracy. Journalists should therefore be in a unique position to disclose, reveal, and convey issues of general interest. Bjerke argues that this is an idealised picture of journalistic practice that should be questioned; most important in this context, however, is that journalism, like any other profession, only possesses real power to the extent that it is trusted. Consequently, the press will only maintain its position, at least in the long term, if it manages to maintain the real confidence of the population in the area it is serving (Bjerke, 2011: 53).

The level of confidence will also largely depend on what readers actually want and expect from the newspaper, and what journalistic ambitions they assign to it. A hyperlocal weekly newspaper (of which there are many in Norway) may be content with reporting about local events in a referential way, and to the extent it thereby meets the expectations of the public, it will also have confidence. Nonetheless, the three papers I discuss in my study seem to have genuinely journalistic objectives with their business, by shaping public opinion and defining the political agenda in their coverage areas. With such ambitions, it will be more of a challenge to gain trust from the readers.

Politics and local media: a mixed bag

The key question when interviewing politicians in Sortland, Bodø, and Alstahaug who participated in the study was how they felt about the importance of the local newspaper in their own work as elected officials. One major impression is that politicians regard the newspaper, primarily the print edition, as being very important for the formation of opinion in the community. This takes place in two ways. (1) Politicians depend on the newspaper in order to reach out with a message and to profile both the party and themselves, either by giving interviews or by using the 'opinion' columns. (2) The paper's overall coverage, and its interpretations and particular angles on what is happening in local politics, are both crucial to how the political processes and decisions appear to the readers.

> [P2, Sl] It is crucially important what the newspaper is able to communicate ...

> [P1, Al] I hurry to buy the paper, to see how the journalist has interpreted what was said at a meeting in the council.

> [P5, Bo] Avisa Nordland reigns supreme, it's the only real market channel we have. We can appeal to our own supporters through various websites and Facebook, but if we want to reach out to new groups, we rely completely on AN, and in particular on the print edition.

> [P3, Sl] Bladet Vesterålen is important to me as a politician because it is found in every home. I am surprised to hear about all the little things in the newspapers people have actually read, as many seem to read every detail.

[P4, Al] Helgelands Blad is certainly interested in politics, and has a strong influence on what we're doing as politicians.

At the same time, most of the politicians have a much more distant relationship with the newspaper as a general source of information for themselves, and they find little information that they can directly use in their political work. It may therefore seem that the most important thing is not what the newspaper conveys, but what effect this may have on the readers:

[P3, Bo] Avisa Nordland is not important at all to me when I have to choose political positions and make decisions because it does not give me the facts I need. Instead, I seek other sources, including those which are directly affected by a political decision.

[P3, Al] Helgelands Blad is completely unimportant as a source of information, except that I look in which way the paper has conveyed what is happening in politics.

Judging by circulation, number of employees, coverage, and frequency of publication, the three newspapers in the study appear as media companies with relatively high journalistic goals and ambitions. When the informants are asked to account for the significance of the newspaper, they inevitably also tended to make an assessment of the quality of local journalism. With a few exceptions, the politicians in all three municipalities state that their relationship with the editorial staff is 'good' or 'OK'. But at the same time, they are also concerned about the way political processes and decisions are rendered in the paper, with a common statement being that the journalism is not sufficiently critical and analytical.

The informants in Sortland state that *Bladet Vesterålen* has a clear editorial profile. They consider the newspaper to be very patriotic and the most committed to conveying positive news. It is sober in its treatment of dramatic events, and never uses sensational headlines on the front page. The paper consistently highlights the importance of primary industries (such as fisheries) in the region, and it is clearly against a future Norwegian EU membership. Even though the politicians obviously only partly agree with what is being expressed in editorials, in general they are satisfied with what the newspaper accomplishes, and they appreciate its clear profile and strong opinions. Even so, they also stress that they would prefer a more assertive, analytical, and critical news journalism. One area some of the respondents regard as neglected is getting the local community and the region (Vesterålen) positioned in the world, so to speak. They call for more of an emphasis on how both national and international conditions may affect the local community, simply because the *local* can no longer be seen as separated from the rest of the world:

[P4, Sl] The focus on the fisheries is OK, but I want a newspaper that is more concerned about possible opportunities and jobs in the future, not just the industries we have today.

[P1, Sl] We would benefit from more critical and informed journalists, we are concerned about getting the best debate on the issues, and we are totally dependent on this fourth estate not being just an intermediary.

There is a need for an editorial staff capable of analysing and disseminating larger complexes of issues than simply the purely local ones. Journalists should therefore draw attention to phenomena – such as structural changes nationally and globally – that affect the local population, often indirectly and in the long term. Politicians in Alstahaug and Bodø call almost unanimously, and in even clearer terms, for a more in-depth, evidence-based, and critical political journalism, and one noted some powerlessness:

[P3, Al] When people read something in the paper that they have knowledge about, they will see that the issue is not rendered properly. But people often read something they have no knowledge about, and they believe what they read! This applies for example in issues regarding municipal finances ...

[P2, Al] When something is repeated often enough, it becomes the truth in the end.

[P5, Bo] Avisa Nordland is not perceptive enough to see the consequences of decisions, which again may contain potential conflicts that are not openly expressed in the city council. A unanimous city council can actually be seriously wrong!

[P1, Al] Helgelands Blad often tries too hard to do critical journalism. We sometimes have issues here that are very complex, requiring journalists

who possess expert knowledge [...] I think Helgelands Blad, like many other local newspapers, is struggling with their ambitions.

[P1, Bo] Both politicians and people in general feed the newspaper with issues. It seems that journalists don't always question what should be crucial: 'Why do I get this information?', and: 'Who is benefitting from it being published?'

Several politicians in Bodø are also critical about key issues not being discovered and reported *earlier* in the political process, before they become official political themes of discussion:

[P3, Bo]: When information about something has been published, the matter may already be settled. This does not stimulate the vital debate and opinion formation before the issues are to be formally discussed in the council.

It is worth noting that, in both Alstahaug and Bodø, many informants are critical about what they consider an excessive focus on persons and conflicts:

[P4, Al] Helgelands Blad is probably doing more critical, political journalism than before, but I often get upset because their angles are so personalised, and they tend to categorise people.

[P3, Al] Helgelands Blad is looking for articulated statements that they then can get an answer to. This is not critical journalism. What about the disclosure of corruption in Norwegian municipalities? The paper doesn't touch a theme like that!

[P5, Bo] When covering politics, the journalistic profile in Avisa Nordland is clearly conflict oriented, especially in cases where there is some disagreement between governing, cooperating parties [...] Still they do have many talented journalists, and I don't understand why this isn't reflected in its political journalism.

As mentioned above, Mathisen (2010) has shown how local newspapers can be caught between two different considerations: on the one hand, they are supposed to reinforce local identity and belonging, while on the other they should be committed to critical, investigative, and independent journalism. The dilemma may occur when the ideals are to be practised in a social context in which there are close relationships between journalists and their sources, and where critical journalism may be instantly regarded as subversive of the interests of the public. The question then is what will serve the community best in the long run: an emphasis on positive news (as Mathisen has shown is actually the case in Norwegian local newspapers), or journalism based on general, professional principles, in which 'localism' is subordinate. While *Bladet Vesterålen* is described as being stable, patriotic, and generally conveying a state of harmony, the informants in Alstahaug and Bodø describe local political journalism as more quasi-critical, with an excessive emphasis on the political game and tactics. They also state that *conflict* as a news criterion, combined with strong personal orientation (especially in Alstahaug), creates a picture of political life that is not always trustworthy.

By and large, the politicians appear to have a somewhat ambivalent relationship with local newspapers. They clearly perceive local media as being essential to maintaining a local public sphere, which is a prerequisite for political processes to be democratic. Nevertheless, many of them are frustrated that the local press as a social institution does not accomplish its function in a sufficiently professional way. If the social contract of the press means that power is delegated to media, this relationship must be based on *trust*. This in turn means that something is at stake; that is, the one delegating runs a risk on whether certain interests and principles are actually taken care of (Grimen, 2009; Luhmann, 2000). When the informants emphasise how important local newspapers are for the flow of information and local political engagement, this apparently is not about obtaining support from voters, their own political career, or the newspaper's well-being. Instead, what is at stake here is the political public and the very legitimacy of the political system. And then the difference between a national and a local context is not as large as one might think; Sortland, Bodø, and Alstahaug have complex social, political, and economic structures as well, all of which require both a journalistic ability and willingness to comprehend and make visible. When politicians require a certain journalistic standard, it suggests that newspapers are regarded as being crucially important. It is also an indication that the politicians do not see any obvious alternatives to the local newspaper as a creator of crucially important sociocultural and sociopolitical values.

As long as the local newspaper is the sole provider of information about rather trivial, though important, events, it will meet an obvious need. But it is not inconceivable that to a large extent this kind of information can be just as easily acquired from the websites of businesses, organisations, and local societies of all kinds, and – not least – via social media. However, what *cannot* be investigated and disseminated by anyone are the more subtle aspects of what is taking place in a community, and this is exactly where journalism as a profession is ultimately justified – in what Alex Jones (2009) calls the 'iron core' of journalism, specifically the ability and willingness to hold those responsible accountable.

Conclusion: a different dance

Newspapers have had a long-lasting golden age, primarily because the industry has been a major advertising channel for businesses, official enterprises, and individuals, in addition to providing journalistic content. However, the industry is now facing a situation in which both media consumers (particularly the young ones) and advertising money tend to move in new directions. This also applies to local newspapers, and they are therefore likely to face some fundamental challenges in the years to come, if they are to retain their position as key political and cultural institutions.

The informants in this study, both youngsters and politicians, are not the most important customer group for local media, numerically and commercially. But each group does represent attitudes, expectations, and behavioural patterns that may indicate something important about what functions local newspapers have today and what is needed in order for them to fill important functions in the future. The printed newspaper is unique because the medium itself, as a physical object, manifests the press as an institution. Even though many of the interviewees from politics do have objections to the quality of local journalism, they still see the newspaper as being fundamentally important to help maintain the flow of information and exchange of views in the public sphere. In other words, they consider themselves and the press parts of the same sociopolitical realm, which in turn defines a democracy based on the legitimate execution of power.

The interview material does not allow for firm predictions about what young people's media usage will be like when they are established in a family context many years from now. One should still note that their relationship with the news media is not ritualised in terms of getting a content regularly presented as a *package* of edited news in print. They may therefore also prefer to deal with a screen in the future, regardless of content, and make their own choices. This provides some opportunities for local media, but it certainly also creates some major challenges for them. Whether local print news will survive is a question in itself which probably depends as much on an economic and media-political framework as on purely editorial innovations. But if the screen (in any shape) proves to be the only viable device in the years to come, this may require a different dance for local journalism. It will then in fact be at the mercy of a channel that is both general and global, that does not favour journalism in the way that print distribution has done, and that conveys content and values of quite a different nature than the specifically local.

Innovations in the local press should therefore above all be proactive, experimental and quality conscious, based on a deep comprehension of what communicative possibilities digital platforms offer. Otherwise, local newspapers may easily end up being minimum solutions, legitimised in a 'crisis discourse' (Schlosberg, 2012), in which the internet basically remains a threat and will be used as The Explanation as to why local newspapers are losing readers. Changeable conditions for local newspapers require broad innovations that include far more than merely technical solutions, utilising what Andrew Hargadon (2003: 13) calls 'existing objects, ideas and people'.

Whatever the medium, ways of communicating, and business model, the question that remains is how local journalism can still construct and maintain a local identity and belonging, facilitate an informed and inclusive public debate, discover and prosecute improprieties, as well as showing how every place is somewhere in the world – now more so than ever. It is hard to see what agencies other than local journalistic media would be able to fill such a role. But then they will have to appear as unique and relevant, with a journalism that fulfils its social responsibilities, thus earning the reader's trust.

Notes

1 Newspapers have historically not been subject to VAT in Norway. Some niche and second-largest papers also get considerable financial support from the government. However, these regulations may be adjusted in the near future.

2   Abbreviations: informant category (U = young person; P = politician); informant number; location (Bo = Bodø, Al = Alstahaug, Sl = Sortland)
3   Interview with Per Arne Skjelvik, Head of Administration in *Avisa Nordland*. 16 November 2012.

Bibliography

Bjerke, P. 2011. *Journalistikkens vekst og fall? Om journalistisk profesjonsmakt.* Kristiansand: IJ-forlaget.

Elvestad, E., and A. Vogt. 2010. *Trenger vi aviser når vi har Facebook? Barn og unges forhold til avis under omstilling.* Kristiansand: IJ-forlaget.

Gentikow, B. 2005. *Hvordan utforsker man medieerfaringer? Kvalitativ metode.* Kristiansand: IJ-forlaget.

Giddens, A. 1991. *Modernity and Self-Identity: Self and Society in the Late Modern Age.* Cambridge: Polity Press.

Grimen, H. 2009. *Hva er tillit?* Oslo: Universitetsforlaget.

Hargadon, A. 2003. *How Breakthroughs Happen: The Surprising Truth about How Companies Innovate.* Boston: Harvard Business School Press.

Hjarvard, S. 2011. *En verden af medier: Medialiseringen af politik, sprog, religion og leg.* Frederiksberg C: Samfundslitteratur.

Høst, S. 2013. *Avisåret 2012.* Rapport 37/2013. Volda: Møreforsking.

Jones, A. 2009. *Losing the News: The Future of the News that Feeds Democracy.* Oxford: Oxford University Press.

Luhmann, N. 2000. 'Familiarity, Confidence, Trust: Problems and Alternatives', in D. Gambetta (ed.), *Trust: Making and Breaking Cooperative Relations.* Department of Sociology: University of Oxford, 94–108. http://www.nuffield.ox.ac.uk/users/gambetta/Trust_making%20and%20breaking%20cooperative%20relations.pdf.

Mathisen, B. R. (ed.) 2010. *Lokaljournalistikk: Blind patriotisme eller kritisk korrektiv?* Kristiansand: IJ-forlaget.

Njaastad, O. 2004. *TV-journalistikk. Bildenes fortellerkraft.* Oslo: Gyldendal Norsk Forlag.

Omdal, S. E. 2012. 'På ryggen av en svart svane', in M. Eide, L. O. Larsen, and H. Sjøvaag (eds), *Nytt på nett og brett.* Oslo: Universitetsforlaget, 23–35.

Picard, R. G. 1989. *Media Economics: Concepts and Issues.* Newbury Park, CA: SAGE.

Schlosberg, J. 2012. 'Co-opting the Discourse of Crisis: Re-assessing Market Failure in the Local News Sector', in J. Mair, N. Fowler, and I. Reeves (eds), *What Do We Mean by Local?* Bury St Edmunds: Abramis, 51–66.

Shirky, C. 2013. *Let a Thousand Flowers Bloom to Replace Newspapers: Don't Build a Paywall around a Public Good.* www.niemanlab.org/2009/09/clay-shirky-let-a-thousand-flowers-bloom-to-replace-newspapers-dont-build-a-paywall-around-a-public-good.

Sjøvaag, H. 2012. 'Journalistisk ideologi', in M. Eide, L. O. Larsen, and H. Sjøvaag (eds), *Nytt på nett og brett.* Oslo: Universitetsforlaget.

Statistics Norway. 2013. 'Population and Population Changes, Q4 2013'. http://ssb.no/en/befolkning/statistikker/folkendrkv/kvartal/2014-02-20 (accessed July 2014).

Part III

New Forms of Local Media

Local journalism is and has been funded first and foremost by local newspapers, whether dailies or weeklies, paid or free. Their coverage has been subject to much criticism, for being too deferential to local elites, for not being local enough, and for prioritising soft stories over more substantial coverage of local problems (e.g. Franklin, 2006). But despite their shortcomings, their importance to local communities has also been highlighted by their decline in recent years as local newspapers have lost print readers and advertisers while only making limited progress online, and have often cut newsrooms in response to declining revenues. This has led to less coverage and a rising local 'news gap' as fewer stories are published (Currah, 2009) and some communities receive little or no attention from journalists, raising the prospects of growing 'news deserts' (Friedland et al., 2012). Other kinds of local media – including public service broadcasters and various forms of mostly volunteer-driven alternative and community media – play an important role in some areas, but newspapers have historically been the most important form of local media, and have in almost all cases been much diminished.

So far, it is unclear whether new forms of local media can make up for the decline of local newspapers. Some have expressed considerable optimism, arguing that the digital environment provides the basis for 'exciting journalistic innovation on the local level' (FCC, 2011: 191) and has 'the potential to support and broaden the range of local media content' (Ofcom, 2012: 103). Much of the conversation is focused on different kinds of so-called 'hyperlocals', digital news operations with a tighter geographical focus than most legacy local media, but more generally we have the seen the emergence of a wider range of locally oriented 'pure players', born-digital local news media including for-profit, non-profit, and citizen journalism initiatives. Legacy media too are experimenting with a variety of often for-profit local sites attached to existing titles and as part of national chains of websites like, for example, Myheimat in Germany,

Local People in the UK and Patch in the US (Thurman et al., 2012), just as existing public service and community media often experiment with new digital locally oriented offerings. But the most interesting and potentially innovative initiatives are generally newly launched, born-digital, local news start-ups, and they are the focus of this section.

In Chapter 7, Nikos Smyrnaios, Emmanuel Marty, and Franck Bousquet examine the journalistic practices and business models of local pure players in Southern France. They show how, while these journalistic start-ups often pursue a closer and more reciprocal relationship with their audience and in some cases provide more independent news coverage than local newspapers – which can seem close to local elites but far from their readers – they struggle to reach a wider audience and especially to generate enough revenues to sustain their reporting. Finding similar economic challenges in their survey of hyperlocal news sites in the Netherlands, Marco van Kerkhoven and Piet Bakker in Chapter 8 turn to examine the motivations, strategies, and forms of engagement of journalistic start-ups there, and show how these struggling sites are typically started by locals concerned over a perceived gap in news coverage of their area, but that the dominant low-cost/no-staff strategy and lack of attention to journalistic ethics and professional practice undermine their ability to carve out a distinct position in local news ecosystems. In Chapter 9, Andy Williams, Dave Harte, and Jerome Turner turn from the question of sustainability and motivation to analysis of the actual content produced by hyperlocal news sites in the UK. They combine content analysis with surveys of and interviews with people behind hyperlocal sites and show how, despite their often precarious economic underpinnings, they in many cases produce news content of real value to local communities, providing coverage that is diverse and genuinely local, even though it is rarely genuinely investigative and independent 'watch-dog' type reporting.

All three chapters show that new forms of local media, for all their differences in terms of content, strategy, and motivation, face a set of shared challenges in terms of (1) defining and legitimising their role in local media ecosystems relative to audiences, advertisers, and authorities, (2) generating enough resources to sustain their work, and (3) maintaining at the same time a degree of autonomy and independence from local elites across politics, business, and civil society. While the platforms involved today – increasingly digital, social, and mobile – are new, these are old challenges that have always accompanied local media.

References

Currah, Andrew. 2009. 'Navigating the Crisis in Local and Regional News: A Critical Review of Solutions'. Working Paper. Oxford: Reuters Institute for the Study of Journalism. http://reutersinstitute.politics.ox.ac.uk/sites/default/files/Navigating%20the%20Crisis%20in%20Local%20%26%20Regional%20News.pdf.

FCC. 2011. *Information Needs of Communities.* http://www.fcc.gov/info-needs-communities.

Franklin, Bob. 2006. 'Preface', in Bob Franklin (ed.), *Local Journalism and Local Media: Making the Local News.* London: Routledge, xvii–xxii.

Friedland, Lewis, et al. 2012. *Review of the Literature Regarding Critical Information Needs of the American Public.* Washington, DC: FCC. http://transition.fcc.gov/bureaus/ocbo/Final_Literature_Review.pdf.

Ofcom. 2012. *The Communications Market Report: United Kingdom.* London: Ofcom.

Thurman, Neil, Jean Christophe Pascal, and Paul Bradshaw. 2012. 'Can Big Media Do Big Society? A Critical Case Study of Commercial, Convergent Hyperlocal News', *International Journal of Media and Cultural Politics*, 8(2): 269–85.

7

Between Journalistic Diversity and Economic Constraints: Local Pure Players in Southern France

Nikos Smyrnaios, Emmanuel Marty, and Franck Bousquet

Introduction

In France, during the last few years, there has been a proliferation of independent news websites. These so-called 'pure players' try to invent a new form of online journalism, partly emancipated from the constraints of traditional news organisations. The particularly rich ecosystem of pure players in France has been likened to a 'nouvelle vague' of journalistic start-ups in the country (Bruno and Nielsen, 2012). Since 2010 this new wave has been sweeping across numerous French cities and rural areas where local journalistic start-ups are challenging established monopolies. Some of these pure players have common points with their national counterparts such as Rue 89 or Mediapart. They cherish their independence from local political and economic elites, if not in fact at least in discourse. They try to innovate journalistically; they engage in intense relations with their public, with whom they share geographical proximity but also often sociological and political closeness. Finally, their presence reinvigorates local public, spaces. Nevertheless they also suffer from weak business models and from a lack of recognition by local institutions and informants.

According to David Domingo (2008), pure players are the result of the junction between two groups who jointly invented the 'myth of online journalism': on the one hand there are experienced journalists who reject traditional media because of their lack of independence and innovation; on the other hand there are digital enthusiasts, carrying a techno-utopian ideology and a specific technological know-how. As

Domingo rightly points out, the initial goal of this junction between experienced professionals and young technophiles is the reinvention of independent journalism in the service of society and democracy. So far, however, empirical evidence suggests that it is very difficult to keep such a commitment while operating under very severe resource constraints (Smyrnaios, 2013). Still, far from economic success as they are, these experiments tell us much about the evolution of contemporary journalism.

Therefore, this chapter explores local online news pure players in Southern France. It is based on the results of a research project that took place between 2010 and 2013 and focused on their editorial strategies, journalistic practices, and business models. The tension between strong economic constraints and the ambition of these new media outlets to provide audiences with in-depth, attractive, and innovative journalism raises several questions. How can they renew relations with the readership? Do they manage to create real online communities around local news? What are their daily journalistic practices and how do they choose to allocate their human and material resources between original reporting, monitoring online material, and enlivening readers' communities through online social networks? Finally, do they manage to generate enough revenue in order to make their editorial project sustainable? And what is the price of successful business models in terms of independence? In order to address these questions, we will first describe the context of online local news and journalism in France. Secondly, we will present our data, method, and theoretical framework. Finally, we will present the results of our empirical research based on the three axes detailed above: relations to the public, journalistic practices, and business models.

General trends of online local news in France

Recent research on local news in France shows that the local and regional media landscape is rapidly evolving (Bousquet and Smyrnaios, 2012). First of all, changing reading habits tend to make it harder for local newspapers to maintain and renew readership. Second, advertising revenue for local newspapers is fading, especially when it comes to classified ads. Third, the local media landscape is subject to increasing concentration of ownership. The latter point is particularly salient in France: the country is partitioned by regional media groups that maintain monopolistic positions in their territories. This situation does not push traditional media to innovate in deploying local journalism on the web, neither from a journalistic nor a business perspective. Web strategies of local monopolies such as *La Dépêche du Midi* in the area of Toulouse (south-western France) tend to concentrate on building audience through classic recipes for advertising-based business models, like intensive search engine optimisation and 'shovelware' publishing (Smyrnaios and Bousquet, 2011). These players tend to reproduce their offline content on the web with no journalistic added value but also with little effort to renew and enrich their relations with the public through interaction and participation. This lack of innovation in the sector of local news is also due to the aforementioned economic crisis of local and regional press. For instance, in the area of Marseille (south-eastern France), despite the existence of two competing local dailies (*La Provence* and *La Marseillaise*) the development of original online reporting is constrained by insufficient resources. On the other hand, local television and radio are underdeveloped in France as broadcast media consumption is concentrated on nationwide (Paris-based) networks. Therefore their online presence is also quite marginal in terms of investment and audience. Consequently, the conservative strategies of traditional media in most French regions – due to lack of competition and/or investment – offer an unprecedented opportunity for independent local news websites to gain popularity. But this opportunity has yet to be seized.

Indeed, in France only two journalistic pure players, Rue 89 (which has been bought by the Nouvel Observateur press group) and Mediapart, are as famous as their US counterparts Politico or the Huffington Post and have some influence in public debates. Numerous local ventures are directly inspired by these two pioneers and some have even been affiliated to Rue 89, like in the cities of Rouen, Strasbourg, and Lyon. Others, like Dijonscope and Télescope d'Amiens, have followed the model of Mediapart, producing investigative journalism available on subscription only. But all of these websites remain unknown to the majority of the public, even at a local level. According to Médiamétrie's audience measurement there are very few Paris-based pure players (among which are Rue 89 and Slate.fr) with more than one million unique visitors a month. None of them is part of the ten most visited news websites in France. These figures are consistent with two sociological surveys on news consumption in France (CEVIPOF, 2010; Granjon and Le Foulgoc, 2010) in which the percentage of people who say they regularly get news on pure player websites is very low, ranging between 3% and 6%. This minority of the population belongs to the upper urban and educated classes and has an extensive daily use of the internet (Comby et al., 2011). Thus, the main target of pure players seems to be confined to a small and relatively homogeneous social group, quite similar to the journalists themselves.

Nevertheless, despite their lack of audience, there is a kind of self-awareness growing stronger among journalistic start-ups in France, based on their common interests. An example of this movement of collective organisation is the foundation of a professional association of journalistic pure players, the Syndicat de la presse indépendante d'information en ligne (Spiil). The goal of this initiative is to increase the visibility of journalistic pure players to authorities, but also to balance the influence of traditional media. For instance, one of the main aims of the Spiil was to convince the French government to lower the VAT on online subscriptions from 19.6% to 2.1%, the rate applied to traditional media. (This was achieved in February 2014.) Another major aim of the Spiil was that independent news websites should be subsidised by the French government like newspapers. President Sarkozy met the latter claim in 2010, even if the sums at stake were much lower than those given to traditional media.

Proof that pure players increasingly organise themselves as a distinct sector of news media can also be found in their few collective partnerships in recent years, even though most of these initiatives have failed. For instance in 2013, through Spiil, local pure players tried to federate themselves in order to create a unified advertising and publishing network called leSquare.info. The concept was to aggregate content from numerous local pure players in order to produce a portal for local news in France and share advertising revenue. The project was abandoned in late 2013 because of lack of investors, but also because of divergences between partners. Another project called Jaimelinfo.fr was launched by Rue 89 in 2010. Jaimelinfo.fr is a crowdfunding platform exclusively dedicated to journalistic start-ups and blogs. The platform still exists but its level of activity is very low and the funding is scarce, showing the general public's lack of interest in financing such ventures.

In summary, the landscape of online media in France offers great opportunities to develop and renew local journalism but also serious difficulties in finding sustainable and sufficient revenue streams. Our empirical research from the south of France will shed more light on that fundamental contradiction.

Positioning theory and method

Our analysis is based on a socio-economic approach. As has already been shown in the past, business models are integral to the editorial strategies and modes of the internal organisation of online media (Boczkowski, 2010). Consequently, in order to understand the evolution of journalism, one has to take into account not only professional practices, but also the economic structure that supports them. Furthermore, by focusing on the case of three French journalistic pure players we strive to go beyond the issue of adapting the traditional media to the web, which has long dominated research (Mitchelstein and Boczkowski, 2010). Even if one should not ignore the fact that online journalism is a part of the media system and very much linked to traditional players such as newspapers and TV networks, pure players are an extremely useful field of observation of innovative trends and new practices.

Local journalism is marked by strong specificities. In France, the physical and geographical proximity between local newspaper representatives and their readership even in the most remote areas is a historic heritage of the press and its main competitive advantage (Ringoot and Rochard, 2005). Traditionally, a journalist of a local newspaper is at the same time a media representative and a member of local society. His 'ideal reader' (Eco, 1979) is his neighbour. Thus, local pure players are a privileged field in which to observe how specificities of local journalism blend with start-up culture and online practices.

To examine the emergence of local pure players, we have researched a sample of three websites: Marsactu.fr, Carredinfo.fr, and Ariegenews.fr (see Table 7.1). In order to grasp the great variety of local journalistic start-ups we decided to compare online news outlets based in two major cities (Marseille and Toulouse) and a small rural town (Foix), within two different administrative regions, Midi-Pyrénées (south-west France) and Provence-Alpes-Côte d'Azur (south-east France). These two regions are currently experiencing important changes in their media landscape, with the development of numerous and diverse new actors, which make them particularly interesting to look at. Far from constituting an exhaustive list of French local pure players our sample is nevertheless quite representative of different geographical, editorial, and economic positions and allows an understanding of some crucial and emblematic issues of contemporary local journalism in France.

Table 7.1 The three pure players that were the focus of research

Name	Founded	Founders	Average monthly audience for 2013	Revenue for 2013	Full-time employees/ journalists	Revenue stream
Marsactu.fr	2009	Pierre Boucaud	200,000 UV	€220,000	10/5	Advertising + PR film production
Carredinfo.fr	2011	X. Lalu X. Druot B. Enjalbal	60,000 UV	€12,000	4/3	Advertising + subscription + teaching
Ariegenews.fr	2007	Philippe Bardou	450,000 UV	€254,000	8/2	Advertising + PR film production

UV = unique visitors

Our method was based on semi-structured interviews and ethnographic observations inside online newsrooms (Domingo and Paterson, 2011). We carried out a dozen interviews with managers and journalists in their workplaces between May 2010 and April 2013. The interviews were accompanied by meticulous observations of their work routines. In supplement we regularly visited the three websites and also collected and analysed a corpus of various internal documents such as financial statements, guides and reports, market research, and readership analyses. This relatively long period of observation allowed us to follow the trajectory of these websites and thus understand how they evolved over time.

Marsactu is a local pure player launched in 2009 and located in the heart of Marseille. The website employs five full-time journalists out of ten employees and aims explicitly to compete with the main local newspaper *La Provence* by deploying investigative journalism especially in the area of local politics. In 2013, Marsactu had 200,000 unique visitors per month on average and an annual revenue of €220,000. Its net income for the same year was negative (–€100,000). Marsactu is published by RAJ Media, owned by Pierre Boucaud (aged 50) who retains 43% of the capital. Other shareholders include local businessman Frédéric Chevalier with 35% and telecom mogul Xavier Niel. Pierre Boucaud has had a long career as an advertising executive (Publicis and Havas) and as head of two local TV stations (TLT in Toulouse and LCM in Marseille). He is therefore an experienced manager and has a very good knowledge of the media market in Marseille. What motivated him in founding Marsactu was on the one hand his desire to head his own business but also the need he felt for Marseille to have an independent journalistic voice able to criticise and denounce corruption and nepotism, which are historically very strong in the city. Each week Marsactu publishes about 30 articles, sometimes with video, and at least one talk-show filmed inside the newsroom's studio.

Carré d'info was created in 2011 by three young professionals with only a few years of experience: journalists Xavier Lalu (aged 30) and Bertrand Enjalbal (aged 31) and manager Xavier Druot (aged 33). In 2012 another young journalist, Pauline Croquet (aged 29), joined the original trio. The four retained 100% of B2X Editions, the publisher of Carré d'info. The team was completed by about a dozen freelance journalists who occasionally collaborated with the website. Throughout 2013, Carré d'info had an average of 60,000 unique visitors per month and generated a little more than €12,000 in revenue for the whole year. The concept of Carré d'info was largely inspired by Rue 89. Like its Parisian model, Carré d'info aimed to produce original news coverage of the metropolitan area of Toulouse with special attention to issues neglected or unexplored by other local media such as culture, ecology, or technology. It also encouraged the participation of its readers. The weekly production of the newsroom was of ten original articles and a few brief news items. By December 2013, and after Bertrand Enjalbal left Toulouse, the remaining partners decided to end the company's activity due to insufficient revenue.

Ariegenews was founded in 2007 in a rural area of south-western France by Philippe Bardou (aged 55) who owns 100% of the publishing company Midinews. Philippe Bardou has had a career as a consultant in digital media and has launched several ventures throughout the 1990s and until the beginning of the 2000s. He was also involved in the initial launching of Dailymotion in 2005. The idea of creating a local news website came to him when he and his family moved from Paris to the Ariège region on the foothills of the Pyrenees mountains and he observed the lack of news coverage of his town. Today Ariegenews is based in Foix, a town of 10,000, and covers the Ariège region with a population of 150,000, whose main occupations are agriculture, tourism, and textile production. Ariegenews employs two full-time journalists, two editors, a webmaster, and two technicians. In 2013 the company had revenue of €254,000 and losses of a few thousand euros while its average monthly audience was about 450,000 unique visitors. Every week the newsroom produces about a dozen original articles and at least three video reports and a news show presented by journalist Laurence Cabrol.

The weekly editorial output of the three newsrooms we examined is variable, from ten original weekly articles for Carré d'info to 30 for Marsactu (in addition to video content for Ariegenews and Marsactu). But it remains quite low compared to legacy media. For instance the main local newspapers of Marseille and of Toulouse, respectively *La Provence* and *La Dépêche du Midi*, each publish more than 200 pieces of news content weekly in their daily editions and at least the same amount online, including a duplication of their printed articles and news feeds from agencies. The low productivity of pure players is mainly due to the economic constraints and limited workforce. But it is also linked, as we detail below, to their specific editorial strategies, that we have previously described as focused on creativity, rather than productivity (Smyrnaios et al., 2010).

Participatory culture and relations to the public

Pure players seem to create stronger and more engaged communities of readers than traditional online media. For instance, Rue 89 and Arrêt sur images have large and well-connected communities of regular commentators who sometimes blog and interact intensely with journalists. These websites also receive a bigger share of incoming traffic from social networks like Facebook and Twitter than from Google, meaning that readers share and strongly promote their content (Smyrnaios, 2013). Thus readers' participation in producing and broadcasting news seems to be a strong feature of these journalistic start-ups. When it comes to our sample of local pure players, two out of three websites – the urban ones, Marsactu and Carré d'info – seem to fit this description. Indeed these websites aim at a readership concentrated in and around two metropolitan areas. Their goal is to try to fill the gap created by the gradual disengagement of local newspapers from inner-city news and the subsequent abandonment of urban readers that can be observed in France since the 1990s (Tétu, 1995). The founders of these two websites believe that urban readers, especially young ones, reject the regional and local daily press but still have an appetite for local news.

Marsactu has a relatively important community of commentators, due to the special attention they are given in the newsroom. This attention requires all journalists' participation in comment moderation and monitoring. All members of the newsroom thus strive to consistently answer questions, comments, and criticisms formulated by readers. This activity is an integral part of their daily work routines. Articles involving local government and politicians are those that give rise to a large number of comments (frequently more than 50, which is quite high compared to the daily audience of the website). Sometimes, people and institutions mentioned in the articles provide clarifications or corrections, or even compliment the journalists. Although Marsactu is not yet open to full contributions from readers, comments on the site and reactions on social networks sometimes push journalists to cover particular issues, revealing a certain degree of public participation in the agenda-building process. For instance, a piece on the closure of numerous museums in Marseille the very year of its promotion as European Capital of Culture – a story taken up by several national media – was the result of readers' complaints.

Social networking sites, mainly Facebook and Twitter, are not only seen as sources of traffic (which can reach 20% for Marsactu) but also the means to interact with readers. With 3,500 likes on Facebook and more than 8,000 followers on Twitter in July 2014, Marsactu is one of the most active local websites on social media. This intense interaction builds up a particular public that can be compared to a sort of 'regulars club'. Marsactu also uses live-blogging, mainly during elections or other important events. However, Pierre Boucaud admits that for the moment live-blogging is more of a gadget. The website is also considering launching a blogging platform, following the model of Mediapart Club, but seems to lack the time, money, and human resources for this project.

Carré d'info also has close but somewhat different relations with its readership. Participation through comments and social networks (1,600 likes and 3,400 followers) is quantitatively smaller than Marsactu's because the overall visibility and audience of the website is lower. Nevertheless, the ideas and the views of the readers are very important for journalists in their selection of issues to cover. Again Facebook (20%) and Twitter (13%) combined accounts for more of the overall traffic than Google does (25%), meaning that stories are very often shared and discussed by readers and that only a quarter of them visit the website at random through a search query. What is particular about Carré d'info compared to Marsactu is that, besides sociological similarity between readers and journalists, there is also political proximity. Carré d'info is openly left leaning, critical of local politics and of traditional local journalism, which it considers to be too reverential. Due to this somewhat radical stance, Carré d'info's journalists refuse, for example, to attend some official events such as press conferences, inaugurations, and so on, but also to cover topics like sports and crime which are considered to be too commercial. According to them, whenever they seem to drift too far from these principles there is always a reader or more to remind them of their commitments through comments or social networks. In this case, as often with politically engaged pure players, the public takes up the role of watchdog defending the values and the principles of the community built around the newsroom. As a result, the level of accountability of the journalists is very high compared to traditional local media online.

Finally, a common trend of the three pure players in our sample is that the physical proximity between journalists and readers, a part of local journalism, influences their relation to the public. The journalists of Carré d'info, Ariegenews, and Marsactu alike have regular encounters with readers, on the street or at particular events. In the case of Carré d'info and Marsactu some of these events, like public debates and conferences, are even hosted by their journalists. Deskwork occupying a relatively small amount of their time compared to online newsrooms of national media, these journalists are really submerged in their social environment during their professional activity and thus get regularly solicited by citizens on local problems or questions. This is particularly true in the case of Ariegenews where journalists do not seem to use comments or social networks as raw material for news production. Indeed, Ariegenews does not have an official Facebook page and has only 270 followers on Twitter. This difference compared to the other two can be linked to the sociological characteristics of the website's readership, which is older and mostly rural. Another reason that explains the low investment of Ariegenews in online interactions with readers is economics. Indeed, for Philippe Bardou, Ariegenews' founder, social networks are not interesting from a business perspective because they harness traffic from all over the country that is not attractive for local advertisers.

Editorial strategies and journalistic practices

Daily production of news at Carré d'info involved field reporting inside the city of Toulouse, mainly in the centre where the newsroom and the main institutions are located. There was no thematic specialisation among the three journalists. After a brief morning discussion, each one of them is free to choose what issues or events to cover for the day. There was also no apparent hierarchy among the journalists, who have equal tasks and obligations. Articles are systematically illustrated with original photographs, mostly by Kevin Figuier, a freelance photographer, but not with videos because, according to the journalists, filming and editing is time consuming. There was a rotation system for desk tasks that go to a different reporter every week. This position involved 'unattractive' but important operations such as proofreading and editing. It also included community management (updating Facebook and Twitter profiles, moderating and replying to comments) and also writing a series of brief news items and operating a selection of links to publish on the website. Monitoring work is done by classic methods such as morning press reviews of local newspapers (*La Dépêche du Midi, La Voix du Midi, 20 Minutes*, etc.) but also quite a lot on the web. Reading RSS feeds was gradually replaced by intensive use of Twitter, more random when it comes to the quality of results but described by the journalists as really excellent for discovering little-known events. For instance, Pauline Croquet always has a tab open on TweetDeck with the search query 'Toulouse', which functions as an alert and provides ideas for stories. Compared to their colleagues who work in big Parisian online newsrooms, the specificity of these journalists was their great amount of fieldwork. But mastering online tools was also essential for these young professionals because it enables them to carry out 'virtual investigations'.

One of the main problems of Carré d'info was the bad relations they had with local authorities and institutions: 'We don't like them and neither do they,' jokes Xavier Lalu. Overall, the feedback they got from the authorities was limited due to the low visibility of the website. However, the staff members of local politicians who monitor everything that is said about them do not hesitate to tackle the journalists about their coverage. The Mayor of Toulouse himself, for example, had already directly expressed his discontent about an article of Carré d'info. The website's journalists also admit to suffering from the treatment they get from PR services that consider them as 'nosy', unlike other media such as La Dépêche du Midi, which the PR people see as more docile and with whom they are used to working. Carré d'info's journalists say they are seen as mere bloggers despite the fact that they are recognised professionals and holders of the press card. Except for making reporting more difficult, these bad relations with local authorities also have direct economic consequences because they are among the main players in the advertising market of Toulouse.

Marsactu, on the other hand, is much more recognisable than Carré d'info in its own city. It aims to compete with the local daily newspaper by proposing 'high quality' content, distinguishing itself from La Provence's coverage of the news, centred on crime and sports (mainly on the local football team Olympique de Marseille). According to Pierre Boucaud the website has the role of a 'news decoder', paying particular attention to topics or issues related to local government policies. Marsactu's journalists imagine that their readers are keen on politics and that they know Marseille's political players and stakes. Thus the coverage of local news is built around investigations into political and financial deviant behaviours. At the same time, the central position of Marsactu's newsroom in the heart of Marseille facilitates on-the-ground reporting and offers the possibility to rapidly access different local political, economic, and social actors.

In Marsactu, field reporting 'in the city' accounts for half of the journalists' working time. The other half is spent inside the newsroom, writing and doing desk tasks such as rewriting wire news, doing research, and interacting with readers. This can be partly explained by the strong digital culture of these young journalists (excepting Pierre Boucaud, the average age is 28), making them more inclined to search for issues and stories online, through digital networks, than their counterparts in traditional media. Deeply acculturated to digital interactions, they use comments and social networking both professionally and personally, as a complementary approach to ground reporting, much like their colleagues at Carré d'info. This trend is made easier by Marsactu's relatively loose hierarchical organisation and highly autonomous working methods inspired by start-up culture and observed also in Paris-based pure players (Damian-Gaillard et al., 2009).

The journalists of Ariegenews, unlike those of Marsactu and Carré d'info, are systematically multitasking, producing on a daily basis photographs, video, and text. The newsroom functions much like a weekly magazine, with a general meeting every Monday morning where journalists discuss the topics to cover under the instructions of Philippe Bardou. When defining the week's agenda, great attention is given to official and public relations events. Thus, the production process is more adapted to 'soft news' as opposed to investigation and breaking-news. Every day Ariegenews journalists are in the field, which is mainly villages and some small towns like Foix, Pamiers, or Lavelanet. Equipped with microphones and cameras they produce at least one or two video reports of a few minutes each on a daily basis. Video content is edited and published online by two dedicated editors. Consequently, the work division in news production is more pronounced in Ariegenews than in the other two websites of our sample, as are hierarchical organisation and productivity constraints. Each video is accompanied by an article, generally short, factual, and neutral in tone, written by the same journalist that filmed the event. Before publication, great attention is given to search engine optimisation, which seems to be quite effective since more than one-third of the website's traffic comes from Google and lands on pages with national or international news where Ariegenews has no expertise whatsoever.

According to Philippe Bardou, the main goal of Ariegenews is not as much to raise its overall traffic as to be 'influential' in the local public sphere. Being influential in his words means gaining the respect of the public in its area for independence by criticising local political and economic elites when necessary. But at the same time it also means being very close to these elites and even promoting their actions. That's because local government and business are also the main sources of revenue for Ariegenews.

Revenue streams and business models

Despite the verve of local pure players in France, few of them have sustainable business models. Indeed, pure players are unable to attract sufficient sums from the two traditional revenue sources of local media: subscription and advertising. One of the most widely known local news websites, Dijonscope in the city of Dijon, terminated operations in May 2013. After being free access between 2009 and 2011, Dijonscope deployed a paywall, making all news available only to subscribers. Its founder Sabine Torres argued that local advertising alone was insufficient to sustain the website as she refused advertorials and other PR work. But with a few hundred subscribers after two years, instead of the 3,500 needed to break even, it was clear that the paywall model was not working. Télescope d'Amiens applied the same recipe with comparable results. Between September 2012 and December 2013 the website gained only 500 subscribers at €4.99 per month, far from the 2,000 necessary. As a result the website terminated operations in April 2014.

Most local pure players – like the three in our sample – have opted for free access. But they too have realised that mere advertising was insufficient and have tried different combinations of revenue streams. Carré d'info's revenue came mainly from advertising (60%) and from its journalists' conferences in a journalism school. The website also had around 50 supporters, mostly friends and relatives of the journalists, who paid a monthly subscription of €5. In an effort to increase its advertising value, the website's manager sold display advertising on the basis of time of exposure and not on cost-per-thousand impressions (CPM). He also limited the number of banners and did not use pervasive formats in order to preserve user experience. In addition to that he tried to negotiate directly with clients rather than using ad networks such as HiMedia. That was because, on the one hand, speaking directly to local clients was a better way to secure long-term partnerships and, on the other hand, doing so avoided the website displaying ads that were not 'in the spirit of Carré d'info'.

Nevertheless, all three revenue sources combined generated about €1,000 per month, which was of course not enough to sustain even a small newsroom. For two years the founders of Carré d'info relied on other resources to make a living (unemployment benefits, welfare, parents' support, etc.) and used their small revenue to pay office and website costs as well as some freelance content. But their business plan proved to be completely wrong. After two years, revenues had not increased as much as the audience did. This failure was mainly due to the lack of experience of the founders, especially in defining an adequate commercial strategy, and their refusal to engage in PR activities. Different solutions were examined, like joining leSquare.info, but none was pursued because of lack of means and motivation. The founders came to the bitter conclusion that local news like that produced by Carré d'info was definitely unprofitable.

Marsactu's business model is also based on advertising. Pierre Boucaud used to have a parallel career as a PR consultant but ended it in order to dedicate himself completely to the website. Its contracts are secured over a long period of time (from several months to more than a year), something that facilitates the deployment of a long-term strategy. What is decisive in the case of Marsactu is the personality and the credibility of its founder as well as his long experience in advertising. Under his lead, Marsactu managed to satisfy the need of local economic and political players for reaching urban, educated upper-class inhabitants of Marseille who do not read local newspapers. Marsactu succeeded in monetising its position by producing advertorial talk-shows in which local business personalities are interviewed, promoting local subsidiaries of companies from different sectors (banking, energy, telecoms, fast-food, etc.). For 2013 this form of advertorial accounts for 80% of the website's revenue. These advertorials are efficient because Marsactu is credible and influential among the 'informed'. In addition to that, Marsactu's CPM for display advertising is quite high (€8) because of the quality of its audience. Pierre Boucaud acknowledges that, even if he aims to increase traffic, his primary goal is to satisfy this particular, educated, and well-off audience rather than the general public. This specific ad-based model allowed Marsactu to almost triple its revenue from €78,000 to €220,000 between 2012 and 2013 and gradually diminish its yearly deficit from €225,000 to €100,000.

Ariegenews' basic revenue stream is also advertising. Its clients are mostly local businesses and institutions. Much like Carré d'info and Marsactu, Ariegenews does not use an advertising network to sell its ads but manages all the phases of a campaign internally (prospecting, producing ads, customer relations). Also, banners are sold on the basis of duration and not CPM. This shows the proximity between local pure players and advertising clients that rarely exists in nationwide news websites. The automated systems of ad networks such as Doubleclick, for instance, are not suitable in this context. Furthermore, the design and production of banners and video clips is a necessary revenue stream for Ariegenews, which functions also as a video producer for municipalities and local government.

But video is also a source of supplementary costs. Unlike Marsactu and Carré d'info who use platforms such as Dailymotion and YouTube, Ariegenews broadcasts video from its own servers. Thus, it has to pay tens of thousands of euros yearly for bandwidth and infrastructure. Philippe Bardou has obtained a subsidy from the government in order to buy a new server. But his main problem when it comes to developing his business is the lack of capital. His search for investors over the past few months has been fruitless. This incapacity to invest impacts human resources. For instance, he is the only one inside the company prospecting for advertising clients. Consequently, Ariegenews seems to be stagnating financially. Between 2011 and 2012, its revenue grew almost 46%, from €172,000 to €251,000. But in 2013 it was merely €254,000 and the yearly deficit remained at around €10,000. This forced the founder to lay off a journalist he had hired in 2012 and to revise his plans for future investment.

Conclusion

We have shown that local pure players function quite differently from nationwide newsrooms and local newspaper websites. Indeed, inside journalistic start-ups, daily operations involve interaction and permanent adjustment between journalists and a particular segment of the public whose members hold the role of expert, informer, commentator, and reader – even if decisions are ultimately made by professionals. This very active segment of readers, a far cry from the average citizen, is characterised by specific features such as possession of a strong cultural capital (embodied by high levels of education) and a keen interest in politics. In the case of local pure players, the sociological and sometimes political proximity between the journalists and the public is also reinforced by geographical and physical vicinity. The sentiment of belonging to a community that is created by intense interactions among journalists and readers inside and around pure players is therefore very strong. Thus, a higher degree of accountability of journalists towards their readers is a structural characteristic of this particular kind of news website.

Indeed, the work practices of journalistic pure players in France illustrate new trends (high degrees of accountability, permanent discussion with the public) and also do away partially or totally with constraints that dominate large online newsrooms (real-time coverage, publishing 'shovelware', etc.). For instance, time constraints in pure player newsrooms are more flexible compared to those of websites of mainstream media which privilege immediacy and hence productivity (Degand, 2011). The latter tend also to be comprehensive in their offer of news, a trend that forces them to rely largely on second-hand material (wire news, PR) and to closely follow the 'official' agenda. Pure players are not obliged to act in the same way, even if some do. In terms of management, pure players' internal organisation is often closer to that of a start-up than to a traditional newsroom. For instance, Marsactu and especially Carré d'info are characterised by loose hierarchy and the requirement of a strong commitment to the project. Finally, at the local level, journalistic pure players tend to practise field reporting at least as much as they do deskwork. This 'outdoor journalism' is for them an essential means to maintain proximity and dialogue with their audience. In this, they differ from Paris-based or local online ventures of legacy media, who do more 'office journalism'.

From a journalistic perspective, all these characteristics are very positive. One can even infer that local pure players might be able to renew and reinvigorate local public spaces and debates. This is true to a certain degree. But our study also identified two important shortcomings. First, the local pure players that we have examined are still addressing themselves to a very small fragment of the public with particular sociological and political characteristics. The overwhelming majority of the population is not familiar with them, so their influence is limited compared to that of traditional players. Second, as we have shown, local pure players like Carré d'info or Dijonscope who based their business models either on traditional advertising or subscriptions have failed to break even. In other words, local online news is not profitable per se. Those that succeed in maintaining important revenue streams, like Marsactu and Ariegenews, draw on non-journalistic activities such as PR film production and advertorials. This in turn jeopardises their independence from local businesses and political power. Therefore, profit remains elusive for local pure players, and there is little support for non-profit journalism in France, so sustainability is a major challenge. Indeed, the state-funded subsidies benefit mostly traditional media and are not adapted to internet ventures, while there is no tradition in the country of non-profit foundations in the news sector. Thus the question of how to fund independently produced local news remains a hard one, underlining the importance of alerting the public to the production cost of quality news and to the active part they have to play in supporting independent journalism.

Bibliography

Boczkowski, P. J. 2010. 'Ethnographie d'une rédaction en ligne Argentine', *Réseaux*, 160–1: 43–78.

Bousquet, F., and N. Smyrnaios. 2012. 'Les Médias et la société locale, une construction partagée', *Sciences de la société*, 84–5: 5–16.

Bruno, N., and R. K. Nielsen. 2012. *Survival is Success: Journalistic Online Start-Ups in Western Europe*. Oxford: Reuters Institute for the Study of Journalism.

CEVIPOF. 2010. Mediapolis research project. http://www.cevipof.com/fr/mediapolis.

Comby, J.-B., et al. 2011. 'Les Appropriations différenciées de l'information en ligne au sein des catégories sociales supérieures', *Réseaux*, 170: 75–102.

Damian-Gaillard, B., F. Rebillard, and N. Smyrnaios. 2009. 'La Production de l'information web: quelles alternatives? Une comparaison entre médias traditionnels et pure players de l'internet'. International conference, New Media and Information, Athens.

Degand, A. 2011. 'Le Multimédia face à l'immédiat: une interprétation de la reconfiguration des pratiques journalistiques selon trois niveaux', *Communication*, 29(1).

Domingo, D. 2008. 'Interactivity in the Daily Routines of Online Newsrooms: Dealing with an Uncomfortable Myth', *Journal of Computer-Mediated Communication*, 13(3): 680–704.

Domingo, D., and C. Paterson (eds). 2011. *Making Online News*, vol. 2: *Newsroom Ethnographies in the Second Decade of Internet Journalism*. New York: Peter Lang.

Eco, U. 1979. *Lector in fabula, le rôle du lecteur*. Paris: Grasset.

Granjon, F., and A. Le Foulgoc. 2010. 'Les usages sociaux de l'actualité: l'expérience médiatique des publics internautes', *Réseaux*, 160: 225–53.

Mitchelstein, E., and P. J. Boczkowski. 2010. 'Online News Consumption Research: An Assessment of Past Work and an Agenda for the Future', *New Media Society*, 12(7): 1085–102.

Ringoot, R., and Y. Rochard. 2005. 'Proximité éditoriale: normes et usages des genres journalistiques', *Mots*, 77: 73–90.

Smyrnaios, N. 2013. 'Les Pure Players entre diversité journalistique et contrainte économique: les cas d'Owni, Rue89 et Arrêt sur images', *Recherches en communication*, 39.

Smyrnaios, N., and F. Bousquet. 2011. 'The Development of Online Local Journalism in South-Western France: The Case of La Dépêche du Midi', in

R. Salaverría (ed.), *Diversity of Journalisms.* Proceedings of the ECREA Journalism Studies Section. Pamplona: ECREA, 347–58.

Smyrnaios, N., E. Marty, and F. Rebillard. 2010. 'Does the Long Tail Apply to Online News? A Quantitative Study of French-Speaking News Websites', *New Media and Society*, 12(8): 1244–61.

Tétu, J.-F. 1995. 'L'Espace public local et ses médiations', *Hermés*, 17–18: 287–98.

8

Hyperlocal with a Mission? Motivation, Strategy, Engagement

Marco van Kerkhoven and Piet Bakker

Identifying the hyperlocal

Hyperlocals are online local initiatives that aim to produce news gathered in and focused on a designated local area. Hyperlocal news operations can be defined as those media that target a geographic area, have a community orientation, contain original news reporting, are indigenous to the web, fill perceived news gaps, and stimulate civic engagement (Kennedy, 2013; Metzgar et al., 2011).

A hyperlocal site is thus not simply a blog (Lowrey, 2012). Publishing local news regularly and frequently sets these sites apart. To do so, hyperlocals need to operate with some sort of business model, usually including some sort of (professional) staff. The operation has to follow some basic journalistic rules as well (Anderson, 2013; Kennedy, 2013). Our focus here is on online news hyperlocals in the Netherlands that cover one or more geographic area, contain original news, and are independent from traditional media operations.

Local online news services have been accompanied by high expectations. They are expected to play a significant role in adding value to local and regional political news ecosystems – defined as the complex infrastructure of competition, municipality, businesses, and all others that are part of dynamic symbiotic or parasitic collectives of interrelated news networks. Hyperlocals are supposed to be more flexible, cheaper to operate, and more innovative, especially in terms of production and distribution. There are also high expectations concerning citizens as contributors. Could these hyperlocals take over the role of traditional media, or is another contribution to a local news ecosystem possible?

The US Federal Communications Commission (FCC) in its report on the future of American journalism (Waldman, 2011), for example, highlights the potential of regional and local community investigative news sites: 'independent non-profit websites are providing exciting journalistic innovation on the local level' (p. 191). The Knight Foundation agrees with the FCC, in expecting more non-commercial local online news websites to be launched in the United States by entrepreneurial journalists (Downie and Schudson 2009; Knight Commission, 2009). These enterprises are expected to have the capacity of combining high-quality journalism with business and technology skills (Knight Foundation, 2011). Bowman and Willis (2003) predicted that in the year 2021 amateur journalists would be responsible for half of all the news produced. But these are all speculations.

Information on the practical consequences of setting up and rolling out an independent hyperlocal, for instance, is scarce. The US FCC is optimistic but also issues a warning: 'a handful [of independent non-profit websites] have created sustainable business models – but most either are struggling to survive or are too small to fill the gaps left by newspapers' (Waldman, 2011: 191). The most viable of the online American non-profit websites have a broad range of revenue sources, Remez (2012) found: foundation funding, grants, donations, corporate sponsorships, selling content to other media, and providing services such as education and training.

A new digital platform without the backing of an experienced editorial and healthy company depends heavily, as one might expect, on its entrepreneurial spirit and ideological foundations. The question for the hyperlocal newcomer on the local media market is: how do entrepreneurial or ideological spirits work out in relation to the hyperlocal's ambitions? How do they affect the organisational and editorial model? And is motivation alone sufficient for maintaining a viable hyperlocal news website that can play a significant role in society? These are the topics we focus on here, where we examine the motivations, strategies, and forms of engagement that characterise independent hyperlocal news websites in the Netherlands.

New(s) business in town

Online news media face difficulties when entering a new market (Bakker, 2009; Harte, 2013; Lowrey et al., 2011; Naldi and Picard, 2012). Since traditional news production is characterised by high start-up costs and fixed costs due to substantial investments in people and technology, only the few companies that can make a profit quickly are able to survive. Due to this 'first-mover effect', newcomers will find little market share left for them (Bakker, 2009). Also, incumbents could lower their prices to keep competitors out, since redistribution costs for news are close to zero. This might be different when online media use business models based exclusively on redistribution of freely gathered news, rather than on being producers themselves – because news production costs are known to form the bulk of operational expenses. The more interesting question, therefore, is why the apparent increase of the news hyperlocal has occurred at all.

Studies on how hyperlocal news sites have been operating, what editorial choices they make, and how successful they are in entering and serving a local news ecosystem have been conducted in Chicago (Churchill and Ubois, 2009), Baltimore (Pew Research Center, 2010), Seattle (Fancher, 2011), and by Radcliffe (2012), who offers an overview of the UK hyperlocal landscape. Metzgar et al. (2011) covers six US initiatives; Thurman et al. (2012) studied the Local People websites. Earlier research worth mentioning here is *We Media* (Bowman and Willis, 2003) and *We the Media* (Gillmor, 2004), which gave insight on the ambitions and editorial strategy of independent news initiatives. The focus of Gillmor, however, was mainly on how new models could offer citizens the possibility to operate their own media by easily accessible technology. It appeared to be a fairly successful strategy. 'The emergence of "we media" has accelerated at a remarkable rate', Gillmor writes (2004: 14). According to Radcliffe (2012: 10), there are 'many reasons why hyperlocal media is gaining popularity'.

It is important to note that not all of these new initiatives are insurgents. An example of hyperlocals associated with established legacy media companies is Examiner.com, owned by Denver media-tycoon Philip Anschutz, with presence in 244 markets in the US (Examiner. com, 2012). Patch was another big player in the US, owned by AOL, and served 800 US communities in 2012 (Patch, 2012). In Europe there is for instance Myheimat.de, which covers Germany and cooperates with more than a dozen major regional publishers. The Belgium Belang van Limburg websites cover all 48 municipalities in the province of Limburg. The 400 Local People websites are part of the media company Local World, owned by Northcliffe Media and Iliffe News and Media. Since June 2009, it serves cities with populations between 10,000 and 50,000 people in the south-west of England and some London boroughs. The Netherlands has

Dichtbij.nl, a product of Telegraaf Media Group (TMG). It operates more than 80 websites, covering all Dutch municipalities.

Mission impossible?

The operation and strategies of hyperlocal news business is the focus of an increasing number of studies, as we have seen. What motivates people to start or participate in a hyperlocal news website, however, is still unmapped territory. Could it be as diverse as the individual characteristics of participatory journalists? Surely, it depends on socio-demographics, expertise, qualification, and gender parameters, as Fröhlich et al. (2012) put it. They asked writers of Myheimat.de sites in Germany what their societal and individual motivations were. The authors found personal motivations such as individually perceived creativeness, the fascination of publishing, and the enjoyment of presenting one's own ideas to a larger public. Typical journalistic motivations mentioned were balancing different perspectives and informing other people (Fröhlich et al., 2012: 1056). Some seek motivation in professional journalistic self-conceptions – often defined by the idea of being a watchdog, playing a role in agenda setting, and informing the public so that people can participate in the democratic process. At the other end of the spectrum, there is the conception of being entertainment journalism, offering advice, showing new trends, being entertaining. The authors state that it is impossible to theoretically predict motivational patterns. 'Motivation has to be measured in the specific context of each journalistic product' (Fröhlich et al., 2012: 1047). In their context they distinguish between intrinsic and extrinsic motivations. In intrinsic motivation, an owner of a hyperlocal website connects to the goals and ideals of an open source community, basically supported by the idea of empowering social contacts, follow-up communication, and belonging to a social group. Extrinsic motivation, on the other hand, is based on a user's need to find a solution for product or service deficiencies. An ideological and a commercial distinction can be identified here, something we will build upon in our own research.

Three local news sites in the US, IN Denver Times, New Jersey Newsroom, and Public Press in San Francisco, were studied and showed that pre-existing expectations (optimistic versus realistic) and experiences of owners can play a decisive role in the future of a website (Naldi and Picard, 2012). Owners can have a very clear idea on what they want with a news site – usually in line with their past experiences – but adapting to the market and changing the model seems to be much harder; the authors call this 'formational myopia', the reluctance of news entrepreneurs to adjust their expectations and learn from new experience as their start-up develops.

Research design and method

Independent online news start-ups seem to be gaining ground in local news ecosystems. The goal of our study is to examine to what extent they seem to have a sustainable business model, adding value to a local news ecosystem. As we have suggested, starting and successfully maintaining an online news website depends on motivation, strategy, and the civic consciousness of the owners. This is why our research questions are:

- What is the motivation of the owners of a hyperlocal website? (RQ1)
- What is the business approach of the owners of hyperlocal news services in terms of their organisational and editorial strategies? (RQ2)
- How do hyperlocals engage with society, the local news ecosystem, and their community in particular? (RQ3)

Interviews were conducted with the owners of hyperlocal websites to find the answers to these questions. For this purpose, all Dutch hyperlocal news websites – independent from traditional media operations – that contained at least some original news reporting and published regularly were taken into consideration. Online platforms of newspapers, weeklies, and local or regional broadcasters were discarded, as were local aggregation sites that only contained news scraped by robots from other sites. This resulted in a database with 123 owners of 350 websites and 74 of them (59%) agreed to be interviewed about our research questions. From website chains we selected the site where the ownership was based, otherwise the largest or the first site. The 74 owners of a hyperlocal website were interviewed in the spring of 2013 by telephone (58) or on camera (16), using the same semi-structured questionnaire.

To address RQ1, all interviewees were asked what the main reasons were for having started their hyperlocal news website. We also used content analyses of all websites to check on additional information on motivation, often found in the 'About' section or in separate files. For RQ2 we inquired about the business approach the owners claimed to have for their hyperlocal news services. Based on a geographically even spread, maximum variation in business scale, and maximum variation in production level, we selected 23 owners for an additional interview to explore journalistic and business ethics. We specifically asked how owners of hyperlocals value and implement journalistic codes of practice, how they combine advertorial-based business models with independent news production, and how they deal with conflicting interests, especially in cases where local economic and political powers seem to interfere. RQ3 was investigated by asking the owners about their involvement and interactions with the community and the news ecosystem. The telephone interviews lasted an average of 17 minutes; the camera interviews took an average of 42 minutes. All the interviews were transcribed afterwards.

Results

The 123 websites we analysed covered 199 municipalities, meaning 1.6 municipality per site. Of these businesses or organisations, 35 operated more than one site; on average these 'chains' owned 7.5 different sites. Figure 8.1 gives an overview of the geographical distribution of the hyperlocals. They are concentrated in the west of the country, which is not unexpected since two-thirds of the population live in the west of the Netherlands, and most of the larger cities are located there.

Motivation (RQ1)

The majority of the owners said they wanted to serve the community and play a social role. 'Doing business' came second. And commercial motives were most often combined with either serving the community or political incentives – often expressed negatively: to compensate for a lack of decent political coverage (Table 8.1). Owners of hyperlocals with different first or dominant reasons, such as gaining experience or being asked to join a start-up, or sites where it remained unclear what motivation played a role, together made up 17% (21 owners) of the sites.

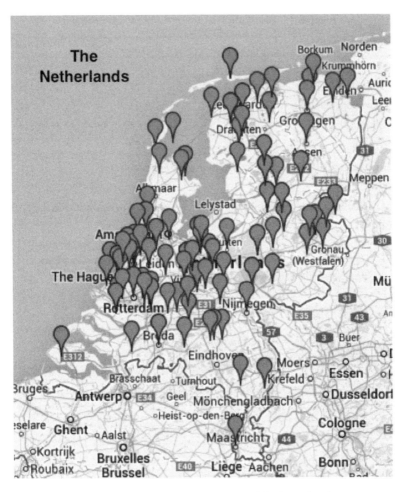

Figure 8.1 Geographical distribution of the hyperlocals.
Map data © Google 2015

From interviews with some owners, it was not clear what motivated them. Other reasons mentioned for starting or operating a hyperlocal were the fact that they were asked to take over from someone else, that they saw it as a way to pass time, and the fact that they missed being a reporter.

Most owners emphasised local cooperation as the most important reason to start a hyperlocal. Reports on art and culture, politics, science, human interest, and the economy were mentioned as inspired by members

Table 8.1   Motivation of owners (123 local models)

	# of owners	%*
Social/community	53	69
Business/financial/commercial	27	35
Providing political news	22	31
Other	8	
Unclear	13	

* Total exceeds 100% as more than one answer was possible.

of the community. Often confidence was expressed – communities are still full of creativity, and people value a new source:

> That might be my ultimate goal: to build bridges between communities. That people understand each other more.

> Our philosophy is that society needs to do more.

> We started with music programmes, later we did more and more: news, and community coverage.

> We started the site to promote community feeling in our city and to help local businesses.

> I started this project when I was a teacher in civic journalism. I believe in community journalism.

Making money was the second most mentioned motive. Financial independence and being able to hire professional journalists and sales staff were considered important. For this category finding subsidies was not the number one goal, but this was mentioned as being part of a commercial business strategy. Most sites were happy to be able to break even, but it is a tough fight still, for all of them:

> If we don't make money at the end of the year I will be pulling the plug.

> Until 2008 I worked for another site that closed because they found out they could not make enough money (also because they had to pay my salary). After that I started this site with volunteers.

Well, things are gradually improving, but it's obviously been a rotten time in recent years in terms of commerce.

Being unhappy with 'traditional' media reporting on mainly political news appeared to be the third important reason to start a hyperlocal. The start-ups felt they had to fill that gap:

Regular media neglected policy and politics.

We just think it's important to let people know what happens in our city.

We started as a response to the disappearance of local newspapers.

Professional journalism was not practised here, so I jumped into that gap.

Business approach/strategy (RQ2)

As we saw, commercial objectives of selling paid content in a news environment are the second most important reason to found and maintain a hyperlocal site. A dominant business strategy is a no-staff/low-budget one. More than 90% of the sites (112) carried advertising (by other sources than the site or its owners) on their homepage in the period under survey. Strangely enough, only 88 of them (72%) offered information on how to advertise on the site (Table 8.2).

Table 8.2 Advertising (123 local models)

	# of (home or central) sites with...	%
Information on advertising	88	72
Sites with ads	112	91
Average # of ads on home page	8.5	
More than 50 ads	1	
Between 41 and 50 ads	-	
Between 31 and 40 ads	3	
Between 21 and 30 ads	2	
Between 11 and 20 ads	22	
Between 1 and 10 ads	84	

Ads are unevenly distributed over the 123 sites. The top five hyperlocal websites contained a third of the total number of ads. Half of the ads were in the top 20 of the sites.

Keeping the costs low as a way of coping with low turnover is a widely embraced practice. Banner advertising dominates, but it is not the only source of income. Crowdfunding had been tried, but has not amounted to considerable sums of money. Some hyperlocals tried selling stories to third parties.

We make money from banner ads and press releases from commercial parties. Non-profit organisations can publish their content for free.

We work without publishers, without subsidies, without subscribers, without a sugar daddy, without guardian angels, yes, even without God. Without your help we will die. So: how can you help? Donate! [...] we also sell some articles to the local newspaper.

We all work for free. We all work for our own CVs.

The lack of money is recognised as a serious risk in terms of sustaining the sites, but for many owners it seems not to seriously jeopardise their optimism:

We are heavily supported by amateur reporters. They deliver the texts and images. That hardly ever goes wrong, since, online, every bullshit story is immediately corrected by the public.

Many retired people are working with us, often with a background in journalism.

People are certainly watching us with some pleasure. They sometimes want to contribute. They are all volunteers, and volunteers who do not worry about their income.

We have an editorial board of freelancers and contributors who have worked in journalism before. And then a group we call co-writers, amateurs who make up for about a quarter of the content.

Other strategies are the cooperation with regional news agencies and building new media tools benefiting from crowdsourcing:

We are a kind of broker between broadcasters and other media.

One of my bloggers has [his] own IT business. He developed an app for us. I knew nothing about it, but I liked it very much.

On most websites amateur reporting seems to be important. Only some of the journalists interviewed had previously worked for traditional news media outlets. Owners were committed to keeping the site lively, and this sometimes means rethinking the editorial strategy and sometimes compromising on journalistic standards:

We work together with the police and the fire department.

You are pondering business-oriented news.

We are careful not to become a 911 [the emergency services number] site. Although we know that this is a market.

For instance by writing articles on assignment, advertorials, but with freedom to choose the content, not necessarily the subject. We think we can maintain journalistic quality, this way.

There is churn in the hyperlocal sector in the Netherlands. As in most other countries, sites are opening, stopping updating, or closing down altogether. In the Netherlands, in 2013, half of the operations (66) were more than five years old. Given the limitations of searching the digital archives of the internet, we found some sites going back as far as 1997. Things changed from 2007 onwards. From then on the number of local news sites increased almost every year. The churn rate over the first period, up to 2007, is hard to establish since definitive data on closings cannot always be obtained from internet archives. But the growth rate, we estimate, decreased from 50% in 2001 and 2002 to 5% in 2012. Comparing the 2012 and 2013 data, we found that almost 10% of the sites closed down within a year.

Ethics

Analysing the websites we found that about 20% state that journalistic codes, either the International Federation of Journalists' Code of Bordeaux or its national derivative, or a self-proclaimed work protocol that involves

Table 8.3   Adaptation of professional ethics

	Yes	No
Using a style book	2	21
Recognising Press Council	10	13
Publish verdict Press Council	14	9
Familiar with ethical code (Dutch)	19 (and sometimes: 1)	3
Implementing ethical code (Bordeaux)	6	16
Hearing both sides	9 (and sometimes: 6)	8
Dealing with complaints	23 (correction afterwards)	-

fact checking and hearing both sides of a story, play a role in daily newsroom routines. The overwhelming majority, however, do not mention any journalism-related goals on their website (see Table 8.3).

Based on the 23 interviews conducted on this issue, ethics do play a role in editorial choices and practical news production, but views and practices differ substantially. The majority of the owners of hyperlocals reject the strict idea of being a journalist, although bringing independent news is still their primary goal. They rather allow themselves the liberty to cross the traditional line between the economic and democratic interests of their business. In half the cases this is said to be a necessary step in order to survive. In three out of our 23 hyperlocals they specifically allow political interests to interfere with journalistic interests.

In 14 of the 23 cases the sites work with journalists who have been active in journalism before, or have had some formal journalism training. In 19 cases the website owners were able to pay contributors some compensation for their work. So, as one owner put it: 'Making them less vulnerable [to] sloppy work'.

None of the owners of hyperlocals said that they regularly considered journalism ethics in their daily routines. Two said they had a journalistic book of codes available. In four cases they said being able to write proper Dutch is the most important code that needs to be addressed.

Interestingly, ten owners of hyperlocals recognise the Netherlands Press Council. Although none of them had had to deal with the Netherlands Press Council so far, 14 would publish a verdict on their website if they were asked to.

The ethical idea of hearing both sides is not commonly practised. All the owners say they would rather publish a story and do the checking afterwards. This also means that stories are corrected after publication. One owner said that in those processes they prefer to rely on their own sources.

> If we have a good news story we simply publish the facts that are known to us, often without checking at the official sources. Recently we heard about a kid that got seriously injured at a soccer dugout. We were the first to report, within 20 minutes. We had two independent sources. We didn't consult the police since their press department is usually later informed than we are.

Ten out of the 23 interviewees say they do not apply hearing both sides of a story as standard procedure. Five hyperlocals say they try to work according to Dutch codes for journalism (*Leidraad voor de Journalistiek*). Seven owners know the Code of Bordeaux, but none of them uses it on a daily basis. Complaints are in all cases handled in the same way: stories are adjusted or corrected if the protest is grounded. One of the hyperlocals has been taken to court over a case.

Engagement (RQ3)

The local news start-ups in our study have difficulties in defining their role in a local news ecosystem. It is usually a small community in which the hyperlocals have to operate – in our study from 7,000 up to a maximum of 300,000 potential news consumers, with an average of 55,000. Relations with local elites, government, and business are sometimes delicate, since hyperlocals often cover the same people that buy ads and make decisions over financial support.

To discern what kind of community roles the hyperlocals want to perform, we specifically looked at how they use social media to connect with audiences, how they use the community as a source, and how their visibility in the community helps them.

Many owners express the ambition to have around-the-clock news on Twitter and Facebook. Facebook is seen as a platform that offers advantages. It is faster and it appeals more to younger people, an audience that is of particular interest for hyperlocals.

Hyperlocals by nature encourage people to get involved. Some of them do it by explicitly stating what the platform is all about, how they operate, and what it can offer people who want to join. Others cooperate with people who already publish online elsewhere. Most sites use volunteers. An experienced copy editor is often necessary – although owners risk discouraging amateur contributors if they correct them too often. Professional contacts with organisations offering content, such as press releases, are common. Interaction is encouraged on most websites. On the majority of sites people can react, although owners say they do not always find the time to respond to those comments or stories. In some cases people can also participate, either on their own initiative or by invitation. Most sites allow people and organisations to post their own unedited press releases. The difference between editorial content, advertorials, and press releases is not always clear.

Hyperlocals treasure their contacts with the municipality. Some are regularly in touch with spokespersons, colleagues from other media, and other key players to establish good relations. Some say they prefer working in anonymity, to guard their independence. And being around all the time is a demanding task. Like going to town hall meetings on a regular basis, as many do not succeed in doing, or being the local 'friend':

> We even help people find their lost cats or dogs. Later they call us and let us know how happy they are. That's also a way to socialise.

> We have people that speak Korean. So we attract people from South Korea too, for instance, if they happen to live in Korea but come from here.

Conclusion and discussion

The *motivation* for starting a local online news website is generally grounded in the perception of a local news gap. But we also found sites predominantly motivated by commercial objectives. These are both what Fröhlich et al. (2012) would call extrinsic motivations. In any case practical and commercial opportunities prevail. In terms of strategy and claimed engagement there are only a few differences between ideologically non-profit hyperlocals and commercial chains.

In all cases a common business *strategy* is that owners operate the service on a 'no-staff, no-budget' basis. Most sites rely on banner advertising. Crowdfunding has been tried on a small scale only. Some sites experiment with other forms of income, including advertorials. Revenues are generally limited.

One of the goals of hyperlocals is *engagement*, a more intense relationship with both the public and advertisers of their community – but without losing independence. Our study showed how the lack of resources has triggered ingenuity, forced owners, employees, and volunteers to commit themselves and to adapt to new situations.

In terms of conventional journalistic ethics, the hyperlocals we have examined are vulnerable. If one is prepared to allow advertorials in between original or independent political news, and if one permits third parties to publish unedited press releases, a news platform risks losing its credibility. This is why there seems to be a gap between noble motives on the one hand and the business approach on the other. Sometimes ideology is getting in the way of sound organisational and editorial decisions. If an owner decides to operate only with qualified staff, for example, but has insufficient revenues to pay for it, then the business is seriously jeopardised economically.

Based on our interviews we conclude that hyperlocals are not particularly concerned about journalistic ethical codes, professional standards, or even practical protocols. They see providing news as their main concern; journalistic practices in this process are instrumental rather than conditional. Checking facts has become part of the follow-up of a story, and does not seem to be an inseparable part of the editorial production process. Ethical behaviour as a quality indicator means that hyperlocals do not live up to expectations and they might risk losing credibility and the trust of the audience. This means that news consumers might start wondering if the news that they are reading is fairly and thoughtfully produced, which might lead to a loss of visitors to the site.

Finally, in general online local news sites in the Netherlands underperform in terms of efficient use of resources, acquisition of readers and advertisers, and in terms of connecting with the audience. Regarding the latter, finding a civic role locally, we signal a discrepancy between ambition and practice. All the participants indicated that their digitally native platform gave them more freedom to experiment with newer technologies in ways they could not have done while working for traditional news outlets. At the same time, taking advantage of all the new tools and ideas is often not considered a priority, mainly due to lack of time and money.

In conclusion, hyperlocals in the Netherlands are often launched with a journalistic motivation – to address a local news gap – but the strategies and forms of engagement employed often undermine their ability to achieve their stated goals.

Bibliography

Anderson, C. W. 2013. *Rebuilding the News: Metropolitan Journalism in the Digital Age*. Philadelphia: Temple University.

Bakker, Gerben. 2009. 'Trading Fact: Arrow's Fundamental Paradox and the Emergence of Global News Networks.' Monograph. London: Department of Economic History, London School of Economics. http://eprints.lse. ac.uk/22519/.

Bowman, Shayne, and Chris Willis. 2003. *We Media: How Audiences are Shaping the Future of News and Information*. Media Center at the American Press Institute. www.hypergene.net/wemedia.

Chen, N. T. N., et al. 2012. 'Building a New Media Platform for Local Storytelling and Civic Engagement in Ethnically Diverse Neighborhoods', *New Media and Society*, 14(6): 931–50.

Churchill, E. F., and J. Ubois. 2009. 'Lead Type, Dead Type: New Patterns of Local News Production and Consumption'. Ethnographic Praxis in Industry Conference, Chicago.

D'heer, Evelien, and Steve Paulussen. 2012. 'The Hyperlocal Online News Project of the Newspaper *Het Belang van Limburg*'. Paper presented at the Etmaal van de Communicatiewetenschap, February, Gent.

Deuze, M. 2004. 'What is Multimedia Journalism 1?', *Journalism Studies*, 5(2): 139–52.

Downie, L., and M. Schudson. 2009. 'The Reconstruction of American Journalism', *Columbia Journalism Review*, 19: 28–51.

Examiner.com. 2012. *Media Kit*. Downloaded from www.examiner.com.

Fancher, M. R. 2011. *Seattle: A New Media Case Study*. Washington, DC: Pew Research Center Project for Excellence in Journalism, The State of the News Media.

Fröhlich, Romy, Oliver Quiring, and Sven Engesser. 2012. 'Between Idiosyncratic Self-Interests and Professional Standards: A Contribution to the Understanding of Participatory Journalism in Web 2.0. Results from an Online Survey in Germany', *Journalism*, 13(8): 1–23.

Gillmor, Dan. 2004. *We the Media: Grassroots Journalism by the People, for the People*. Sebastopol: O'Reilly.

Groves, J. 2014. 'Book Review: Dan Kennedy The Wired City: Reimagining Journalism and Civic Life in the Post-Newspaper Age', *Journalism*, 15(1): 130–1.

Harte, David. 2013. 'One Every Two Minutes: Assessing the Scale of Hyperlocal Publishing in the UK', *JOMEC Journal* [online], 1(3). http://www.cardiff.

ac.uk/jomec/research/journalsandpublications/jomecjournal/3-june2013/
index.html.

Kennedy, D. 2013. *The Wired City: Reimagining Journalism and Civic Engagement in the Post-Newspaper Age.* Amherst: University of Massachusetts Press.

Kik, Quint, Piet Bakker and Laura Buijs. 2013. 'Meer lokaal nieuwsaanbod, meer van hetzelfde nieuws' (More local news models, more of the same news), *Tijdschrift voor Communicatiewetenschap.* http://www.journalismlab.nl/publicatie/meer-lokaal-nieuwsaanbod-meer-van-hetzelfde-nieuws/.

Knight Commission on the Information Needs of Communities in a Democracy. 2009. *Informing Communities: Sustaining Democracy in the Digital Age.* October. Washington, DC: Aspen Institute.

Lowrey, Wilson. 2012. 'Journalism Innovation and the Ecology of News Production: Institutional Tendencies', *Journalism and Communication Monographs*, 14(4): 214–87.

Lowrey, Wilson, Scott Parrott, and Tom Meade. 2011. 'When Blogs Become Organizations', *Journalism*, 12(3): 243–59.

Metzgar, E., D. Kurpius, and K. Rowley. 2011. 'Defining Hyperlocal Media: Proposing a Framework for Discussion', *New Media and Society*, 13(5): 772–87.

Naldi, Lucia, and Robert G. Picard. 2012. '"Let's start an online news site"': Opportunities, Resources, Strategy, and Formational Myopia in Startups', *Journal of Media Business Studies*, 9(4): 69–97.

Patch. 2012. *Niemanlab.* www.niemanlab.org.encyclo/path.

Pew Research Center. 2010. *How News Happens: A Study of the News Ecosystem of One American City.* Washington, DC: Pew Research Center's Project for Excellence in Journalism.

Radcliffe, D. 2012. *Here and Now: UK Hyperlocal Media.* London: Nesta.

Remez, M. 2012. 'How Community News is Faring', *State of the News Media, 2012.* Washington, DC: Pew Research Center's Project for Excellence in Journalism. http://stateofthemedia.org/2012/mobile-devices-and-news-consumptionsome-good-signs-for-journalism/how-community-news-is-faring.

Thurman, N., J. C. Pascal, and P. Bradshaw. 2012. 'Can Big Media Do Big Society? A Critical Case Study of Commercial, Convergent Hyperlocal News', *International Journal of Media and Cultural Politics*, 8(2–3): 269–86.

Waldman, S. 2011. *The Information Needs of Communities: The Changing Media Landscape in a Broadband Age.* Washington, DC: FCC. www.fcc.gov/info-needs-communities#download.

9

Filling the News Hole? UK Community News and the Crisis in Local Journalism

Andy Williams, Dave Harte, and Jerome Turner

Introduction

The public interest value of news is often viewed through the prism of its relationship to democracy (McNair, 2009). Key to this is the idea that representative democracy enables good government most effectively if citizens' decisions are based on accurate and reliable (and where necessary oppositional) information (Chambers and Costain, 2001; Habermas, 1989). McNair identifies four principal (and interrelated) democracy-enabling roles for the news. He sees news as

(1) a source of accurate information for citizens;
(2) a watchdog/fourth estate;
(3) a mediator and/or representative of communities (a role which can help with community cohesion); and
(4) an advocate of the public in campaigning terms (McNair, 2009: 237–40).

The value of local news has been defined similarly, as indicated by Franklin when he writes, 'local newspapers should offer independent and critical commentary on local issues, make local elites accountable, [and] provide a forum for the expression of local views on issues of community concern' (Franklin, 2006a: xix).

However, numerous studies have found the ongoing crisis in the UK news industry is endangering the 'local-ness', quality, and independence of local news (Fenton, 2011; Franklin, 2006b). These studies find that, as revenues fall and staff are cut, workloads increase and mainstream local news relies more on official sources and PR, and that only a very narrow range of sources are routinely cited (Davis, 2008; Franklin, 1988; Franklin and Van Slyke Turk, 1988; O'Neill and O'Connor, 2008). This news becomes less local in focus as editions are cut, high-street offices are closed, and the use of cheap news agency filler becomes more prevalent (Davies, 2008; Franklin, 2011; Hamer, 2006; Williams and Franklin, 2007). This has all led to increasing concerns about the industry's ability to play its democracy-enabling roles.

Harrison, echoing others' findings (Franklin, 1988; Franklin and Van Slyke Turk, 1988), found that local newspapers' reliance on sources in local government means that 'local newspapers are unlikely to be able to perform their role as principal institutions of the public sphere' (Harrison, 1998). O'Neill and O'Connor find that local and regional journalists in the north of England rely very heavily on a relatively small range of official sources, usually those with the most resources to devote to media relations (O'Neill and O'Connor, 2008). Official sources are quoted the most often, and very few members of the public or local activists were cited at all (O'Neill and O'Connor, 2008: 491–2). They also note with alarm that the majority of stories (76%) relied on single sources, with less than a quarter of stories employing secondary sources who may provide alternative, opposing, or complementary information to that provided by primary sources (p. 492). This suggests a local press that takes too much information on trust, is too uncritical, and provides readers with limited access to the range of the (often competing) voices and perspectives actually present in local public debates. Scholars have reached similarly gloomy conclusions about the range of topics covered by UK local newspapers. In-depth coverage of local politics and the governance of local communities has gradually given way to a more tabloid-oriented spread of news (Franklin, 2005, 2006b). Since the mid-1980s the local press in the UK has reduced coverage of local elections, produced fewer election stories with distinct local angles, and put a 'growing emphasis on trivial and entertaining coverage rather than a sustained discussion of policy concerns' (Franklin et al., 2006).

The rise of hyperlocal community news

However, the web has enabled a new generation of community-oriented local news outlets, often termed hyperlocal news (Kurpius et al., 2010; Metzgar et al., 2011). In the USA, as early as 2007, Schaffer produced survey-based research on 500 hyperlocal citizen media sites which found this kind of news outlet to be 'a form of "bridge" media, linking traditional forms of journalism with classic civic participation' (2007: 7). By 2009, distinguished commentators had already accepted that such community news operations had a role to play in sustaining US democracy (Downie and Schudson, 2009). Although the market for local news in the USA is still in steep decline, and community news start-ups face many challenges around future economic sustainability, there have recently been some signs that smaller local news publishers may be weathering the storm better than some of their mainstream counterparts. The Pew Research Center recently identified 438 digital organisations that produce original news regularly, most of them local in orientation, and found that these smaller, often non-profit, news sites are the biggest component of a growing US digital news sector (Jurkowitz, 2014). Contrasting somewhat with this more mature and established hyperlocal media market, hyperlocal community news media are also a part of distinct European national media systems. Fröhlich et al. (2012), along with Bruns (2011), have researched the large German community news network MyHeimat. In 2010, Fröhlich's team found a national network of 37,000 citizen journalists collaborating with a number of regional news operations as well as publishing directly to a series of hyperlocal audiences (Fröhlich et al., 2012). In the Netherlands, Kerkhoven and Bakker identified 350 hyperlocal news websites publishing in 199 municipalities (Kerkhoven and Bakker, 2014). These sites offer diverse, and often very locally relevant, news, but in common with many community news outlets worldwide, they often struggle to maintain themselves financially.

In the UK hyperlocal community, news is less well understood but still attracts sustained interest from the news industry, investors, and policy-makers. In their 2012 overview of the emerging network of hyperlocal websites the communications regulator Ofcom claimed that these sites have 'the potential to support and broaden the range of local media content available to citizens and consumers at a time when traditional local media providers continue to find themselves under financial pressure' (Ofcom, 2012: 103). Ofcom data show that 7% of UK adults currently access these sites once a week or more, and 14% at least monthly. By contrast, three years previously Ofcom described the hyperlocal sector as nascent when compared with a stronger US scene.

Many have suggested, often without adequate data to back this up, that some of the problems associated with the contraction of mainstream local news publishers can be solved with the advent of online local citizen news.

Eulogising about a 'blossoming of hyper-local online ventures', Beckett and Hevre-Azevedo claim that 'hyper-local journalism is not simply a hobby or a pleasant localist addition. It is a potential amelioration of the drastic problem of declining professional regional and local news media' (2010: 11). In 2009, the then Labour Government, in its *Digital Britain* report, cited the 'medium-term potential of online hyperlocal news' to contribute to a gap in the provision 'between the old and new' news media (DCMS, 2009: 150). Writing about the US context, Metzgar et al. build on accounts of how the internet facilitates new forms of news participation, and argue that hyperlocal news can contribute to undermining, but also adding public value to, the kinds of news provision normally offered to communities, specifically in the way they are often intended 'to fill perceived gaps in coverage of an issue or region and to promote civic engagement' (2011: 774). It is the filling of such real or perceived 'gaps' that concerns Ofcom and other actors who are keen to scrutinise the development of hyperlocal media in light of the decline of commercial local news (Ofcom, 2012: 103). Our research was designed, in part, to test empirically whether, in what ways, and to what extent hyperlocal community news can plug the holes left by the retreat of local news from many UK communities.

Methods

We have focused most of our research on the *content* of local community news, along with its *production*. More specifically, we did a large content analysis of UK hyperlocal news, along with an online survey of, and semi-structured interviews with, producers of such news.

Content analysis

Our sample consists of posts published on the sites of members of the UK's Openly Local news network between 8 and 18 May 2012 (Openly Local, 2014). There were 3,819 posts published on 313 active websites during this period, and we coded every other story (odd numbers) on each site, a total of 1,941 posts (more detailed information about the generation of the sample can be found in Harte, 2013a). We coded each story 'live' on the sites in question and did not generate our own archive of this material.

Openly Local does not comprise a full list of hyperlocal publishers in the UK, and we are aware that many are not included. There is, as yet, no comprehensive list of community journalists in the UK because the sector is so young, informal, and subject to such rapid change. The network is embodied in an openly accessible online map to which local news producers can add their sites should they wish to – it is, in essence, a self-selecting sample. But even with this limitation in mind, we are confident that this large sample allows us the most comprehensive insight yet into the unstable and shifting cultural form of the UK hyperlocal news blog.

In line with our wish to produce findings which are comparable with historical content analyses of mainstream local news in the UK, our content analysis pays particular attention, among other things, to: sources (who gets to define hyperlocal news?); topics (what news is covered?); the 'local-ness' of this news; and the civic value of the news (principally, here, in relation to coverage of politics). The detailed content analysis coding frame was drawn up inductively after immersion in the sample.

Interviews

We conducted 36 semi-structured interviews with hyperlocal news publishers in the UK. We interviewed producers from a range of different hyperlocal outlets in terms of: the geographic areas served (urban, rural, wealthy, poor, etc.); the longevity of the site (some are new, some very long-established); the professional backgrounds of producers (some with varying levels of journalistic training and/or experience, some with none); and approaches to sustaining their operations (some who see their sites as hobbies, some as businesses).

Interviews were conducted and recorded over the telephone between October 2013 and May 2014 and later fully transcribed for analysis. They lasted 64 minutes on average, and were designed to gather information about: motivations for doing this kind of work; the day-to-day practice of hyperlocal news work; workloads; relations with audiences; uses of social media; principal challenges faced; and the economic value of hyperlocal news. Here we focus on findings which relate to motivations, sourcing strategies, opinions of and relations with local mainstream media outlets, and discourses about and examples of campaigning, critical, and investigative hyperlocal journalism, in order to triangulate our findings with relevant parts of the content analysis.

Online survey

The survey data interrogated here focuses principally on the content of community news in order to supplement, contextualise, and explain gaps in knowledge generated from the content analysis. More broadly, our survey was split into sections which covered the running of the site; site reach; site content (split into three categories: information, campaigns, and investigations echoing the democratic roles for local news outlined by McNair); site sustainability and profitability; and economic and human resources expended on community news sites. The range of questions invited single and multiple responses, as well as more expansive qualitative answers in selected cases, principally to elicit examples of practice. This gave us a good quantitative overview in key areas, but also allowed participants to submit longer discursive answers which, in some cases, we subjected to a secondary level of coding and categorisation. It was also important that questions were worded so as to gather insights which would give us a more longitudinal perspective on the subject matter than the short-term snapshot of community news our content analysis allowed.

Conducted using the online survey tool Survey Monkey, it sampled active sites on the Openly Local network and members of the Talk About Local mailing list (Talk About Local is a hyperlocal advocacy and consultancy group which now manages and updates the Openly Local map).[1] The design and circulation of the survey was a collaboration between our own research team, Steven Barnett and Judith Townend at the AHRC Media Plurality and Power Project at Westminster University, and Will Perrin and Mike Rawlins at Talk About Local. Firstly, an online request was delivered from Talk About Local to 455 members of its email list. Secondly, a more personalised online request was successfully delivered to 216 sites listed on Openly Local, either via email or the contact box on their sites. Finally, we advertised the survey on our blogs and Twitter accounts, which generated 24 additional responses. A total of 183 responses were received altogether (76% finished the survey).[2] We therefore achieved a response rate of around one-third of the original target population (based on Harte's figure of 496 active hyperlocal sites in the UK), making this the most extensive survey of hyperlocal media in the UK to date (Harte, 2013b).

Findings and discussion

What gets covered?

In terms of the topics covered by hyperlocal publishers we found that the largest category of news in the sample related to local community activities (13%). This is, on the whole, a very geographically focused, community-oriented, journalistic form. This category includes stories about local non-political civil society groups (e.g. the WI, community groups, local clubs and societies) as well as stories about community events like local festivals.

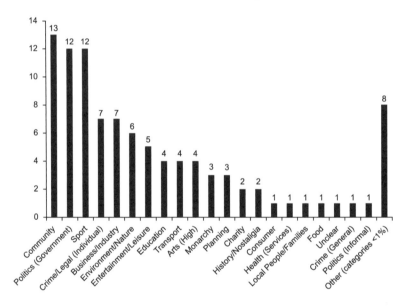

Figure 9.1   What gets covered? Percentage of topics covered by hyperlocal blog posts

We also found many stories about local councils and the services they provide (11.7%), so we know that hyperlocal audiences are getting a lot of information that in principle could be of civic value. Indeed, this would have been our largest category if we had not separated out stories about local planning (3.3%) which falls under the remit of local government in the UK. This kind of coverage of local politics contrasts somewhat with the UK's mainstream local and regional news media, which have scaled back such coverage in recent years. Other notably large categories included crime and business news entertainment, and the arts.

Putting the 'local' back in local news

We have seen clearly from the data on story topics that readers of hyperlocal news are getting a large amount of information about politics, particularly the politics of local government, which relates to the news' ability to foster informed citizenship. To investigate this further using content analysis we looked for stories that made any reference to politics and determined whether or not they had an angle that was explicitly locally relevant. Here we generated further indications of the strength of this kind of news when it comes to reporting about local mainstream political spheres. More than a third of stories in our sample make reference to politics (39.1%), and most reference local politics (26.9%). This is encouraging, especially because many of these sites exist in places where depleted local newspapers are operating on skeleton staffs, where they have already been closed down, or where there was never much local news coverage to speak of in the first place. One of the complaints made about the decline of local and regional mainstream news in the UK is that it is becoming increasingly less local in its orientation, at least in part because of the continuing cuts to newsroom resources and the increasingly deskbound nature of local and regional journalism work. This is not a charge which can be levelled at hyperlocal news.

Who gets to speak?

We coded for all directly quoted sources, but also all examples of indirect reported speech.

When we compare our broad findings on sources with studies of mainstream local news there are some continuities, but also important differences. As in the commercial local news, official sources in government, business, and the police are very important: politics at various levels accounts for around a quarter of all sources cited (27%), with business (14%) and the police (6%) also being very influential. But a key difference is the expanded role afforded to members of the general public and to representatives of local civil society groups in this emergent sector (12% and 7%, respectively). We expected to find more influence for members of the public actively organised in political struggles or campaigns, but explicitly political activists and trade unionists were thin on the ground in this sample, with each group making up just 1% of sources cited.

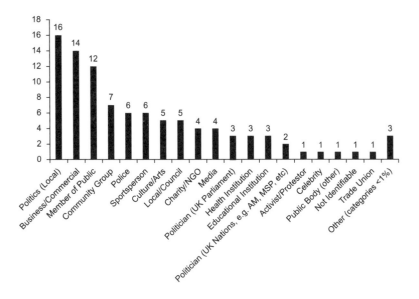

Figure 9.2   Who gets to speak? Percentage of sources either quoted or indirectly cited in UK hyperlocal news

A plurality of voices?

The overall number of news sources found in the sample was quite low, and this seems to signal a difference in practice between these emergent community news sites and more established providers of local news. Just over half of the posts cited any news sources (56.3%), meaning that many did not contain source input at all. Just as importantly only around a fifth (21.7%) cited more than one source. Studies of traditional news have been critical of such under-sourcing, worrying that it leads to a lack of transparency, a lack of plurality in the sources of information to which audiences are exposed, and a lack of opportunity for audiences to learn about conflicting perspectives on particular issues.

We also set out to track the different functions of secondary source intervention, and asked whether each utterance from such sources was: corroboratory (in broad agreement with the primary source); contextual (adding further information to that provided by the first-quoted source); and/or oppositional (expressing disagreement with the first source).

Table 9.1   Functions of secondary source intervention in UK hyperlocal blog posts

	Frequency	Percentage of whole sample
Contextualisation	358	18.4
Corroboration	304	15.7
Oppositional	60	3.1

Overall the sourcing of UK hyperlocal news in this sample seems to display a high level of consensus. In terms of the level of debate and the amounts of alternative viewpoints presented on any given story, this journalism, on the evidence of this content sample, seems quite uncritical. Most of the interventions of secondary sources added context and further information to that provided by the first source. Many were in broad agreement with primary sources, giving corroboratory information; only 3% of all stories in our sample included disagreement between social actors. This further suggests that, when it comes to sourcing, audiences are not being exposed to a wide range of alternative viewpoints in relation to the news they read. But the seemingly uncritical nature of the news in this sample needs to be understood in the context of our interview and survey findings.

Balancing sources is, of course, one of the principal ways in which mainstream professional journalists have performed their commitment to airing a plural range of perspectives on issues of public importance. However, hyperlocal news outlets take a variety of different positions on the issue of providing journalistic balance. First, many hyperlocal news producers have journalistic training and experience, and interview data suggest these are more likely than others to both quote and balance news sources. But we were also told on numerous occasions that not *all* local news *demands* the use of multiple, or even single, sources. A key role that many (perhaps even most) hyperlocal sites play is the provision of often quite uncontroversial information about everyday life and activity in their communities. For instance, we found many posts consisted of promotional trails for, or *post facto* accounts of, events organised by broadly non-political community groups. In the words of one interviewee, 'If I'm telling people about a local event I don't need to be getting extra quotes for balance. I don't need to be quoting people.' We also found some evidence that this apparent 'under-sourcing' of individual posts represents a (sometimes unconscious) rejection, or a critique in praxis, of some elements of mainstream journalistic sourcing strategies (Forde, 2011: 118–40). For example, Daniel Ionescu, the editor of the Lincolnite, told us of an example of a contentious story where he felt his team achieved fair coverage of key differing perspectives by covering competing local points of view in different stories, on different days.

Others, especially those who produce critical investigative hyperlocal news, take a much less conciliatory stance when it comes to providing space for the perspectives of those they critique. For instance, Quentin Kean of the Leeds Citizen, a retired journalist who describes himself as someone who produces critical news the mainstream local media 'haven't got either the resources or, in some cases, the interest to cover', is clear in his rejection of the need to offer an automatic right to reply in his coverage of local government.

> I'm scrupulous that everything I write is always accurate, nobody has ever challenged me about the accuracy of a story I've written. I'm choosing stories that are nearly always about the way interest groups, or political power, works. [But], for example, if I have a story about council stuff, I don't immediately slap off an email to them [at] the press office for them to give me a quote because they've got plenty of outlets for all of their stuff.

This unwillingness to balance sources in critical reporting is rooted, in part, in a pragmatic expectation that the PR office in question will not take any questions or allegations seriously (Kean talks of 'bland meaningless responses'), but also in a certain amount of contempt for the uncritical way in which local newspapers already routinely provide a mouthpiece for the output of local government communications officers. Mark Baynes, of campaigning London blog Love Wapping, shares these critiques. When asked whether he balances his critical coverage of Tower Hamlets Council with quotes from relevant officers he told us:

> I don't see why I should, as a resident, ring the town hall up or anybody else [...] Because I know all they're going to give me is the usual bullshit. So what's the point? And they've got a huge media machine. [...] I don't see, to be quite honest, why any hyperlocal should. Because if you look at it in the broader context of media and communications in our society: if Tower Hamlets wants to get on TV, they can get on TV. They can send a press release to the East London Advertiser [the local weekly newspaper] [...] and they literally print the press release.

Steven Downes, freelance sports journalist and editor of local investigative site Inside Croydon, elaborated on this, suggesting that the journalistic norm of providing balance through a right to reply sometimes offers council PR offices a way to 'close down' critical reporting by simply refusing to comment. In such cases these hyperlocals have borrowed from the approaches of professional investigative reporting by relying on the quality of their documentary evidence as a way of guaranteeing accuracy and fairness. Referring to balance, and in common with others, Downes told us, 'I've adopted a different attitude. [...] In the end, it comes down to editorial judgement in terms of how you assess a source and the documentation [...] documents are the thing. If you get the document, you're away.'

Hyperlocal campaigning

The dearth of non-party-political activists and campaigners cited in our content analysis sample initially led us to suspect that campaigns may be under-represented in hyperlocal news. We were wrong, however. Survey and interview data suggest there are two broad ways that hyperlocal news outlets cover campaigns: they actively campaign for change themselves; and/or they cover existing local campaigns. In order to glean a fuller picture of hyperlocal news practice in this area we asked our survey respondents whether they had started campaigns, or covered the campaigns of others in the last two years (n = 159). We found that most UK hyperlocals have joined in, supported, or publicised the campaigns (73.3%) of others, and a substantial minority (40%) have taken part in their own originally instigated campaigning journalism (Barnett and Townend, 2014). We also asked them how often they undertook such journalism. The average number of campaigns instigated by hyperlocals themselves in the last two years is 3.3 (n = 55), and the average number of campaigns they have 'joined in or supported' was 5.07 (n = 81). It is clear from the interviews, as well as the more qualitative survey answers, that the subjects of these campaigns vary greatly in size, range, and impact. Some are very local, in their focus on issues likely to affect a small number of people, often in quite minor ways, and other issues are more wide-ranging in their effects and more explicitly political in focus.

The raw figures only tell us part of the story. We also asked survey participants to give us a qualitative insight into the campaigns they have run on their community news sites by noting examples of the most recent and the most important campaigns they have initiated and supported. These qualitative responses were then analysed, categorised, and coded.

Campaigns around planning and licensing are both supported *and* initiated by community news producers, and mainly consisted of planning issues around contentious local developments. Many also included an environmental aspect to do with the protection of local green spaces, or were related to local businesses (e.g. local opposition to the proposed opening of chain supermarket outlets), but a few were about minor local issues such as the granting of alcohol or take-away food licences. Campaigns around local public services (largely in opposition to *cuts* to such services) were also common in both categories. For instance, there were many campaigns against library closures, and a significant number around perceived threats to the provision of healthcare and education services. Campaigning for improvements to local infrastructure were more commonly supported rather than initiated, either calling on authorities to make – or lobbying against – substantial changes to local roads, train lines, or provision for cyclists. Local business campaigns normally involved calls to promote local independent shops and restaurants, and included numerous 'shop local' campaigns.

Numerous 'community action' campaigns were either in favour of, against, or linked to the activities of local neighbourhood plans and neighbourhood forums, entities enabled under the Localism Act which are designed to enable more democratic control of planning issues. The numerous campaigns against these bodies, however, suggest concern in some communities about how democratic they actually are in practice. Community news producers were quite likely to initiate campaigns which called for improvements to local amenities such as signage, local parks, car parking, play areas, or the cleanliness of a local area (e.g. in relation to those favourite UK hyperlocal preoccupations: litter and dog poo). A number of campaigns dealt specifically with local council responsibilities. Several called for greater transparency and accountability from local government institutions, calling on councils to allow the filming, recording, or live coverage of meetings. It is perhaps unsurprising that these were among the most likely to be initiated by community journalists, as restrictions on reporting directly affect their abilities to cover the affairs of local political institutions. There were also a few instances of much more serious council-related malpractice, such as campaigns around the misuse of public funds, or illegal payments made to local businesses.

Hyperlocal coverage of many of these issues, it is claimed, was instrumental in numerous full or partial victories by the campaigners, but even when campaigns were unsuccessful much of this coverage is likely to have led to an enriched local public sphere in the affected communities. There is also evidence to suggest that coverage of campaigns, tapping in as it does to existing networks of active citizens with an interest in local public life, and covering issues which are of common concern to many, can help hyperlocal producers gain wider audiences, generate social standing, trust, and respect from official sources, and become more visible in their communities.

Hyperlocal accountability reporting: investigations

Our findings relating to the lack of conflicting perspectives among sources, as well as those which indicate low numbers of non-party grassroots or alternative campaigners, raise the possibility that UK hyperlocal news, on aggregate, may be unlikely to undertake very much critical accountability journalism. But a more nuanced and differentiated picture can be obtained when triangulating these research findings with those from the survey and interviews, which allowed us to investigate two broad areas of hyperlocal practice in this regard: investigative hyperlocal news; and non-investigative news which is nonetheless critical of local institutions.

In order to address the issue of investigative hyperlocal news, and to interrogate hyperlocal producers' willingness or ability to carry out this form of watchdog reporting, we asked survey respondents whether they had carried out investigations in order to uncover controversial information of local concern in the last two years. It seems that a substantial proportion of hyperlocal news producers are carrying out investigations. Indeed, around the same proportion (42%), and similar numbers (55), of survey respondents who have started local campaigns also undertake this kind of critical journalistic research (Barnett and Townend, 2014). As before, respondents were asked for brief details of their most recent, and their most important, investigations.

Examples of investigations survey respondents cited included: environment stories such as a waste incinerator breaching emissions guidelines and plans to develop land poisoned by previous industrial owners; council stories about lack of transparency, or involving (documented) secret or illegal payments; planning issues around supermarket developments, the proposed High Speed 2 railway line, and green field sites being reallocated as brown field in order to allow developments; as well a range of data-led stories about issues as diverse as parking fines, environmental enforcement activities, numbers and rates of crimes solved by local police, use of local libraries in order to argue against cuts to services, and lift failures in council-owned flats.

As well as there being generalist hyperlocals which occasionally carry out investigations, there is a small but influential group of community news sites in the UK which devote themselves almost exclusively to the production of critical and investigative news. Examples include Inside Croydon and Broken Barnet in London, the Leeds Citizen in the north of England, Carmarthenshire Planning Problems and More from rural West Wales, and Real Whitby, the seaside town in North Yorkshire. All of these sites have investigated and broken stories of local and national significance, chiefly about political corruption and transparency issues. One might expect, given the demanding, risky, and resource-intensive nature of the research needed to take on local elites, that all of these hyperlocal producers would be trained journalists – this is not the case. The most commonly cited methods used in hyperlocal investigations during our interviews are: the careful analysis of public institutional documents and data; Freedom of Information Requests to public bodies (mostly councils) to obtain unpublished documents, data, and correspondence; and leaks and tip-offs (mainly from within local councils, occasionally from private bodies). More risky methods such as undercover work were not encountered.

Hyperlocal accountability reporting: critical news

In order to explore the production of *non-investigative* news which nonetheless still includes source input critical of local institutions, or which may take an explicitly critical editorial stance, we asked a series of open questions in the interviews about producers' day-to-day practice, how their work relates to the output of other local news producers, as well as their aims and motivations. Many were unequivocal about the need for local news producers to ask awkward questions, to air difficult issues, and hold elites to account. Rachel Howells of the Port Talbot Magnet in South Wales told us 'Somebody's got to be there asking those questions […] saying, "Well, hang on a minute you've broken the air quality limits three times this month, what's going on?" […] You've got to have somebody there [to] hold these people to account and have a public forum for that debate.' Howells also told us that the production of such watchdog news can also lead to hyperlocal news outlets being taken more seriously by official sources: 'What we've found to be generally true is that the more firm and journalistic we are, the more critical we are, the more seriously they take us'.

One striking trend in our interview findings, however, does initially seem to lend credence to the suggestion in our content analysis data that this is a largely uncritical, and non-progressive, form of news. There is a very common tendency among hyperlocals to want to portray the place they live in a positive light. Pamela Pinski from the Birmingham blog Digbeth Is Good, for instance, is motivated by 'improving perceptions of Digbeth', a suburb of which she is 'very proud' and for which she is a 'passionate' advocate. Anna Williams, the editor of Northumberland seaside town Amble's 14-year-old community newspaper and website, the *Ambler*, similarly speaks of a conscious editorial decision to 'promote the good things that were happening in Amble'. It may be tempting to see this widespread trend as evidence of toothless local news producers who are unlikely to fulfil the critical watchdog function of accountability news. In many cases this would be a mistake. Closer examination of the interview data suggests this tendency is in many cases more accurately interpreted as a reaction to the perceived practice of journalists in the local and regional newspaper industry. It is not just the practice of balancing with which many hyperlocal news producers are uncomfortable. When prompted, many define themselves, their working practices, and the news they produce, explicitly against the working routines and news output of mainstream professional local news companies. This is expressed in (sometimes quite vehement) critiques of: local press intrusion; exploitative treatment of community members at the centre of human interest stories; distant coverage which is not reflective enough of community life, is too reliant on press releases, and is too deferential to authority; and coverage which is sensationalist and overly negative. Anna Williams echoes the sentiments of many interviewees: 'The only time you ever read anything in the local mainstream press [about Amble] was when some things had been vandalised, or some kids had been nabbed for doing something. It was always doom and gloom.'

Many of those who express a wish to represent their communities to themselves, and to the outside world, in a positive light are also keen to point out that this does not imply they shy away from critical coverage where they feel it is appropriate. Gareth Jenkins, who edits the Kirkbymoorside Town Blog, from the edge of the North York Moors in northern England, for instance, discussed how he was partly motivated to set up the blog to collate information about 'all the things you could get involved in' in the 'buzzy little town' he clearly loves. But this does not, however, mean he is reticent to cover, and facilitate debate about, controversial issues in public life. During our interview he cited numerous examples of news stories which included negative comment and critique, including around a controversial housing development, the arrival of a new Tesco supermarket, and divisive and expensive plans to convert a disused library building into new offices for the town council.

Conclusion: the democratic value of hyperlocal news

In terms of UK community news' ability to (at least partially) plug the ever-widening gaps in UK local and regional news provision we have generated some promising, and some less clearly encouraging, findings. Hyperlocal news, on the whole, is very community- and locally oriented. By contrast with much professional commercial news, which has become progressively less local in its focus and depth of coverage as resources decline, hyperlocal audiences get lots of locally sourced stories with strong local news angles. Members of the public and local community groups tend to get more of a say as news sources than in the mainstream local and regional news. Official sources in local government, business, and the emergency services still get a platform, but so do many local citizens. These blogs produce and circulate a lot of news about politics, civic life, local economies, and the business of local government (which is an area of life in the UK that has been under-reported as the crisis in local commercial news has developed).

While some of our findings seem to suggest a rosy picture in terms of hyperlocal news' ability to foster citizenship, democracy, and local community cohesion, others were less unequivocally positive. One of the ways professional journalists provide us with a plurality of perspectives on local life is to speak to numerous news sources to gather the raw materials of news, many of whom they go on to quote in their stories. In our sample, many hyperlocal news producers quote relatively few news sources, and when they *are* used they rarely provide conflicting or oppositional viewpoints in the same posts. But our interviews suggest that some hyperlocal producers have developed alternative means to foster and inform plural debate around contentious local issues, for example opting to enact source balance by spreading interventions from opposing voices out across different stories. In the case of more overtly critical investigative hyperlocal sites, the practice of balancing sources is often rejected on practical and ideological grounds: because council PR departments cannot be relied upon to engage meaningfully with questions, or they use the expectation of being given a right to reply as a tactic to close down debate by stonewalling journalists; because balance is a practice associated with a largely uncritical local mainstream press; and because local elites have enough of a platform for their carefully crafted communications messages in mainstream commercial news media anyway.

Whilst our content analysis findings seem to suggest a lack of critical, investigative, and campaigning journalism, the interviews and survey yielded clear data to the contrary. Many hyperlocal news producers cover the campaigns of others and a significant minority have initiated their own campaigns. Critical investigations are also carried out by a (perhaps surprisingly) large number of UK community journalists on a wide variety of issues of public concern, and a small but effective group of hyperlocal sites devote themselves almost entirely to this kind of public interest news production. There is a strong tendency among many of these sites to want to produce news that paints their local areas in a positive light, but this does not generally mean they shy away from writing critical stories where necessary. Many hyperlocals are, on the contrary, committed to producing news which fulfils the watchdog function of holding local elites to account. Indeed, many are also producing news about their local areas that could fulfil many of McNair's above-mentioned commonly accepted social and political roles for journalism.

Notes

1   'Active' was defined as 'a website having posted a news story at least once in the 5 months prior to the sample period'. Inactive sites had either closed, or had not published in the five months prior to his sampling (Harte 2013b).

2   The response rate was higher from the list compiled from the Openly Local directory (86 of 216: 39.8%) than from the Talk About Local mailing list (69 of 455: 15.2%). There are two main reasons that could explain the low response to the Talk About Local mailing list. Firstly, the request for participation took the form of a generic newsletter (only 115 of 455 recipients opened the email); and secondly, the mailing list contained contact details for people who were interested in hyperlocal media, but do not publish sites themselves.

Bibliography

Barnett, Steven, and Judith Townend. 2014. 'Plurality, Policy and the Local,' *Journalism Practice*: 1–18. doi: 10.1080/17512786.2014.943930.

Beckett, Charlie, and Jayme Herve-Azevedo. 2010. *The Value of Networked Journalism*. London: London School of Economics and Political Science.

Bruns, Axel. 2011. 'Citizen Journalism and Everyday Life: A Case Study of MyHeimat.de', in Bob Franklin and Matt Carlson (eds), *Journalists, Sources, and Credibility: New Perspectives*. London: Routledge, 182–94.

Chambers, Simone, and Anne Costain (eds). 2001. *Deliberation, Democracy, and the Media*. London: Rowman and Littlefield.

Davies, Nick. 2008. *Flat Earth News*. London: Chatto and Windus.

Davis, Aeron. 2008. 'Public Relations in the News', in Bob Franklin (ed.), *Pulling Newspapers Apart: Analysing Print Journalism*. London: Routledge, 256–64.

Department for Culture, Media and Sport (DCMS). 2009. *Digital Britain*. London: HMSO.

Downie, Leonard, and Michael Schudson. 2009. *The Reconstruction of American Journalism*. New York: Columbia University Publications.

Fenton, Ben. 2008. 'Bad Ad News Ripples across the Sector', *Financial Times*, 1 July.

Fenton, Natalie. 2011. 'Deregulation or Democracy: New Media, News, Neoliberalism and the Public Interest', *Continuum: Journal of Media and Cultural Studies*, 25(1): 63–72.

Forde, Susan. 2011. *Challenging the News: The Journalism of Alternative and Community Media*. Basingstoke: Palgrave Macmillan.

Franklin, Bob. 1988. *Public Relations Activities in Local Government*. London: Charles Knight.

Franklin, Bob. 2005. 'McJournalism: The Local Press and the McDonaldization Thesis', in Stuart Allen (ed.), *Journalism: Critical Essays*. Milton Keynes: Open University Press, 137–51.

Franklin, Bob. 2006a. 'Preface', in Bob Franklin (ed.), *Local Journalism and Local Media: Making the Local News*. London: Routledge, xvii–xxii.

Franklin, Bob. 2006b. 'Attacking the Devil? Local Journalists and Local Papers in the UK', in Bob Franklin (ed.), *Local Journalism and Local Media: Making the Local News*. London: Routledge, 3–15.

Franklin, Bob. 2011. 'Sources, Credibility, and the Continuing Crisis of UK Journalism', in Bob Franklin and Matt Carlson (eds), *Journalism, Sources, and Credibility*. London: Routledge, 90–106.

Franklin, Bob, and Matt Carlson. 2011. 'Introduction', in Bob Franklin and Matt Carlson (eds), *Journalism, Sources, and Credibility*. London: Routledge, 1–18.

Franklin, Bob, Geoff Court, and Stephen Cushion. 2006. 'Downgrading the "Local" in Local Newspapers' Reporting of the 2005 UK General Election', in Bob Franklin (ed.), *Local Journalism and Local Media: Making the Local News*. London: Routledge, 256–69.

Franklin, Bob, and Judy Van Slyke Turk. 1988. 'Information Subsidies: Agenda Setting Traditions', *Public Relations Review*, Spring: 29–41.

Fröhlich, Romy, Oliver Quirling, and Sven Engesser. 2012. 'Between Idiosyncratic Self Interest and Professional Standards', *Journalism*, 13(8): 1041–63.

Habermas, Juergen. 1989. *The Structural Transformation of the Public Sphere: An Inquiry into a Category of Bourgeois Society*. Cambridge, MA: MIT Press.

Hamer, Martin. 2006. 'Trading on Trust: News Agencies, Local Journalism, and Local Media', in Bob Franklin (ed.), *Local Journalism and Local Media: Making the Local News*. London: Routledge, 210–18.

Harrison, Shirley. 1998. 'The Local Government Agenda: News From the Town Hall', in Bob Franklin and David Murphy (eds), *Making the Local News: Local Journalism in Context*. London: Routledge, 157–69.

Harte, Dave. 2013a. 'One Every Two Minutes: Assessing the Scale of Hyperlocal Publishing in the UK'. *JOMEC Journal* [online], 1(3). http://www.cardiff. ac.uk/jomec/research/journalsandpublications/jomecjournal/3-june2013/ index.html.

Harte, Dave. 2013b. 'Hyperlocal Publishing in the UK – A 2013 Snapshot'. 11 October. http://daveharte.com/hyperlocal/hyperlocal-publishing-in-the- uk-a-2013-snapshot/ (accessed July 2014).

Hartley, John. 2009. *The Uses of Digital Literacy*. New Brunswick, NJ: Transaction.

Jurkowitz, Mark. 2014. *The Growth in Digital Reporting*. Pew Journalism Research Project, 26 March. http://www.journalism.org/2014/03/26/the-growth-in- digital-reporting (accessed July 2014).

Kerkhoven, Marco, and Piet Bakker. 2014. 'The Hyperlocal in Practice: Innovation, Creativity, and Diversity', *Digital Journalism*, 2(3): 296–309.

Kurpius, David, Emily Metzgar, and Karen Rowley. 2010. 'Sustaining Hyperlocal Media: In Search of Funding Models', *Journalism Studies*, 11(3): 359–76.

McNair, Brian. 2009. 'Journalism and Democracy', in Karin Wahl Jorgensen and Thomas Hanitsch (eds), *The Handbook of Journalism Studies*. New York and London: Routledge, 237–49.

Metzgar, Emily, David Kurpius, and Karen Rowley. 2011. 'Defining Hyperlocal Media: Proposing a Framework for Discussion', *New Media and Society*, 13(5): 772–87.

Ofcom. 2009. *Local and Regional Media in the UK*. London: Ofcom.

Ofcom. 2012. *The Communications Market Report: United Kingdom*. London: Ofcom.

O'Neill, Deidre, and Catherine O'Connor. 2008. 'The Passive Journalist: How Sources Dominate Local News', *Journalism Practice*, 2(3): 487–500.

Openly Local. 2014. 'Hyperlocal Sites in UK and Ireland'. http://openlylocal.com/hyperlocal_sites (accessed July 2014).

Radcliffe, Damian. 2012. *Here and Now: UK Hyperlocal Media Today*. London: Nesta.

Schaffer, Jan. 2007. *Citizen Media: Fad or the Future of News? The Rise and Prospects of Hyperlocal Journalism*. http://www.j-lab.org/_uploads/downloads/citizen_media-1.pdf (accessed July 2014).

Taggart, Chris. 2010. 'Yet Another UK Hyperlocal Directory ... But This Time it's Open Data', *CounterCulture*, 13 January. http://countculture.wordpress.com/2010/01/13/yet-another-uk-hyperlocal-directory-but-this-time-its-open-data (accessed July 2014).

Thurman, Neil, Jean Christophe Pascal, and Paul Bradshaw. 2012. 'Can Big Media Do Big Society? A Critical Case Study of Commercial, Convergent Hyperlocal News', *International Journal of Media and Cultural Politics*, 8(2): 269–85.

Williams, Andy, and Bob Franklin. 2007. *Turning around the Tanker: Implementing Trinity Mirror's Online Strategy*. Cardiff: Cardiff University School of Journalism Media and Cultural Studies. http://image.guardian.co.uk/sys-files/Media/documents/2007/03/13/Cardiff.Trinity.pdf (accessed July 2014).

Index

RISJ/I.B.TAURIS PUBLICATIONS

CHALLENGES

Journalism and PR: News Media and Public Relations in the Digital Age
John Lloyd and Laura Toogood
ISBN: 978 1 78453 062 4

Reporting the EU: News, Media and the European Institutions
John Lloyd and Cristina Marconi
ISBN: 978 1 78453 065 5

Transformations in Egyptian Journalism
Naomi Sakr
ISBN: 978 1 78076 589 1

Climate Change in the Media: Reporting Risk and Uncertainty
James Painter
ISBN: 978 1 78076 588 4

Women and Journalism
Suzanne Franks
ISBN: 978 1 78076 585 3

EDITED VOLUMES

Media, Revolution and Politics in Egypt: The Story of an Uprising
Abdalla F. Hassan
ISBN: 978 1 78453 217 8 (HB); 978 1 78453 218 5 (PB)

*The Euro Crisis in the Media: Journalistic Coverage of Economic Crisis and European
Institutions*
Robert G. Picard (ed.)
ISBN: 978 1 78453 059 4 (HB); 978 1 78453 060 0 (PB)

Local Journalism: The Decline of Newspapers and the Rise of Digital Media
Rasmus Kleis Nielsen (ed.)
ISBN: 978 1 78453 320 5 (HB); 978 1 78453 321 2 (PB)

Media and Public Shaming: The Boundaries of Disclosure
Julian Petley (ed.)
ISBN: 978 1 78076 586 0 (HB); 978 1 78076 587 7 (PB)

Political Journalism in Transition: Western Europe in a Comparative Perspective
Raymond Kuhn and Rasmus Kleis Nielsen (eds)
ISBN: 978 1 78076 677 5 (HB); 978 1 78076 678 2 (PB)

Transparency in Politics and the Media: Accountability and Open Government
Nigel Bowles, James T. Hamilton and David A. L. Levy (eds)
ISBN: 978 1 78076 675 1 (HB); 978 1 78076 676 8 (PB)

The Ethics of Journalism: Individual, Institutional and Cultural Influences
Wendy N. Wyatt (ed.)
ISBN: 978 1 78076 673 7 (HB); 978 1 78076 674 4 (PB)